WHAT AM I DOING HERE

Bruce Chatwin was born in Sheffield in 1940. After attending Marlborough School he began work as a porter at Sotheby's. Eight years later, having become one of Sotheby's youngest directors, he abandoned his job to pursue his passion for world travel. Between 1972 and 1975 he worked for the *Sunday Times*, before announcing his next departure in a telegram: 'Gone to Patagonia for six months.' This trip inspired the first of Chatwin's books, *In Patagonia*, which won the Hawthornden Prize and the E.M.Forster award and launched his writing career. Two of his books have been made into feature films: *The Viceroy of Ouidah* (retitled *Cobra Verde*), directed by Werner Herzog, and the British Film Institute's *On The Black Hill*. On publication *The Songlines* went straight to No. 1 in the *Sunday Times* bestseller list and stayed in the top ten for nine months. His novel, *Utz*, was shortlisted for the 1988 Booker Prize.

He died in January 1989.

ALSO BY BRUCE CHATWIN

In Patagonia
The Viceroy of Ouidah
On the Black Hill
The Songlines
Utz
Photographs and Notebooks

with Paul Theroux
Patagonia Revisited

'His last book, a "personal selection" of essays, portraits, meditations, travel writing and other unclassifiable Chatwinian forms of prose, was put together during his final, terrible year of wasting away...one of its chief delights is that it contains so many of its author's best anecdotes, his choicest performances'

Salman Rushdie, *Observer*

'It is a personal collection of travel pieces, profiles, stories and essays, and as one reads it one cannot forget it was compiled by a uniquely gifted writer in the face of death, urgently pinning down experiences important to him. All that might suggest a scrapbook, but as a legendary traveller and observer of people Chatwin had more to put into his than most'

Mail on Sunday

'Each of his books, in its distinctness from the others, mirrored his evident fear of being categorised by critics or publishers, and this sense of wanting to surprise went hand in hand with the power to create a collusion with the individual reader, as though you and he alone knew where the work's real thrust lay'

Jonathan Keates, *The Independent*

'Bruce Chatwin's posthumously published volume of articles and stories is both a marvellous introduction to his work and a memorial to a great writer...It is a remarkable collection, and a fitting postscript to a distinguished career'

Today

'All the writing in this volume demonstrates Bruce Chatwin's loathing of the humdrum, the dreary, the predictable. What attracted him was the unusual, the weird and wonderful. Wherever he was, he would respond to odd news items he read, like the day he was in Benares and read that a wolf-child had been found near Sultanpur. Most people would think how interesting and turn the page but not Chatwin. He caught a train at once and within twenty four hours was travelling on by rickshaw to where the boy was. The journalist in him (strongly present) knew a good story when it heard one'

Margaret Forster, *The Guardian*

'Bruce Chatwin's originality as a writer is that he uses accepted means, sharpened and pared down admittedly, to express unlikely material. If there was a barrier or inhibition, he just crashed it as he would in life; the resources of language had to take the strain he put on them without distortion. That is Tolstoy's formula, and almost every great writer's. It is like the best letter-writing only more artful, and as with the best letter writers there was a competence, almost a smoothness about Bruce'

Peter Levi, *The Spectator*

'When I read *The Songlines* I felt that his most engrossing character was himself, and that the unknown land which most fascinated him remained, as it had been since childhood, his own imagination. That is true in this book too. There are a dozen autobiographical articles about his father, about undergoing tests in hospital and his feelings about death, about his visit to the location where Herzog was filming *The Viceroy of Ouidah*. Pieces like these show us that human existence – at least as Chatwin sees it – is gloriously open-ended, unpredictable and exotic. The more he assures us that he is telling the truth, the more wonders we can expect'

Kenneth McLeish, *The Sunday Times*

'He was a great traveller and a fine stylist, a good companion, an original nomad, and clearly a nice man. His work will last'

Philip Howard, *The Times*

'*What Am I Doing Here* (the question Rimbaud asked in Ethiopia), because it is more ragged than anything else he wrote, tells us more about him – his interests and friends, if not his passions. He writes of his father, of his friend, the distinguished painter Howard Hodgkin, and his *tête-à-têtes* with André Malraux and Nadezhda Mandelstam...Ideally he gets a really bizarre bee in his bonnet, such as the rumour of a "wolf-boy" in India, or a Chinese *fengshui* geomancer in Hong Kong, or the idea of looking for a Yeti, and he sets off and deals with it. At its most successful his travel is a search for an unholy grail – something freakish, plainly an excuse – and off he goes, and the piece is a winner. More than half of those in this book are winners, and the others can be classified as Anecdotes, Fragments, Assignments, and Bits of Odd Lore. This latter category is a Chatwin speciality'

Paul Theroux, *The Telegraph*

'"My whole life," said Chatwin in 1983, "has been a search for the miraculous." There have been few writers better qualified to seek it, or better able to distinguish the fake from the genuine article'

Punch

'These essays cover the whole of his short writing life and they get better and better. The many little pieces he composed in the last year of his life are the best of all...Chatwin's travels had left him with both rich eyes and rich hands and he had only begun to dispense the results to his readers'

Sean French, *New Statesman & Society*

'The effect ought to be disjointed; yet the recurrent theme of Chatwin's own insatiable wanderlust ultimately knits this unlikely assortment of people and places into an absorbing whole'
Daily Mail

'Nobody is as good as Chatwin at evoking a whole atmosphere just through putting down exactly what he saw because what he did see was always the telling detail'
Margaret Forster, *Guardian*

'Bruce could tell stories like the poet Byron, like the poet of *Don Juan,* and like him he lived what he wrote'
Peter Levi, *Spectator*

Bruce Chatwin

WHAT AM I
DOING HERE

VINTAGE

Published by Vintage 1998

4 6 8 10 9 7 5

First published in Great Britain by
Jonathan Cape Ltd in 1989

Vintage
Random House, 20 Vauxhall Bridge Road,
London SW1V 2SA

Random House Australia (Pty) Limited
20 Alfred Street, Milsons Point, Sydney
New South Wales 2061, Australia

Random House New Zealand Limited
18 Poland Road, Glenfield, Auckland 10,
New Zealand

Random House (Pty) Limited
Endulini, 5A Jubilee Road, Parktown 2193,
South Africa

The Random House Group Limited Reg. No. 954009
www.randomhouse.co.uk

A CIP catalogue record for this book
is available from the British Library

ISBN 0 09 976981 6

Papers used by Random House are natural, recyclable
products made from wood grown in sustainable forests.
The manufacturing processes conform to the environ
mental regulations of the country of origin

Printed and bound in Great Britain by
Cox & Wyman, Reading, Berkshire

I

WRITTEN FOR FRIENDS AND FAMILY

ASSUNTA
A Story

What am I doing here? I am flat on my back in a National Health Service hospital hoping, praying, that the rigors and fevers which have racked me for three months *will* turn out to be malaria — although, after many blood tests, they have not found a single parasite. I have been on quinine tablets for thirteen hours — and my temperature does seem to be sliding down. I feel my ears. They are cold. I feel the tip of my nose. It is cold. I feel my forehead. It is cool. I feel inside my groin. Not too bad. The excitement is enough to send my temperature soaring.

In comes one of the people I most adore on the ward, Assunta, the cleaning lady and tea-maker.

She comes from Palermo and has married an Englishman. She works here, not so much for money, as for love. I rejoice at the sight of Assunta because she fills the room with Southern warmth.

She has come with a mop to swab the floor.

'Oh, my God!' she says. 'The snake! . . . My daughter, she go to the police about the snake.'

'What snake?'

'Puppet.'

'Puppet?'

'No. No. Poppet.'

'Assunta, what *are* you talking about?'

3

She takes a deep breath and speaks in grim and halting sentences:

'Mister Bruce . . . I have this next-door neighbour . . . She is an evil woman . . . My kids, they play in the garden and she scream, "Your kids make too much noise. Take them in the house" . . . She not believe in God or nothing . . . She have two abortions . . . All she love is animals . . . She have dog . . . She have cat . . . She have rabbits . . . and she have Poppet . . . '

'The snake?'

'So she knock on my door and she say, "Have you seen Poppet? She got out of her cage . . . " "No, I no see . . . Look for Poppet yourself . . . " I *shut* the windows . . . I lock the door . . . I say the kids, you no go in the garden until she find Poppet . . . She not find Poppet . . . Anywhere! . . . Then I must go my garden shed to get something . . . Comes this terrible noise, "*Sssss*! . . . *Ghrr*! *Sssss*!" I slam the door . . . I shout, "Your Poppet is in my shed!" She come over . . . She open the door . . . And this snake jump out . . . And go round and round her body five, six times . . . And lick all over her face . . . '

'How big is this snake?'

'BIG!' says Assunta. 'Big as this room . . . '

She waves the mop-handle diagonally across the room. The snake must be a python or a boa constrictor over twenty feet long.

'And the head!' she says. Her hands gesture to something the size of a small honeydew melon. 'And horrible red eyes!

'So she say, "Can I bring Poppet through the house? . . . " "No," I say. "You go over the wall."'

'You should have gone to the police long ago.'

'And the little kids playing in the street! . . . English people is mad . . . Now she knock on my door. She say, "My Poppet, she have a baby" . . . She pay £17 for artificial insemination . . . Disgusting! . . . My daughter, she go to the police.'

1988

4

ASSUNTA 2
A Story

It may be malaria. The temperature *has* gone down. Young doctors smile and ask how I feel. Now it's my turn to be sceptical: 'You tell *me* how I feel.' I pestered them to put me on quinine but they were reluctant. If it *is* malaria, I know where I got it. Last spring, having recovered from a very rare Chinese fungus of the bone-marrow, I went to Ghana where a film-director friend was making a film based on one of my books.

There were no hotel beds in Accra because the city was host to a Pan-African Ladies' Congress. The film crew had moved to the North. My friend regretted there might be no one reliable to meet me. We called the British Council representative who volunteered to find something. I once spent a night in Accra, in the bus-park.

Outside the airport building there were *two* reception committees, not one: the boys of Ghana Film Industries, the girls of the British Council. They waved bits of white cardboard: 'Mr Chatwin . . . Mr Chatwin . . . ' We drove off in the British Council's white station-wagon. The boys followed in their tumbledown cars. We came to the hotel, which I think was called Liberty Hall. I was really too tired to take in the name, and I left at five in the morning. I gave the boys and girls beer and lemonade, and they shyly answered questions. I heard a loud and angry commotion at the reception desk. A lady was shouting, in French, 'Madame, est-ce que je peux vous aider?'

There were many hungry ladies in the dining-room. They were the delegation from Guinea and they only spoke French. I assumed the role of head waiter and my English-speaking assistant took notes on a pad.

I announced the menu: steak, kid, guinea-fowl, chicken, fish. The ladies were very particular. One wanted her steak 'not too cooked'. One wanted chicken with *akassas* and a chile sauce 'not too strong'. The waiter went to the kitchen and the ladies clapped. Here was life again!

I had not noticed that my face was covered with mosquito bites.

I flew to the North in a chartered plane. I felt the film was going to *look* spectacular but was not much to do with my book. The star did not look like a Brazilian slave trader as much as a bad-tempered European woman. I mistimed one of my anti-malarials and forgot about it.

A week after coming back to England I took another prophylactic and had a seizure: shivers followed by a temperature. It was not serious. I thought nothing of it.

A week later I took another pill and this time had a shaking fit and raging fever. I had recovered by the morning. The doctors and I agreed it was probably a reaction to the pill.

The young doctors were reluctant to put me on quinine without a go-ahead from the Professor. He is one of the most brilliant clinical physicians in this country — which leads the world. In the Far East he has made advances in the study of cerebral malaria. He dazzles me with his mind and his wisdom.

He comes into the room with a stethoscope round his neck:
'How are you?'
'Look at the temperature chart.'
He looks at the chart, he looks up and grins:
'I'm always mistrustful of patients who diagnose their own

6

diseases. I suspect they may have healing powers, or self-healing powers, of which we know nothing.'

He goes. I lie back on the pillow and shut my eyes. The Professor has made me happier than he can imagine.

He is a world authority on snake-bites.

In comes Assunta with the morning tea.

'Like a cup-a-tea, Bruce?'

'I'd love a cup of tea, Assunta.'

She brings the tea and we settle in for our daily morning talk.

'You know, Assunta, it may be malaria after all.'

'These doctors,' she sighs. 'They not always know . . . Sometimes you know and they not know . . . I have terrible time with my last child . . . '

'When was that, Assunta?'

'My little girl is fourteen.'

She is going to tell me another story.

'My husband and I . . . we have three children . . . so I take the pill . . . and I get fat . . . I get so fat people say: "Assunta you're pregnant" . . . I say, "I can't be pregnant . . . I take the pill . . . I have my periods . . . Regular . . . " But I feel something inside . . . It is not a baby . . . It not move . . . I have three babies and they move . . . So my husband, he take me to hospital . . . They make more scan . . . And one day doctor and nurses come . . . My husband come . . . He white like a sheet . . . The doctor hold my hand . . . He say, "Be calm, Assunta. Be calm . . . " I *NOT* calm! "Assunta," he say. "You really want this baby?" "Yes, now I want baby . . . " Now really I worry . . . "What the matter?" "Be calm, Assunta," he say. "Be calm . . . Assunta, the baby in your body have no arms and no legs. You not want child like that . . . "

'I go up and down . . . I go up . . . I go down . . . I no breathe . . . The nurse she have needle and I sleep . . . So I wake in morning and I am drunk . . . "Where am I?" I say the nurse . . . "Assunta, you still in hospital . . . " And the nurse . . . she put in front of me piece paper . . . "Please sign" . . . I

7

am so drunk I sign . . . O my God I sign away baby . . . O Mary forgive me! But no . . . I stay in hospital three months . . . The baby not move . . . Every week . . . Scan . . . Scan . . . Scan . . . Back . . . front . . . side . . . Always same: "Assunta, your baby, it have no arms and no legs . . . " So comes time for baby to be born. The doctors say me, "Assunta, you want injection? . . . You not want to see baby? . . . " "*NO!*" I shout. "I want see baby . . . *MY* baby! I see my baby! . . . With my eyes! . . . ' So the baby come . . . And I look . . . And I see the little hand . . . My baby is normal! Normal . . . '

I am crying. I find it hard to cry, but I am crying.

'I look at doctor and I say, "You, you, you . . . you . . . you fuckin' bastard! You tell me my baby have no arms and no legs . . . " The doctor . . . he go away . . . I am happy . . . Happy, Bruce . . . So happy! . . . I hold my child . . . I thank the Virgin . . . I crying . . . So comes next morning . . . the nurses all around . . . I still crying . . . "Please, please tell doctor forgive what I say him . . . " The nurses say, "No, Assunta. You are right . . . All hospital know you right . . . " "But tell doctor forgive me!" I still crying . . . So comes the morning . . . The doctor, he knock my door . . . He bring *BIG* bouquet of flowers . . . I never saw flowers like . . . BIG, BIG coronations! . . . And big box chocolates and little clothes for my baby. He take my hand . . . He smile . . . "Assunta, you right to call me fucking bastard!"

1988

YOUR FATHER'S EYES
ARE BLUE AGAIN

My mother has come back from her cataract operation. For years she has felt hemmed in by the murk. The colours amaze her.

'Your father's eyes are blue again.'

My father has the most beautiful blue eyes I have ever seen in a man. I do not say this because he is my father. They are mariner's eyes, level and steady. On the Malta convoys they scanned the surface of the sea for mines, or the horizon for an enemy warship. They are the eyes of a man who has never known the meaning of dishonesty. They have never tempted him to anything mean or shoddy.

My mother's eyes are brown and lively, with suggestions of Southern ancestry.

When my mother, Margharita, was in hospital he found a photograph I had feared was lost. He had it taken at Hove in 1940 before going to sea. The photo shows the clear blue eyes, that can only be blue, gazing squarely at the camera from under the patent leather peak of his naval officer's cap. My mother kept it by her bedside. I would kiss it before going to bed. My first memory of him is on my third birthday, the 13th of May 1943. He took us bicycling near Flamborough Head, the grey Yorkshire headland that Rimbaud may have seen from a brig and put into his prose-poem *Promontoire*.

He rigged up an improvised saddle for me on his crossbar,

with stirrups of purple electric wire. I pointed to a squashed brown thing on the road.

'What's that, daddy?'

'I don't know.'

He did not want me to see something dead.

'Well, it looks to me like a piece of hedgehog.'

My father was not looking in the box of old photos for the one of himself, but for one of his father's yacht, the *Airey-mouse*. In the Twenties and Thirties my grandfather, a Bir-mingham lawyer, owned a vessel of legendary beauty. She was a teak, clipper-bowed ketch built at Fowey in Cornwall in 1898; she had once been rigged as a cutter. An aireymouse is a bat and, under her bowsprit, there was the figurehead of a bat with outstretched wings. The bat had disappeared by my father's day. *Aireymouse* had brown sails dyed with cutch-bark, a brass ship's bell, and a gold line from stem to stern.

My grandfather died in 1933, and *Aireymouse* had to be sold. She needed expensive repairs to her stanchions. Neither my father nor his brothers and sister could afford them. They sold her for £200. For my father alone it was the loss of a lover.

He had other boats — the *Nocteluca*, the *Dozmaree*, the *Nereid*, the *Sunquest* — but he shared them with others, and none matched the boat of his dreams.

I do not think he could bring himself to find out what had happened to *Aireymouse*. He heard rumours. In Guernsey a car had driven over the pier and landed on her deck — without doing too much damage. Or she was a rotting house-boat in the mud of a West Country creek. Or an incendiary bomb had hit her in the War. He came to accept that she was gone, but never quite believed it. On our sailing holidays we all believed that one golden evening, off Ushant or in the Race of Alderney, two sails would appear on the horizon and the ethereal craft would heave into view. My father would raise his binoculars and say the words he yearned to say: 'It's *Aireymouse*.'

He became resigned. My parents no longer went to sea.

They bought a camping van and travelled all over Europe. My father kept a sailor's log-book of their journeys, and read road-maps as if they were charts.

He had also dreamed of making one trade-wind passage to the West Indies. He never found the time to get away. Too many people depended on his legal advice. He would come home exhausted in the evenings after grappling with the problems of National Health Service hospitals. After his retirement, he had an arthritic hip and I feared he would go into decline. Once the operation had been performed, he was young again.

Four years ago my brother took him on the trade-wind passage. The boat was a modern yacht to be delivered to Antigua. But the owners had made her top-heavy with expensive junk. In a following sea, she did a fifty-degree roll and they had to turn back to the Cape Verde Islands. My father looked younger than ever after his adventure, but it was a disappointment.

Three days before Margharita went to hospital, he found himself talking on the phone to a man who said: 'I've been looking for you for a long time.' Was Charles Chatwin related to the pre-war owners of *Aireymouse*?

'I am,' said my father. 'She was our boat.'

'I've bought her,' the man said.

The man had found her up the River Dart. He fell in love with her and bought her. He took her to a yard in Totnes. The deck was gone. Many of the oak timbers were gone. But the teak hull was in perfect condition.

'I'm going to reconstruct her,' the man said. Could he count on Charles's help?

Charles will be eighty this year.

Let us pray he will sail on *Aireymouse*.

1988

2

STRANGE ENCOUNTERS

A COUP
A Story

The coup began at seven on Sunday morning. It was a grey and windless dawn and the grey Atlantic rollers broke in long even lines along the beach. The palms above the tidemark shivered in a current of cooler air that blew in off the breakers. Out at sea — beyond the surf — there were several black fishing canoes. Buzzards were circling above the market, swooping now and then to snatch up scraps of offal. The butchers were working, even on a Sunday.

We were in a taxi when the coup began, on our way to another country. We had passed the Hôtel de la Plage, passed the Sûreté Nationale, and then we drove under a limply-flapping banner which said, in red letters, that Marxist-Leninism was the one and only guide. In front of the Presidential Palace was a road-block. A soldier waved us to a halt, and then waved us on.

'Pourriture!' said my friend Domingo, and grinned.

Domingo was a young, honey-coloured mulatto with a flat and friendly face, a curly moustache and a set of dazzling teeth. He was the direct descendant of Francisco Felix de Souza, a Brazilian slave-dealer about whom I was writing a book.

Domingo had two wives. The first wife was old and the skin hung in loose folds off her back. The second wife was hardly more than a child. We were on our way to Togo, to watch a football game, and to visit his great-uncle who knew a lot of old stories about the slaver.

The taxi was jammed with football fans. On my right sat a very black old man wrapped in green and orange cotton. His teeth were also orange from chewing cola nuts, and from time to time he spat.

Outside the Presidential Palace hung an outsize poster of the Head of State, and two much smaller posters of Lenin and Kim Il Sung. Beyond the road-block, we took a right fork, on through the old European section where there were bungalows and balks of bougainvillaea by the gates. Along the sides of the tarmac, market-women walked in single file with basins and baskets balanced on their heads.

'What's that?' I asked. There was some kind of commotion, up ahead, towards the airport.

'Accident!' Domingo shrugged.

The women were screaming, and scattering their yams and pineapples, and rushing for the shelter of the gardens. A white Peugeot shot down the middle of the road, swerving right and left to miss the women, and then, we heard the crack of gunfire.

'C'est la guerre!' our driver shouted, and spun the taxi round.

'I knew it.' Domingo grabbed my arm. 'I knew it.'

The sun was up by the time we got to downtown Cotonou. In the taxi-park the crowd had panicked and overturned a brazier. A stack of crates had caught fire. A policeman blew his whistle and bawled for water. Above the rooftops, there was a column of black smoke, rising.

'They're burning the Palace,' said Domingo. 'Quick! Run!'

We ran, bumped into other running figures, and ran on. A man shouted, 'Mercenary!' and lunged for my shoulder. I ducked and we dodged down a sidestreet. A boy in a red shirt beckoned me into a bar. It was dark inside. People were clustered round a radio. Then the bartender screamed (wildly, in African) at me. And suddenly I was out again on the dusty red street, shielding my head with my arms, pushed and pummelled against the corrugated building by four hard, acridly-sweating men until the gendarmes came to fetch me in a jeep.

'For your own proper protection,' their officer said, as the handcuffs snapped around my wrists.

The last I saw of Domingo he was standing in the street, crying, as the jeep drove off, and he vanished in a clash of coloured cottons.

In the barracks guardroom a skinny boy, stripped to a pair of purple underpants, sat hunched against the wall. His hands and feet were bound with rope, and he had the greyish look Africans get when they are truly frightened. A gecko hung motionless on the whitewash. Outside the door there was a papaya with a tall scaly trunk and yellowing fruit. A mud-wall ran along the far side of the compound. Beyond the wall the noise of gunfire continued, and the high-pitched wailing of women.

A corporal came in and searched me. He was small, wiry, angular, and his cheekbones shone. He took my watch, wallet, passport and notebook.

'Mercenary!' he said, pointing to the patch-pocket on the leg of my khaki trousers. His gums were spongy and his breath was foul.

'No,' I said, submissively. 'I'm a tourist.'

'Mercenary!' he shrieked, and slapped my face — not hard, but hard enough to hurt.

He held up my fountain-pen. 'What?'

'A pen,' I said.

'What for?'

'To write with.'

'A gun?'

'Not a gun.'

'Yes, a gun!'

17

I sat on a bench, staring at the skinny boy who continued to stare at his toes. The corporal sat cross-legged in the doorway with his sub-machine-gun trained on me. Outside in the yard, two sergeants were distributing rifles, and a truck was loading with troops. The troops sat down with the barrels sticking up from their crotches. The colonel came out of his office and took the salute. The truck lurched off, and he walked over, lumpily, towards the guardroom.

The corporal snapped to attention, and pointed to me. 'Mercenary, Comrade Colonel!'

'From today,' said the colonel, 'there are no more comrades in our country.'

'Yes, Comrade Colonel,' the man nodded; but checked himself and added, 'Yes, my Colonel.'

The colonel waved him aside and surveyed me gloomily. He wore an exquisitely-pressed pair of paratrooper fatigues, a red star on his cap, and another red star in his lapel. A roll of fat stood out around the back of his neck, his thick lips drooped at the corners. He looked, I thought, so like a sad hippopotamus. I told myself I mustn't think he looks like a sad hippopotamus. Whatever happens, he mustn't think I think he looks like a sad hippopotamus.

'Ah, monsieur!' he said, in a quiet dispirited voice. 'What are you doing in this poor country of ours?'

'I came here as a tourist.'

'You are English?'

'Yes.'

'But you speak an excellent French.'

'Passable,' I said.

'With a Parisian accent I should have said.'

'I have lived in Paris.'

'I, also, have visited Paris. A wonderful city!'

'The most wonderful city.'

'But you have mistimed your visit to Benin.'

'Yes,' I faltered. 'I seem to have run into trouble.'

'You have been here before?'

18

'Once,' I said. 'Five years ago.'

'When Benin was Dahomey.'

'Yes,' I said. 'I used to think Benin was in Nigeria.'

'Benin is in Nigeria and now we have it here.'

'I think I understand.'

'Calm yourself, monsieur.' His fingers reached to unlock my handcuffs. 'We are having another little change of politics. Nothing more! In these situations one must keep calm. You understand? Calm!'

Some boys had come through the barracks' gate and were creeping forward to peer at the prisoner. The colonel appeared in the doorway, and they scampered off.

'Come,' he said. 'You will be safer if you stay with me. Come, let us listen to the Head of State.'

We walked across the parade-ground to his office where he sat me in a chair and reached for a portable radio. Above his desk hung a photo of the Head of State, in a Fidel Castro cap. His cheeks were a basketwork of scarifications.

'The Head of State', said the colonel, 'is always speaking over the radio. We call it the *journal parlé*. It is a crime in this country *not* to listen to the *journal parlé*.'

He turned the knob. The military music came in crackling bursts.

Citizens of Benin . . . the hour is grave. At seven hours this morning, an unidentified DC-8 jet aircraft landed at our International Airport of Cotonou, carrying a crapulous crowd of mercenaries . . . black and white . . . financed by the lackeys of international imperialism . . . A vile plot to destroy our democratic and operational regime.

The colonel laid his jowls on his hands and sighed, 'The Sombas! The Sombas!'

The Sombas came from the far north-west of the country. They filed their teeth to points and once, not so long ago, were cannibals.

'. . . launched a vicious attack on our Presidential Palace
. . .'

I glanced up again at the wall. The Head of State was a
Somba — and the colonel was a Fon.

'. . . the population is requested to arm itself with stones
and knives to kill this crapulous . . .'

'A recorded message,' said the colonel, and turned the
volume down. 'It was recorded yesterday.'

'You mean . . .'

'Calm yourself, monsieur. You do not understand. In this
country one understands nothing.'

Certainly, as the morning wore on, the colonel understood
less and less. He did not, for example, understand why, on the
nine o'clock communiqué, the mercenaries had landed in a
DC-8 jet, while at ten the plane had changed to a DC-7
turboprop. Around eleven the music cut off again and the
Head of State announced a victory for the Government
Forces. The enemy, he said, were retreating *en catastrophe* for
the marshes of Ouidah.

'There has been a mistake,' said the colonel, looking very
shaken. 'Excuse me, monsieur. I must leave you.'

He hesitated on the threshold and then stepped out into the
sunlight. The hawks made swift spiralling shadows on the
ground. I helped myself to a drink from his water-flask. The
shooting sounded further off now, and the town was quieter.
Ten minutes later, the corporal marched into the office. I put
my hands above my head, and he escorted me back to the
guardroom.

It was very hot. The skinny boy had been taken away, and on
the bench at the back sat a Frenchman.

Outside, tied to the papaya, a springer spaniel was panting
and straining at its leash. A pair of soldiers squatted on their
hams and tried to dismantle the Frenchman's shotgun. A third
soldier, rummaging in his game-bag, was laying out a few
brace of partridge and a guinea-fowl.

'Will you please give that dog some water?' the Frenchman asked.

'Eh?' The corporal bared his gums.

'The dog,' he pointed. 'Water!'

'No.'

'What's going on?' I asked.

'The monkeys are wrecking my gun and killing my dog.'

'Out there, I mean.'

'*Coup monté*.'

'Which means?'

'You hire a plane-load of mercenaries to shoot up the town. See who your friends are and who are your enemies. Shoot the enemies. Simple!'

'Clever.'

'Very.'

'And us?'

'They might need a corpse or two. As proof!'

'Thank you,' I said.

'I was joking.'

'Thanks all the same.'

The Frenchman was a water-engineer. He worked up-country, on Artesian wells, and had come down to the capital on leave. He was a short, muscular man, tending to paunch, with cropped grey hair and a web of white laugh-lines over his leathery cheeks. He had dressed himself *en mercenaire*, in fake python-skin camouflage, to shoot a few game-birds in the forest on the outskirts of town.

'What do you think of my costume?' he asked.

'Suitable,' I said.

'Thank you.'

The sun was vertical. The colour of the parade-ground had bleached to a pinkish orange, and the soldiers strutted back and forth in their own pools of shade. Along the wall the vultures flexed their wings.

'Waiting,' joked the Frenchman.

'Thank you.'

'Don't mention it.'

Our view of the morning's entertainment was restricted by the width of the doorframe. We were, however, able to witness a group of soldiers treating their ex-colonel in a most shabby fashion. We wondered how he could still be alive as they dragged him out and bundled him into the back of a jeep. The corporal had taken the colonel's radio, and was cradling it on his knee. The Head of State was baying for blood — '*Mort aux mercenaires soit qu'ils sont noirs ou blancs* . . . ' The urchins, too, were back in force, jumping up and down, drawing their fingers across their throats, and chanting in unison, '*Mort aux mercenaires! . . . Mort aux mercenaires! . . .* '

Around noon, the jeep came back. A lithe young woman jumped out and started screeching orders at an infantry platoon. She was wearing a mud-stained battledress. A nest of plaits curled, like snakes, from under her beret.

'So,' said my companion. 'The new colonel.'

'An Amazon colonel,' I said.

'I always said it,' he said. 'Never trust a teenage Amazon colonel.'

He passed me a cigarette. There were two in the packet and I took one of them.

'Thanks,' I said. 'I don't smoke.'

He lit mine, and then his, and blew a smoke-ring at the rafters. The gecko on the wall hadn't budged.

'My name's Jacques,' he said.

I told him my own name and he said, 'I don't like the look of this.'

'Nor I,' I said.

'No,' he said. 'There are no rules in this country.'

Nor were there any rules, none that one could think of, when the corporal came back from conferring with the Amazon and ordered us, also, to strip to our underpants. I hesitated. I was unsure whether I was wearing underpants. But a barrel in the small of my back convinced me, underpants or no, that my trousers would have to come down — only to find that I did, after all, have on a pair of pink and white boxer shorts from Brooks Brothers.

Jacques was wearing green string pants. We must have looked a pretty couple — my back welted all over with mosquito bites, he with his paunch flopping over the elastic — as the corporal marched us out, barefoot over the burning ground, and stood us, hands up, against the wall which the vultures had fouled with their ash-white, ammonia-smelling droppings.

'*Merde!*' said Jacques. 'Now what?'

What indeed? I was not frightened. I was tired and hot. My arms ached, my knees sagged, my tongue felt like leather, and my temples throbbed. But this was not frightening. It was too like a B-movie to be frightening. I began to count the flecks of millet-chaff embedded in the mud-plaster wall . . .

I remembered the morning, five years earlier, my first morning in Dahomey, under the tall trees in Parakou. I'd had a rough night, coming down from the desert in the back of a crowded truck, and at breakfast-time, at the café-routier, I'd asked the waiter what there was to see in town.

'Patrice.'

'Patrice?'

'That's me,' he grinned. 'And, monsieur, there are hundreds of other beautiful young girls and boys who walk, all the time, up and down the streets of Parakou.'

I remembered, too, the girl who sold pineapples at Dassa-Zoumbé station. It had been a stifling day, the train slow and the country burnt. I had been reading Gide's *Nourritures terrestres* and, as we drew into Dassa, had come to the line 'Ô cafés — *où notre démence s'est continuée très avant dans la nuit* . . .' No, I thought, this will never do, and looked out of the carriage window. A basket of pineapples had halted outside. The girl underneath the basket smiled and, when I gave her the Gide, gasped, lobbed all six pineapples into the carriage, and ran off to show her friends — who in turn came skipping

23

down the tracks, clamouring, 'A book, please? A book? A book!' So *out* went a dog-eared thriller and Saint-Exupéry's *Vol de nuit*, and *in* came the 'Fruits of the Earth' — the real ones — pawpaws, guavas, more pineapples, a raunch of grilled swamp-rat, and a palm-leaf hat.

'Those girls', I remember scribbling in my notebook, 'are the ultimate products of the lycée system.'

And now what?

The Amazon was squawking at the platoon and we strained our ears for the click of safety catches.

'I think they're playing games,' Jacques said, squinting sideways.

'I should hope so,' I muttered. I liked Jacques. It was good, if one had to be here, to be here with him. He was an old Africa hand and had been through coups before.

'That is,' he added glumly, 'if they don't get drunk.'

'Thank you,' I said, and looked over my shoulder at the drill-squad.

'No look!' the corporal barked. He was standing beside us, his shirt-front open to the navel. Obviously, he was anxious to cut a fine figure.

'Stick your belly-button in,' I muttered in English.

'No speak!' he threatened.

'I won't speak.' I held the words within my teeth. 'But stay there. Don't leave me. I need you.'

Maddened by the heat and excitement, the crowds who had come to gawp were clamouring, '*Mort aux mercenaires!* . . . *Mort aux mercenaires!*' and my mind went racing back over the horrors of Old Dahomey, before the French came. I thought, the slave-wars, the human sacrifices, the piles of broken skulls. I thought of Domingo's other uncle, 'The Brazilian', who received us on his rocking-chair dressed in white ducks and a topee. 'Yes,' he sighed, 'the Dahomeans are a charming and intelligent people. Their only weakness is a certain nostalgia for taking heads.'

No. This was not my Africa. Not this rainy, rotten-fruit Africa. Not this Africa of blood and slaughter. The Africa I loved was the long undulating savannah country to the north, the 'leopard-spotted land', where flat-topped acacias stretched as far as the eye could see, and there were black-and-white hornbills and tall red termitaries. For whenever I went back to that Africa, and saw a camel caravan, a view of white tents, or a single blue turban far off in the heat haze, I knew that, no matter what the Persians said, Paradise never was a garden but a waste of white thorns.

'I am dreaming,' said Jacques, suddenly, 'of perdrix aux choux.'

'I'd take a dozen Belons and a bottle of Krug.'

'No speak!' The corporal waved his gun, and I braced myself, half-expecting the butt to crash down on my skull.

And so what? What would it matter when already I felt as if my skull were split clean open? Was this, I wondered, sun-stroke? How strange, too, as I tried to focus on the wall, that each bit of chaff should bring back some clear specific memory of food or drink?

There was a lake in Central Sweden and, in the lake, there was an island where the ospreys nested. On the first day of the crayfish season we rowed to the fisherman's hut and rowed back towing twelve dozen crayfish in a live-net. That evening, they came in from the kitchen, a scarlet mountain smothered in dill. The northern sunlight bounced off the lake into the bright white room. We drank akvavit from thimble-sized glasses and we ended the meal with a tart made of cloudberries. I could taste again the grilled sardines we ate on the quay at Douarnenez and see my father demonstrating how his father ate sardines à la mordecai: you took a live sardine by the tail and swallowed it. Or the elvers we had in Madrid, fried in oil with garlic and half a red pepper. It had been a cold spring morning, and we'd spent two hours in the Prado, gazing at the Velasquezes, hugging one another it was so good to be alive: we had cancelled our bookings on a plane that had crashed. Or the lobsters we bought at Cape Split Harbour, Maine. There was a notice-board in the shack on the jetty and, pinned to it, a card on which a widow thanked her husband's friends for their contributions, and prayed, prayed to the Lord, that they lashed themselves to the boat when hauling in the pots.

How long, O Lord, how long? How long, when all the world was wheeling, could I stay on my feet . . . ?

How long I shall never know, because the next thing I remember I was staggering groggily across the parade-ground, with one arm over the corporal's shoulder and the other over Jacques's. Jacques then gave me a glass of water and, after that, he helped me into my clothes.

'You passed out,' he said.

'Thank you,' I said.

'Don't worry,' he said. 'They *are* only playing games.'

It was late afternoon now. The corporal was in a better mood and allowed us to sit outside the guardroom. The sun was still hot. My head was still aching, but the crowd had simmered down and fortunately, for us, this particular section of the Benin Proletarian Army had found a new source of amusement — in the form of three Belgian ornithologists, whom they had taken prisoner in a swamp, along with a Leica lens the shape and size of a mortar.

The leader of the expedition was a beefy, red-bearded fellow. He believed, apparently, that the only way to deal with Africans was to shout. Jacques advised him to shut his mouth; but when one of the subalterns started tinkering with the Leica, the Belgian went off his head. How dare they? How dare they touch his camera? How dare they think they were mercenaries? Did they look like mercenaries?

'And I suppose they're mercenaries, too?' He waved his arms at us.

'I told you to shut your mouth,' Jacques repeated.

The Belgian took no notice and went on bellowing to be set free. *At once! Now! Or else! Did he hear that?*

Yes. The subaltern had heard, and smashed his fist into the Belgian's face. I never saw anyone crumple so quickly. The blood gushed down his beard, and he fell. The subaltern kicked him when he was down. He lay on the dirt floor, whimpering.

'Idiot!' Jacques growled.

'Poor Belgium,' I said.

The next few hours I would prefer to forget. I do, however, remember that when the corporal brought back my things I cursed, 'Christ, they've nicked my traveller's cheques' — and Jacques, squeezing my arm very tightly, whispered, 'Now *you* keep your mouth shut!' I remember 'John Brown's Body' playing loudly over the radio, and the Head of State inviting the population, this time, to gather up the corpses. *Ramasser les cadavres* is what he said, in a voice so hoarse and sinister you knew a great many people had died, or would do. And I remember, at sunset, being driven by minibus to the Gezo Barracks where hundreds of soldiers, all elated by victory, were embracing one another, and kissing.

Our new guards made us undress again, and we were shut up, with other suspected mercenaries, in a disused ammunition shed. 'Well,' I thought, at the sight of so many naked bodies, 'there must be some safety in numbers.'

It was stifling in the shed. The other whites seemed cheerful, but the blacks hung their heads between their knees, and shook. After dark, a missionary doctor, who was an old man, collapsed and died of a heart-attack. The guards took him out on a stretcher, and we were taken to the Sûreté for questioning.

Our interrogator was a gaunt man with hollow temples, a cap of woolly white hair and bloodshot slits for eyes. He sat sprawled behind his desk, caressing with his fingertips the blade of his bowie-knife. Jacques made me stand a pace behind him. When his turn came, he said loudly that he was employed by such and such a French engineering company and that I, he added, was an old friend.

'Pass!' snapped the officer. 'Next!'

The officer snatched my passport, thumbed through the pages and began blaming me, personally, for certain events in Southern Africa.

'What are you doing in our country?'

'I'm a tourist.'

'Your case is more complicated. Stand over there.'

I stood like a schoolboy, in the corner, until a female sergeant took me away for fingerprinting. She was a very large sergeant. My head was throbbing; and when I tried to manoeuvre my little finger onto the inkpad, she bent it back double; I yelled 'Ayee!' and her boot slammed down on my sandalled foot.

That night there were nine of us, all white, cooped up in a ramshackle office. The President's picture hung aslant on a bright blue wall, and beside it were a broken guitar and a stuffed civet cat, nailed in mockery of the Crucifixion, with its tail and hindlegs together, and its forelegs splayed apart.

In addition to the mosquito bites, my back had come up in watery blisters. My toe was very sore. The guard kicked me awake whenever I nodded off. His cheeks were cicatrised, and I remember thinking how remote his voice sounded when he said, '*On va vous fusiller.*' At two or three in the morning, there was a burst of machine-gun fire close by, and we all thought, This is it. It was only a soldier, drunk or trigger-happy, discharging his magazine at the stars.

None of us was sad to see the first light of day.

It was another greasy dawn and the wind was blowing hard onshore, buffeting the buzzards and bending the coco palms. Across the compound a big crowd was jamming the gate. Jacques then caught sight of his houseboy, and when he waved, the boy waved back. At nine, the French Vice-Consul put in an appearance, under guard. He was a fat, suet-faced man, who kept wiping the sweat from his forehead and glancing over his shoulder at the bayonet points behind.

'Messieurs,' he stammered, 'this situation is perhaps a little less disagreeable for me than for you. Unfortunately, although we do have stratagems for your release, I am not permitted to discuss your liberty, only the question of food.'

'*Eh bien!*' Jacques grinned. 'You see my boy over there? Send him to the Boulangerie Gerbe d'Or and bring us sandwiches of jambon, paté and saucisson sec, enough croissants for everyone, and three petits pains au chocolat for me.'

'*Oui,*' said the Vice-Consul weakly.

I then scribbled my name and passport number on a scrap of paper, and asked him to telex the British Embassy in Lagos.

'I cannot,' he said. 'I cannot be mixed up in this affair.'

He turned his back, and waddled off the way he'd come, with the pair of bayonets following.

'Charming,' I said to Jacques.

'Remember Waterloo,' Jacques said. 'And, besides, you may be a mercenary!'

Half an hour later, Jacques's bright-eyed boy came back with a basket of provisions. Jacques gave the guard a sandwich, spread the rest on the office table, sank his teeth into a petit pain au chocolat, and murmured, '*Byzance!*'

The sight of food had a wonderfully revivifying effect on the Belgian ornithologist. All through the night the three had been weepy and hysterical, and now they were wolfing the sandwiches. They were not my idea of company. I was left alone with them, when, around noon, the citizens of France were set at liberty.

'Don't worry,' Jacques squeezed my hand. 'I'll do what I can.'

He had hardly been gone ten minutes before a big German, with a red face and sweeps of fair hair, came striding across the compound, shouting at the soldiers and brushing the bayonets aside.

He introduced himself as the Counsellor of the German Embassy.

'I'm so sorry you've landed in this mess,' he said in faultless English. 'Our ambassador has made a formal protest. From what I understand, you'll have to pass before some kind of military tribunal. Nothing to worry about! The commander is a nice chap. He's embarrassed about the whole business. But we'll watch you going into the building, and watch you coming out.'

'Thanks,' I said.

'Anyway,' he added, 'the Embassy car is outside, and we're not leaving until everyone's out.'

'Can you tell me what *is* going on?'

The German lowered his voice: 'Better leave it alone.'

The tribunal began its work at one. I was among the first prisoners to be called. A young zealot started mouthing anti-capitalist formulae until he was silenced by the colonel in charge. The colonel then asked a few perfunctory questions, wearily apologised for the inconvenience, signed my pass, and hoped I would continue to enjoy my holiday in the People's Republic.

'I hope so,' I said.

Outside the gate, I thanked the German who sat in the back of his air-conditioned Mercedes. He smiled, and went on reading the *Frankfurter Zeitung*.

It was grey and muggy and there were not many people on the street. I bought the government newspaper and read its account of the glorious victory. There were pictures of three dead mercenaries — a white man who appeared to be sleeping, and two very mangled blacks. Then I went to the hotel where my bag was in storage.

The manager's wife looked worn and jittery. I checked my bag and found the two traveller's cheques I'd hidden in a sock. I cashed a hundred dollars, took a room, and lay down.

I kept off the streets to avoid the vigilante groups that

roamed the town making citizens' arrests. My toenail was turning black and my head still ached. I ate in the room, and read, and tried to sleep. All the other guests were either Guinean or Algerian.

Around eleven next morning, I was reading the sad story of Mrs Marmeladov in *Crime and Punishment*, and heard the thud of gunfire coming from the Gezo Barracks. I looked from the window at the palms, the hawks, a woman selling mangoes, and a nun coming out of the convent.

Seconds later, the fruit-stall had overturned, the nun bolted, and two armoured cars went roaring up the street.

There was a knock on the door. It was the manager.

'Please, monsieur. You must not look.'

'What's happening?'

'Please,' he pleaded, 'you must shut the window.'

I closed the shutter. The electricity had cut off. A few bars of sunlight squeezed through the slats, but it was too dark to read, so I lay back and listened to the salvoes. There must have been a lot of people dying.

There was another knock.

'Come in.'

A soldier came into the room. He was very young and smartly turned out. His fatigues were criss-crossed with ammunition belts and his teeth shone. He seemed extremely nervous. His finger quivered round the trigger-guard. I raised my hands and got up off the bed.

'In there!' He pointed the barrel at the bathroom door.

The walls of the bathroom were covered with blue tiles, and on the blue plastic shower-curtain was a design of tropical fish.

'Money,' said the soldier.

'Sure!' I said. 'How much?'

He said nothing. I glanced at the mirror and saw the gaping whites of his eyes. He was breathing heavily.

I eased my fingers down my trouser pocket: my impulse was to give him all I had. Then I separated one banknote from the rest, and put it in his outstretched palm.

'*Merci, monsieur!*' His lips expanded in an astonished smile. '*Merci,*' he repeated, and unlocked the bathroom door. '*Merci,*' he kept repeating, as he bowed and pointed his own way out into the passage.

That young man, it struck me, had very nice manners.

The Algerians and Guineans were men in brown suits who sat all day in the bar, sucking soft drinks through straws and giving me dirty looks whenever I went in. I decided to move to the Hôtel de la Plage where there were other Europeans, and a swimming-pool. I took a towel to go swimming and went into the garden. The pool had been drained: on the morning of the coup, a sniper had taken a pot-shot at a Canadian boy who happened to be swimming his lengths.

The frontiers of the country were closed, and the airport.

That evening I ate with a Norwegian oil-man, who insisted that the coup had been a fake. He had seen the mercenaries shelling the Palace. He had watched them drinking opposite in the bar of the Hotel de Cocotiers.

'All of it I saw,' he said, his neck reddening with indignation. The Palace had been deserted. The army had been in the barracks. The mercenaries had shot innocent people. Then they all went back to the airport and flew away.

'All of it', he said, 'was fake.'

'Well,' I said, 'if it was a fake, it certainly fooled me.'

It took another day for the airport to open, and another two before I got a seat on the Abidjan plane. I had a mild attack of bronchitis and was aching to leave the country.

On my last morning I looked in at the 'Paris-Snack', which, in the old days when Dahomey was Dahomey, was owned by a Corsican called Guerini. He had gone back to Corsica while the going was good. The bar-stools were covered in red leather, and the barman wore a solid gold bracelet round his wrist.

Two Nigerian businessmen were seated at lunch with a pair of whores. At a table in the corner I saw Jacques.

'*Tiens?*' he said, grinning. 'Still alive?'

'Thanks to you,' I said, 'and the Germans.'

'*Braves* Bosches!' He beckoned me to the banquette. 'Very intelligent people.'

'*Braves* Bosches!' I agreed.

'Let's have a bottle of champagne.'

'I haven't got much money.'

'Lunch is on me,' he insisted. 'Pierrot!'

The barman tilted his head, coquettishly, and tittered.

'Yes, Monsieur Jacques.'

'This is an English gentleman and we must find him a very special bottle of champagne. You have Krug?'

'No, Monsieur Jacques. We have Roerderer. We have Bollinger, and we have Mumm.'

'Bollinger,' I said.

Jacques pulled a face: 'And in Guerini's time you could have had your oysters. Flown in twice a week from Paris . . . Belons . . . Claires . . . Portugaises . . . '

'I remember him.'

'He was a character.'

'Tell me,' I leaned over. 'What *was* going on?'

'Sssh!' His lips tightened. 'There are two theories, and if I think anyone's listening, I shall change the subject.'

I nodded and looked at the menu.

'In the official version,' Jacques said, 'the mercenaries were recruited by Dahomean émigrés in Paris. The plane took off from a military airfield in Morocco, refuelled in Abidjan . . . '

One of the whores got up from her table and lurched down the restaurant towards the Ladies.

''66 was a wonderful year,' said Jacques, decisively.

'I like it even older,' I said, as the whore brushed past, 'dark and almost flat . . . '

'The plane flew to Gabon to pick up the commander . . . who is supposed to be an adviser to President Bongo . . . ' He then explained how, at Libreville, the pilot of the chartered DC-8 refused to go on, and the mercenaries had to switch to a DC-7.

'So their arrival was expected at the airport?'

'Precisely,' Jacques agreed. 'Now the second scenario . . . '

The door of the Ladies swung open. The whore winked at us. Jacques pushed his face up to the menu.

'What'll you have?' he asked.

'Stuffed crab,' I said.

'The second scenario', he continued quietly, 'calls for Czech and East German mercenaries. The plane, a DC-7, takes off from a military airfield in Algeria, refuels at Conakry . . . you understand?'

'Yes,' I said, when he'd finished. 'I think I get it. And which one do you believe?'

'Both,' he said.

'That', I said, 'is a very sophisticated analysis.'

'This', he said, 'is a very sophisticated country.'

'I know it.'

'You heard the shooting at Camp Gezo?'

'What was that?'

'Settling old scores,' he shrugged. 'And now the Guineans have taken over the Secret Police.'

'Clever.'

'This is Africa.'

'I know and I'm leaving.'

'For England?'

'No,' I said. 'For Brazil. I've a book to write.'

'Beautiful country, Brazil.'

'I hope so.'

'Beautiful women.'

'So I'm told.'

'So what is this book?'

'It's about the slave-trade.'

'In Benin?'

'Also in Brazil.'

34

'*Eh bien!*' The champagne had come and he filled my glass. 'You have material!'

'Yes,' I agreed. 'I do have material.'

1984

THE LYMAN FAMILY
A Story

I have a friend called Jack who has been writing articles on the alternative society for the *Boston Globe*. Mel Lyman, who is, I believe, a scion of Old Boston, spent time in California as a guitarist. He has returned to his native city where, in the thrall of lysergic acid, he has persuaded himself and the 'Family' that he is Christ.

The Lyman Family publishes a broadsheet called *Avatar*. It usually contains a photo of the Saviour, with his triangular jaw and crooked grin, floating through the galaxies in the lotus position. Here are some specimens of his prose:

'I'm Christ. I swear to God, in person, and I'm about to turn this foolish world upside down.'

'I am here as the World Heart and I am not alone.'

'I am master of my own fate.'

'What they fail to realise is that the 20th-century Saviour is going to outfox them all — yes — he's going to crucify HIMSELF.'

He has also put out an album for children: 'Puff the Magic Dragon.'

I was a bit apprehensive about going to the Lyman Family. The Saviour is very shy and doesn't have any teeth at present. Besides, another friend who went there found his orange juice had been laced with LSD. He was taken into a 'sacrament chamber' where there was a light-show and stereophonic sound. At the end of the 'trip' the Saviour appeared in person.

You can see Roxbury Hill for miles because a tall monument crowns it, built to commemorate Boston's gallant defence against the British. A hundred years ago this was a fashionable neighbourhood: now it is in the black section. The houses of the Lyman Family adjoin an area of rough ground below the monument.

It was a windy winter afternoon. Smutty icicles hung from the eaves. All the doors and windows were boarded-up, and the doorbells ripped out. The garden was surrounded by a high wall, roughly built of re-used stone blocks, column bases, pilasters and fragments of decorative marble which the Family had looted from the grander houses of Roxbury Hill. The wall had the superficial appearance of an early Christian church built out of Roman ruins.

Jack led the way to a wooden trap-door in the garden. He hammered out a signal and it opened. We climbed down some steps, past the guard, into a subterranean passage. Arranged in a rack there was an arsenal of repeater rifles with telescopic sights. The passage took us into the nursery.

It was a warm and comfortable room, and small children were playing despondently on the floor. There were no toys. A mother-to-be in a cotton house-coat had spread herself on the stairs. She didn't move.

Jack showed me into the kitchen.

'Burgeoning domesticity,' he said. 'They do all their own woodwork.'

A small boy, about four or five, rushed in from another room and hugged my knees.

'Daddy,' he shouted, 'Daddee . . . !'

I unclasped his arms and knelt down.

'I'm not Daddy,' I said.

'Oh!' He walked away in silence.

'That child's drugged,' I said to Jack.

'Sure he's drugged,' he said.

On the wall there hung a poster of Charles Manson, in brilliant day-glo pink, with a lighted candle beneath it.

It was a Saturday, and on Saturdays the Lyman Family watches the ball game on television.

'They're all in Number 6,' volunteered the mother-to-be, and still she didn't move.

Jack and I, following the arrows as bidden, threaded our way along another underground passage and came up under the Viewing Room. We had arrived just in time for the opening of the Super Bowl game in the Tulane Stadium, New Orleans. On the screen the drum-majorettes were marching; the band played 'America, America', and the Lyman Family — thirty or more of them — sitting on a tier of benches — were bawling their heads off: 'America! America!'

When not used for viewing, the room converts into a school for children. Two charts plotted the axis of American History. The Stars and Stripes hung from the ceiling. The Third Coming was for white Anglo-Saxons only.

There were three televisions, one in colour. We sat on one of the benches.

'Who are you?' asked the boy on my left. He was in his late twenties, fair-haired with watery eyes and pimples.

'I'm from England,' I said. 'I've come with Jack here.'

'Who's Jack?' he said, disagreeably.

'He's a friend of Wayne.'

'Well, that's all right then.' He continued to munch his popcorn.

'Oh! I'm glad you're here right now,' he burst out abruptly. 'You've certainly picked the best time to be here. It's so beautiful when we're all together watching the ball game. You really get an idea how beautiful it is to live in a commune. I came back from Wisconsin for the ball game. I couldn't miss it. Man, I'm glad to be back. I am *certainly* glad to be back.'

The Saviour was sprawled over the biggest, plushest arm-chair like a movie mogul. An angular girl nestled her curls in his lap. From time to time he flicked himself into the lotus position on the wing of the chair. He operated the three TV sets with remote-control switches. He had scraped his hair forward to conceal the beginning of baldness.

A member of the Family complained he couldn't see the screen because the Saviour's reading-lamp was in the way.

'Too bad,' said the Saviour. 'I have to see to write. How about a beer everybody? How many beers in the fridge?'

'Zero beers,' a voice called from the back.

'Zero beers! Somebody's going to be sorry. Very sorry!'

On the Saviour's left there was a table cluttered with almanacs, note pads and a chart pinned to a board. Now and then he picked up the board and jotted down a few quick notes.

The Kansas City Chiefs were in red. The Family cheered wildly as they ran onto the field. The Minnesota Vikings were in white with rainbow stripes down the sides of their trousers. The Family cheered again.

The Saviour frantically scribbled notes and consulted the almanac. I noticed that the Family were focused on Him rather than on the ball game. It then dawned on me that this was some kind of divinatory exercise. He had consulted the horoscopes of all the players and would predict the result of the game. There seemed to be some significance as to who passed the ball to whom.

The Minnesota Vikings and the Kansas City Chiefs rambled about the field, which had been dyed mauve and yellow.

'I've had a wild conviction,' the Saviour screamed with prophetic fury. 'It just came to me. Minnesota will lead Kansas 13–10 in the first half.'

It soon became apparent that the wild conviction was misguided. The Minnesota Vikings failed to score but the Kansas City Chiefs scored with convincing regularity.

'It's that rule,' he shrieked. 'That damn rule! I've been hating that rule all season. I hate that rule. I HATE THAT RULE!

Why doesn't someone do something about it? It stops me getting through.'

Half-time was called: the Saviour was thoroughly depressed. Jack and I followed the Family members as they dispersed through the house. On the door of the community living room there was a notice. TAKE YOUR SHOES OFF. DON'T DIRTY THE CARPET.

The carpet was new and bright red. The walls were dark red, and the furniture dark, late nineteenth-century and art nouveau. The curly-headed blonde was scraping at the varnish of the dining-room table.

'What did I tell you?' Jack said. 'Home handicrafts.'

The Saviour and his bodyguard bore down on us and asked Jack, unpleasantly, why the hell he'd come back. He acknowledged the explanation and turned to me.

'Who's that?'

'An English friend of mine,' said Jack.

'What's his name?'

'Bruce.'

'What's your sign, Bruce?'

'Taurus.'

'Taurus? D'ya mean Taurus?'

'Yes. May 13.'

'You're a liar, Bruce.'

'I was born on May 13.'

'Look at him.'

The bodyguard, in a black sweat-shirt, flexed his biceps.

'He's Taurus. Now look at yourself. You're a wimp!'

I was very relieved when a big-breasted girl interrupted the interview.

'Where am I going to sit for my neck massage?' the Saviour asked.

'Here on the chaise-longue,' she answered sullenly and began the work.

In another room Jack and I talked to another of the girls. She said the Family were saving up to buy Him a new set of teeth:

'He lost his own set when he went on speed.

'A trip with Him', she droned on, 'is a very moving and beautiful experience. If you've never been on acid before, it would be that much more beautiful . . . and the most beautiful moment of all is when he rescues you . . . you then *know* he's the Saviour. And I used to think he was mad!'

'Let's get out of here,' I said to Jack.

I overheard three young men discussing guard duty — against the blacks.

One of them escorted us down the passage, opened the trap-door, and we were out in the cold.

The sun had left an afterglow and the buildings of downtown Boston were turning from ultramarine to black.

'Whew!' I inhaled the freezing air. 'Never again!'

From the *New York Times* the next day:

'Kansas City was all Chiefs and no Indians in the field today as the American League Champions upset the Minnesota Vikings 23–7 in the Super Bowl game at the Tulane Stadium.'

1988

UNTIL MY BLOOD IS PURE
A Story

There was another Englishman staying at the Hôtel Beau-regard. His khaki trousers were big in the seat and narrow at the ankles. He spent a lot of time talking to the boy at the reception desk. The boy wore a thick silver name-bracelet around his very slender wrist, and was acting coy.

The Englishman was writing a history of the German Colonial Empire. He had been investigating the activities of the Black African Nazi Movement, here in Douala, in the late Thirties. Black men in black shirts with red armbands and black swastikas. The idea made him very excited.

The owner of the hotel, Monsieur Anatole, was a man in his sixties who always wore a grey double-breasted suit and two-tone shoes. He was a member of the Bamiléké tribe. He also owned a fleet of taxis and the Confidence Trading Company. Monsieur Anatole had the idea of going to Rhodesia to fight for his black brothers. He told me he would go, personally, to Rhodesia, and thumped his hand hard on his chest, and held it there.

None of the waiters at the Hôtel Beauregard was a Bamiléké. But almost all the guests were.

They drove down from the hills in Monsieur Anatole's taxis, and came in powdered from head to foot with red dust. They made straight for the shower upstairs. When they came out, they were black and gleaming, and over the floor of the shower there was a thin layer of mud.

After dark they put on tight white shirts and bright blue suits and went up onto the roof to drink Monsieur Anatole's whisky. Later in the evening, they would lounge about the bar and look over the whores.

The other foreign guest was a Chinese who went everywhere clutching a black attaché case.

It was hot and airless in the bar. All the lights were red. The one white light came from the door leading into the hall, where the Englishman was still chatting to the receptionist. It was almost ten o'clock. The boy would soon be off duty.

A man beside me was pretending to read a newspaper, but the pages glowed red and the print was unreadable. Over the bar there was an advertisement for Guinness and a slogan: *Le Qualité de l'Homme Fait Son Trésor*. In the Republic of Cameroon Guinness is thought to be an aphrodisiac. The barmaid wore a green plastic harp in her hair.

The waiter had spilled a can of pineapple juice on the floor, the smell of pineapple mixed with the smell of disinfectant and the smell of Guinness and sweat. The seats were covered in warm red plastic. Your back stuck to it and came away with the sound of sticking-plaster.

Three Bamilékés came in with two girls and sat at the next table. Like most Bamilékés, they were big men with very round mouths. They were swimming in sweat. Grey patches gradually spread over their shirts. They ordered two beers and a whisky, and soft drinks for the girls.

The waiter moved clumsily. His arm muscles bulged out from under his shirt sleeves, and were netted with thick veins. He was a simple, placid boy and he smiled easily. He thought he had understood the order, but he came back and asked them to repeat it. One of the men went over it slowly, in French. His companion turned to me.

'*Lui,*' he pointed to the waiter. '*Lui, il ne comprend pas. Il est sous-developpé parce qu'il a été né dans la zone britannique.*'

The waiter came from West Cameroon, which was once a

British Protectorate.

His face puckered with furious concentration. He looked along his biceps muscle at the tray with empty glasses on it. Then he grinned. And the grin grew and grew and the red light caught his teeth and made them glow.

'Sir!' he said to me. 'Dis people dey be fashun no fine. Dey was fashun by de Frenchman and dey hab no mannars.'

There were five whores attached to Monsieur Anatole's hotel — five permanents with rooms of their own — and several transients who took their customers out with them. Four of the residents were thin, but Big Mary was the biggest whore I have ever seen.

Her shoulders heaved like a volcano when she laughed, and her smile lit up white and gold. She lumbered from table to table, wisecracking with the men, who creased up and cried out loud and hung onto their stomachs for laughing.

'That', said one of the Roundmouths, 'is the *première putain du Beauregard*.'

'So I see.'

'You like her?'

'Not for me.'

'Ha!' said Roundmouth, who, having discovered I didn't like fat women, assumed I did like thin women, and decided to take me in hand. He enumerated the charms of all present and selected for me a fifteen-year-old, all arms and legs in a dress of see-through pink. She sat alone in a corner, chewing something.

I walked over in her direction and pretended to take a look.

'Don't touch them, Sir!'

The Chinese was at my elbow.

'Don't touch them. There will be diseases.'

The girl sat up, interested, and looked me up and down with sad, amused eyes.

'*Qu'est-ce que c'est?*' She thumbed the Chinese.

'*C'est un Chinois.*'

'What she say?' asked the Chinese.

'She asked who you were and I said you were Chinese.'

'*Mais qu'est-ce que c'est?*'

'*Un Chinois,*' I repeated.

'*Chinois?*' she stuck out her lower lip. '*Connais-pas Chinois! C'est garçon ou fille ou quoi?*'

'*Garçon.*'

'*Et ce n'est pas beau,*' she said, definitely.

'Did she ask you?' asked the Chinese.

'For what?'

'Sexuality.'

'Not yet.'

'Don't touch her.' He clawed at my sleeve. 'I touch girl twice in life. Never touch girl again.'

'I won't touch her,' I said. 'I'm tired. I'm going to bed.'

It was equally hot at breakfast, although the fans in the restaurant were ruffling the grimy white curtains. The Chinese came in, smiled nervously and asked if he could sit at my table. He had on a freshly laundered shirt. His hair was slicked across his forehead. He put the attaché case on a free chair and ordered coffee and fried eggs.

He was tired, he said. He had worked all night on his order book. He was a travelling salesman from Hong Kong. Selling poplins was his family business and now it was bad business, because Hong Kong poplins were undercut by cheaper poplins from Colombia, North Korea, Poland and China.

'Bad situation,' he said. 'My poplin ten pence yard forty-eight inch wide and black man want pay seven half pence only. Not possible continue.'

He blinked through his horn-rimmed spectacles at the waiter who brought the eggs.

'Cameroonian people,' he whispered. 'Bad! All want is money. Money and not work. Black man not like yellow man.'

He reached for the tomato sauce bottle and unscrewed the lid. His hand was shaking.

45

'Yellow man not like black man,' he went on. 'Cameroon bad, but no so bad. Nigeria very bad! Bad trouble with customs. Customs officer make me pay on samples only and keep money for self.'

And it was sad and lonely, he said, alone in Africa, away from his family, so long away on the world tour. Married one year only, the wife and the mother living together, and the baby boy born two days before he left.

'She kill me,' he said.

He was close to tears. He held onto the sauce bottle. He had not poured from it and the eggs were going cold.

'My wife kill me if she find out.'

'Kill you?'

'I cannot return until my blood is pure. I not go with girls again. Not never. One emission only. One half minute only!'

'How long ago?'

'Five week.'

'In Douala?'

'In Fleetown. I have one friend in Fleetown. Nepalese. Also merchant. He giving drink. He getting girls. I write him what he has done.'

I asked for clinical details and, assuming a cheerful manner, assured him that syphilis in its primary stage was a complaint that well-travelled men, such as himself, took in their stride. A blood-test, a course of injections, another blood-test. The cure, I said, was final. No reason for his wife to find out. No reason why he shouldn't father lots more baby boys.

'All I want is certificate of pure blood.'

'You want a cure,' I said. 'A certificate is paper and syphilis is syphilis. You have been to a doctor?'

'He gave me paper of pure blood but the wound not go.'

'Who recommended him?'

'Confidence Trading Company. Give me no confidence at all! No confidence in African doctor. He take the money and the wound not go.'

46

'Some African doctors are excellent,' I said, 'but there are different kinds of doctor. I hope he gave you an injection?'

'He gave me remedies. Please, Sir! You come with me! You explain doctor. Speak French with him.'

We went out into the street. It was grey with the sky overcast. There were shabby concrete buildings, some limp-leaved trees coated with dust, tangles of electric wires and kite-hawks hovering over the refuse dumps. There were ash-grey puddles, iridescent at the edges, and pot-bellied children with green mucus round their noses. There were men going in and out of bars, and old women shuffling round shacks that had been bashed out of oil-drums. Near the railway station, the Chinese found the pharmacy of Dr Shere Malhalua Meji.

I looked at the billboard that advertised the doctor's Isis Pins and 'other celebrated remedies for modern men and women'.

We did not go to that doctor.

We turned up a tree-lined avenue, past the old Lutheran Cathedral, its granite tombs untended now; past the newer Catholic Cathedral; past houses with well-kept gardens and red front gates, and cafés with awnings and bookshops full of students. In the big shopping street, Germans were buying safari equipment and Belgian art dealers were buying old fetish figures, piled head first and feet first like the photos of bodies in Belsen. There were shop-signs announcing the latest imports — Belons, Camemberts, haricots verts — and in that street there were other kinds of doctor.

The Chinese winced when the doctor said how much the injection would cost. But I said something about secondary and tertiary stages and, in the end, he took it well, the injection and the payment. He was very methodical. He made notes in Chinese about the timing of future doses.

Afterwards, over coffee, he brightened up and talked about the baby boy. From Douala he was going to Yaoundé, and from Yaoundé to Bangui. Then he'd go downriver to Kinshasa and drive across Zaire by car. Zaire was a bad place.

47

Bad people and lions in jungle. I said he might have to watch for elephants on the road. The idea of elephants alarmed him, but somehow he'd get through to Lusaka, and up to Dar es Salaam, and along the coast to Mombasa and inland to Nairobi. Kenya was a not-so-bad place. Other Chinese merchants in Kenya. And from Nairobi he'd fly back home if, by that time, his blood was clean and pure.

1977

THE CHINESE GEOMANCER

The man I had arranged to meet was standing by one of the two bronze lions that snarl in the forecourt of the new Hongkong and Shanghai Bank. He wore a blue silk Nina Ricci tie, a gold wristwatch with a crocodile strap, and an immaculate worsted grey suit.

He handed me his card on which was written, in embossed letters:

LUNG KING CHUEN
Geomancer

Searching and fixing of good location for the burial of passed-away ancestors; surveying and arranging of good position for settling down business and lodging places, in which would gain prosperity and luck in the very near future

The building — to which workmen were adding the final touches — has forty-seven storeys (including the helipad on the roof) and stands on the site of the Bank's former Head Office — overlooking the Cenotaph, on the south side of Victoria Square. It is the work of the English architect, Norman Foster, and is, by any standards, an astonishing performance.

I heard the bank called, variously, 'The shape of things to come'; 'An act of faith in Hong Kong's future'; 'Something out of *Star Wars*'; 'A cathedral to money'; 'A maintenance nightmare', and 'Suicides' leap'.

Having exceeded its budget three times over, to the tune of $600 million U.S., the new Hongkong and Shanghai Bank has also earned the distinction of being the most expensive office block ever built.

Architecturally, I felt it was less a 'vision of the future' than a backward, not to say nostalgic look at certain experiments of the Twenties (when buildings were modelled on battleships, and Man himself was thought to be a perfectible machine): buildings such as the PROUNS of El Lissitzky; Vesnin's project for the offices of *Pravda* — the unrealised dreams of the Early Soviet Constructivists.

Mr Lung, on the other hand, is a modest practitioner of the venerable Chinese art of geomancy, or *feng-shui*. At the start of the project, the Bank called him in to survey the site for malign or demonic presences, and to ensure that the design itself was propitious. Whichever architect was chosen, there was bound to be some anxiety; for the Hongkong and Shanghai Bank is the pivot on which Hong Kong itself stands or falls. With 1997 in sight, prosperity and luck must either come 'in the very near future' — or not at all.

The afternoon was overcast and a sharp wind was blowing off the harbour. We rode the escalator to the first floor, and took shelter in the Cash Department. It was like entering a war-machine: the uniform grey, the absence of 'art', the low hum of computerised activity. It was also cold. Had the building been put up in Soviet Russia there would at least have been a touch of red.

Behind a gleaming black counter sat the tellers — unscreened and unprotected, since, in the event of a bank-raid, a kind of portcullis slices sideways into action, and traps the raiders inside. A few potted palms were positioned here and there, apparently at random.

I sat down on a slab of black marble which, in less austere surroundings, might have been called a banquette. Mr Lung was not a tall man. He stood.

Obviously, the surroundings were too austere for many of

the Bank's personnel, and already — in the executive suites on high — they had unrolled the Persian carpets, and secretaries sat perched on reproduction Chippendale chairs.

'This', Mr Lung began, in a proprietorial tone, 'is one of the Top Ten Buildings of the World. Its construction is particularly ingenious.'

'It is,' I nodded, glancing up at the cylindrical pylons and the colossal X-shaped cross-braces that keep the structure rigid.

'So first,' he continued, 'I would like to emphasise its good points. As far as *feng-shui* is concerned, the situation is perfect. It is, in fact, the best situation in the whole of Hong Kong.'

Feng-shui means 'wind-and-water'. From the most ancient times the Chinese have believed that the Earth is a mirror of the Heavens, and that both are living sentient beings shot through and through with currents of energy — some positive, some negative — like the messages that course through our own central nervous systems.

The positive currents — those carrying good '*chih*', or 'life force' — are known as 'dragon-lines'. They are thought to follow the flow of underground water, and the direction of magnetic fields beneath the Earth's surface.

The business of a geomancer is to make certain, with the help of a magnetic compass, that a building, a room, a grave or a marriage-bed is aligned to one or other of the 'dragon-lines' and shielded from dangerous cross-currents. Without clearance from a *feng-shui* expert, even the most 'westernised' Chinese businessman is apt to get the jitters, to say nothing of his junior staff.

At a lunch I happened to tell an 'old China hand', an Englishman, that the Bank had taken the advice of a geomancer.

'Yes,' he replied. 'It's the kind of thing *they* would believe in.'

Yet we all feel that some houses are 'happy' and others have a 'nasty atmosphere'. Only the Chinese have come up with cogent reasons why this should be so. Whoever presumes to mock *feng-shui* as a superstitious anachronism should recall its vital contribution to the making of the Chinese landscape, in which houses, temples and cities were always sited in harmony with trees and hills and water.

Perhaps one can go a step further? Perhaps the *rootedness* of Chinese civilisation; the Chinese sense of belonging to the Earth; their capacity to live without friction in colossal numbers — have all, in the long run, resulted from their adherence to the principles of *feng-shui*?

'Now it so happens,' Mr Lung said, 'that no less than five "dragon-lines" run down from The Peak and converge on the Central Business District of Hong Kong.'

We looked across the atrium of glass, towards the sky-scrapers of the most expensive patch of real estate in the world.

Some of the lines, he went on — not by any means all — were punctuated here and there with 'dragon-points' or 'energy-centres', like the meridian-points known to acu-puncturists: points at which a particularly potent source of *chih* was known to gush to the surface.

'And the site on which the bank stands', he added, 'is one of them. It is, in fact, the only "dragon-point" on the entire length of the line.'

Other lines, too, were known to have branches, like tap-roots, which tended to siphon off the flow of *chih*, and diminish its force.

'But this line', he said, 'has no branches.'

Yet another favourable point was the bank's uninterrupted view of the mountain. Had there been naked rocks or screes, they might have reflected bad *chih* into the building.

'But The Peak', he said solemnly, 'is covered in trees.'

Similarly, because the new building was set well back from the waterfront — and because the sun's course passed to landward — no malign glitter could rise up from the sea.

Mr Lung liked the grey colour which, he felt, was soothing

to the nerves. He also liked the fact that the building absorbed light, and did not reflect glare onto its neighbours.

I questioned him carefully on the subject of reflected glare, and discovered that glass-curtain-wall buildings which mirror one another — as they do in every American city, and now in Hong Kong — are, from a *feng-shui* point of view, disastrous.

'If you reflect bad *chih* onto your neighbours,' Mr Lung said, 'you cannot prosper either.'

He also approved of the two bronze lions that used to guard the entrance of the earlier building. During the War, he said, the Japanese had tried to melt them down:

'But they were not successful.'

I said there were similar lions in London, outside the Bank of England.

'They cannot be as good as these two,' he answered sharply: so sharply, in fact, that I forgot to ask whether the lions had been put away in storage three years ago, when Mrs Thatcher made her first, ill-informed foray into Chinese politics — and gave the Hong Kong Stock Exchange its major nervous breakdown.

The result, of course, was the historic slap from Deng Xiao-ping himself.

'So what about the bad points?' I asked Mr Lung.

'I'm coming to them now,' he said.

The Hong Kong waterfront was built on reclaimed land and there were stories . . . No. He could not confirm them but there were, nevertheless, stories . . . of sea-monsters and other local ghouls, who resented being dumped upon and might want to steal into the building.

This was why he had recommended that the escalator to the first floor — which was, after all, the main public entrance — should be so angled, obliquely, that it ran along a 'dragon-line'. The flow of positive *chih* would thus drive the demons back where they belonged.

Furthermore, since all good *chih* came from the landward, he had advised that the Board Room and Chief Executive offices should turn away from the sea: away, that is, from the view of Kowloon and the mountains of China; away from the cargo-ships, tugboats, ferries, drifters, coaling-barges, junks; away from the White Ensign, Red Ensign and that 'other' red flag — and turn instead to face the 'Earth Spirit' descending from The Peak.

The same, equally, applied to the underground Safe Deposit — which has the largest, circular, stainless-steel door ever made.

Finally, Mr Lung said, he had to admit there were a number of danger zones in the structure — 'killing-points' is what he called them — where, in order to counteract negative *chih*, it had been necessary to station living plants: a potted palm at the head of the escalator 'in case of a fall'; more potted palms by the lift-shafts; yet more palms close to the pylons to nullify the colossal downward thrust of the building.

'Right,' I said. 'I'd like to ask you one thing. I believe that "dragon-lines" never run straight, but are curved.'

'True,' he said.

'And isn't it also true that traditional Chinese buildings are almost always curved? The roofs are curved? The walls are curved?'

'Yes.'

Chinese architecture — like Chinese art, Chinese language and the Chinese character — abhors the rigid and rectilinear.

'Now, as a *feng-shui* man,' I persisted, 'how would you interpret this rigid, straight-up-and-down Western architecture? Would say it had good or bad *chih*?'

He blanched a little, and said nothing.

'These cross-braces, for example? Good or bad? Would you consider putting plants underneath them?'

'No,' he said, blandly. 'Nobody sits there.'

My question, I have to confess, was most unfair, for I had heard on the grapevine that the cross-braces were terribly bad *feng-shui*.

It was obvious I had overstepped the mark. At the mere

mention of cross-braces, Mr Lung moved onto the defensive. He back-pedalled. He smiled. He re-emphasised the good points, and glossed over the bad ones. He even left the impression that there were no bad ones.

At the foot of the escalator he shook my hand and said:

'I have done *feng-shui* for Rothschilds.'

1985

3

FRIENDS

GEORGE ORTIZ

For Olivier on his twenty-first birthday

Olivier, your father and I have known each other since I was eighteen and he was thirty-one and I always associate him with hilarious moments. None was more hilarious than our visit to the Soviet Union which coincided with your arrival.

You will have been told a thousand times how your great-grandfather was a Bolivian *hacendado*, who, one day, found two American trespassers with bags of mineral specimens on their backs. He locked them in a stable, thinking the minerals might be gold or silver. Finally they confessed the specimens were tin. That is one side of your family history.

In the spring, twenty-one years ago, your father learned that I had an official invitation to visit archaeological museums in the Soviet Union and also to meet Soviet archaeologists. The man who invited me I had met the year before in Sofia where I assured him that a treasury supposed to have been found at Troy was either a fake or a fake on paper. The rest of the party was to include my professor of archaeology and a lady Marxist archaeological student from Hampstead.

We met in Leningrad. G.O. was Doctor O of the Basel Museum. For the first days he behaved like Dr O. He listened patiently — although he nearly exploded afterwards — to the rantings of an orthodox Marxist archaeologist. The museum impressed him greatly. He saw Greek objects, but he saw objects he had never seen before, treasures from the frozen tombs of Siberia, objects from the Siberian taiga.

On our last day in Leningrad we had an interview with the Deputy Director of the Hermitage Museum. The Director himself was away in Armenia excavating the site of Urartu. It would not be fair to say that your father only reached the door handle, but he is not a tall man, and the space suited him ideally. We were, after all, in the Tsar's reception room. The Deputy Director greeted us with great kindness, but was plainly shocked by his previous visitor. As we entered a notorious pedlar of fakes from Madison Avenue went out. He had told the Deputy Director, in the name of his own foundation for the investigation of forgeries, that the celebrated Peter the Great Gold Treasure had been made by a jeweller in Odessa in 1898. Your father rose to the occasion and assured the man that his visitor had been a complete fraud. He then got carried away. The mask of Dr O vanished. He said, 'This is the greatest museum in the world, right? I am the greatest collector of Greek bronzes in the world. If I leave you my collection in my will, will you appoint me Director of this museum for a number of years?'

We went on to Moscow and stayed at the Metropol Hotel. Dr O reasserted his identity. Again, in the Russian Historical Museum, he saw objects he had never dreamed of. We went to a reception to meet seventy Soviet scholars and had to stand in line having our hands crushed. Our host, the top archaeologist of the Soviet Union and my friend from Sofia, was there to greet us. By the window, G.O. and I saw a pair of very cheerful figures looking at us with amusement. I said, 'One is an Armenian, the other a Georgian.' When our fingers stopped being crushed, we went over to these two gentlemen. I was right about the Armenian. The other, with a huge black moustache, was a Greek from Central Asia. I asked what they were laughing about. They said they had just been paid for their doctoral thesis and were deciding if they had enough money to go to the Moscow food market and buy a whole sheep for a barbecue.

G.O. passed the test of being a great Greek scholar. On our last evening in Moscow we were invited by the top archaeologist himself to an Uzbeg banquet. The only dish was a lamb stuffed with rice, apricots and spices. The whole party became extremely drunk on wine, on champagne and, worst of all, on brandy. I was very drunk myself, but threw every second glass on to the floor. The Soviet academicians went under the table one by one. G.O., the Marxist lady archaeologist and the professor went off to the lavatory and were sick. The top archaeologist, in a steel-grey suit, was drunk and the only survivor except for his sister, who did not drink. She asked me to recite speeches from Shakespeare. I stood up: 'If music be the food of love, play on. Give me excess of it.

> That surfeiting, the appetite may
> Sicken and so die.
> That strain again.
> It had a dying fall.
> It came o'er mine ears like the sweet
> Smell that breathes upon a bank of violets . . .
> The quality of mercy is not changed . . .
> I come to wive it wealthily in Padua,
> If wealthily then happily in Padua . . .
> Once more unto the breach,
> Dear friends, once more, or close the
> Wall up with our English dead. In
> Peace there's nothing so becomes
> A man as modest stillness and humility:
> But when the blast of war blows in our
> Ears then summon up the action of a tiger.
> Stiffen the sinews, summon up the flood.
> Disguise fair nature with hard bitten rage . . . '

The top archaeologist finally went under the table like a grey sea-lion who could stand the open air no longer. It was time to go. The Western party had revived. I was still very drunk.

In Moscow it was the time of white nights. A large Volga limousine taxi appeared to be waiting for us. We drove back to the hotel. I lay down on the bed which was furthest from the bathroom. 'You were wonderful,' said your father. 'You showed them what Englishmen are made of.'

'Look, I'm going to be sick. Get the woman to bring a basin.'

'Now I know why England won the war.'

'Get me a basin, quickly!'

'Do you think I should send my son to Eton?'

'Watch out,' I cried — and a column of vomit fell diagonally across his bed.

'Look what you've done to my Charvet dressing-gown!'

I think this was the end of the Soviet Union for your father. He survived a day in Kiev but his thoughts were on Catherine and your birth. I feel I should record this on paper and offer it to you as a twenty-first birthday present.

1988

KEVIN VOLANS

In the summer of 1986 I completed my book *The Songlines* under difficult conditions. I had in fact picked up a very rare fungus of the bone-marrow in China. Certain I was going to die, I decided to finish the text and put myself into the hands of doctors. My work would then be done.

The last third of the manuscript was a commonplace book of quotations and vignettes intended to back up the main line of argument. I put this into shape on sweltering summer days, wrapped in shawls, shivering with cold in front of the kitchen stove. It was a race for time.

The Songlines starts with an investigation into the labyrinth of invisible pathways which Australian Aboriginals call the 'Footprints of the Ancestors' or 'The Way of the Law'. Europeans know them as 'Songlines' or 'Dreaming Tracks'.

Aboriginals believe that the totemic ancestor of each species creates himself from the mud of his primordial waterhole. He takes a step forward and sings his name, which is the opening line of a song. He takes a second step which is a gloss on the first line and completes the linked couplet. He then sets off on a journey across the land, footfall after footfall, singing the world into existence: rocks, escarpments, sand-dunes, gum trees and so on.

I hoped to use this astonishing concept as a springboard from which to explore the innate restlessness of man.

I made a miraculous recovery. The book came out in June 1987. On the day of publication there was a French air controllers' strike and we had to cross the Channel by hover-craft. We were four hours late. I promised myself *not* to buy the newspapers and read the reviews. I relented and bought the *Independent*: I think I am quoting the reviewer correctly by saying he found my work 'unbearably pretentious'.

We took the slow train from Boulogne to Paris. On the seat behind, two musicians were working on a score. Their instruments were on the rack above their heads. They were Rostropovic and Anne-Sophie Mutter. It was a good omen.

The book did well. When it appeared on top of the bestseller list, I had a crisis of confidence. Had I at last joined the trash artists?

Early on I saw it was useless to lay down the law on a subject so tenuous and decided to write an imaginary dialogue in which both narrator and interlocutor had the liberty to be wrong. This was a difficult concept for English-speaking readers. I had a running battle as to whether the book should be classified as fiction or non-fiction. 'Fiction,' I insisted. 'I made it up.' A Spanish reviewer had no such difficulty. A *libro de viaje* was a travel book and a *novela de viaje* . . . there was *Don Quixote*.

Understandably, the academics were cautious. But I refused to budge from the basic tenets I aired in the book:

As a South African palaeontologist, Dr Elizabeth Vruba, said to me, 'Man was born in adversity. Adversity, in this case, is aridity.' *Homo sapiens* evolved once and once only, in Southern Africa sometime after the First Northern Glaciation (*circa* 2,600,000 years ago), when the North Pole formed, the sea level fell, the Mediterranean became a salt lake and the mixed South African forest gave way to open savannah scrub.

Homo sapiens was migratory. He made long seasonal journeys interrupted by a phase of settlement, a 'lean season' like Lent.

The males of *Homo sapiens* were hunters and the women were gatherers of vegetable food and small game. But the function of their journeys was to make friendly contact with neighbours near and far. Men talk their way through the problem of inbreeding. Animals fight to achieve this.

Man is 'naturally good' in Rousseau's sense and the sense of the New Testament. There is no place for evil in evolution.

The fighting impulse in men and women was designed as a protection from wild beasts and other terrors of the primeval bush. In settlement these impulses tend to get thrown out of gear. Compare the story of Cain the settler and Abel the wanderer.

Man is a talking creature, a singing creature. He sings and his song echoes up and down the world. The first language was in song. Music is the highest of the arts.

There is no contradiction between the Theory of Evolution and belief in God and His Son on earth. If Christ were the perfect instinctual specimen — and we have every reason to believe He was — He must be the Son of God. By the same token, the First Man was also Christ.

I had many letters from readers of *The Songlines*. Occasionally the morning post would throw up some miraculous treasure. A lady from Connecticut sent me a photostat from Anne Cameron's *Daughters of the Copper Woman* in which an old Nootka woman describes how her forebears would navigate their ocean-going canoes.

The Nootka, the Bela Coola, the Haida and the Kwakiutl were technically in the hunting and gathering stage but the sea so teemed with salmon and the forests with game that they settled in large timber houses and had classes of nobles, workers and slaves.

This is the text of the steerswoman:

'Everythin' we ever knew about the movement of the sea was preserved in the verses of a song. For thousands of years we went where we wanted and came home safe because of the song. On clear nights we had the stars to guide us and in the fog we had the streams and creeks that flow into and become Klin Otto . . . '

Klin Otto was the salt water current that ran from California to the Aleutian Islands.

'There was a song for goin' to China and a song for goin' to Japan, a song for the big island and a song for the smaller one. All she had to know was the song and she knew where she was. To get back, she just sang the song in reverse . . . '

One morning last February, during a very bad bout of malaria, the post brought a most intriguing letter from a South African composer I had never heard of: Kevin Volans.

'I have been meaning to write to you for some time, but the temptation of adding some presumptuous invitation . . . to come with me on a recording trip to Lesotho . . . held me back.'

His titles were wonderful: White Man Sleeps, She Who Sleeps with a Small Blanket, Cover him with Grass, Studies in Zulu History, Kneeling Dance, Leaping Dance, Hunting; Gathering.

I was too feverish to play Volans's tape at once but finally summoned the strength to put it on the tape deck. It was a dazzling, frosty day and my bedroom, with its white walls and white Venetian blinds, was slatted with sunlight. I was boiling hot. I lay back and could not believe my ears. I was listening to 'White Man Sleeps' scored for two harpsichords, viola da gamba and percussion. It was a music I had never heard before or could have imagined. It derived from nothing and no one. It had arrived. It was free and alive. I heard the sounds of thorn-scrub Africa, the insects and the swish of wind through grass. But there was nothing that would have been foreign to Debussy or Ravel.

I called him up in Belfast where he was Composer-in-Residence at Queen's University. Mine was the first call on his new answering-machine. Within a very few days he was at my bedside. I had a friend for life.

Kevin comes from Pietermaritzburg, the most English city in South Africa, and is thirty-eight years old. His parents owned a dry-cleaning business. When he was ten his mother bought a piano. By the time he was fourteen he was playing Lizst's Piano Concertos and wanted to be a concert pianist. He was terrorised by the other boys on the school bus, and would walk home in temperatures of 105°, in a black flannel blazer, grey flannel trousers, spit-and-polished shoes and a boater hat. On the way he passed Africans sheltering under the trees, hearing the people's song, guitar music and work of rhythms.

He went to Johannesburg to study Western music without yet being aware that he loved the sounds of Africa.

He came to Europe in 1973 and studied with Karlheinz Stockhausen, later becoming his teaching assistant. He studied piano with Aloys Kontarsky and music theatre with Mauricio Kagel. He began to realise that what distinguished African music from European (except perhaps for early music like that of Hildegard of Bingen) was its unawareness of proportion. African music is not deliberately asymmetric, it has no precise proportions: patterns are created by addition, not subdivision. In many cases repetition is not perceived. The music ends as abruptly as it begins, like birdsong. No rhythm is arrived at by calculation — Stockhausen calculates everything.

Arriving fresh from a field trip in the mountains of Lesotho, Kevin made straight for a Cologne première by the German composer and was struck by the conviction that the language of serialism was dead. Western music was always architectural: he wanted a music in which the roof floated free.

Kevin had two colleagues, Walter Zimmerman, the son of a Nuremberg baker, and Clarence Barlow, who was born in Calcutta.

They decided to return home and investigate the relation of music to its geographical source. This was not shopping around the world of ethnomusicology. Zimmerman produced what he called *Lokale Musik*, with the implication that the local was the universal: he composed a series of works which would define aspects of his tradition. One of these was an orchestral work in which he mapped features of his native landscape onto the orchestration of some two hundred rustic waltzes (*Ländlertopographien*).

Clarence Barlow came back from Calcutta with a twenty-four-hour cycle of street-sounds, and an analysis of harmonic and rhythmic consonance and dissonance in Indian music.

Kevin made several recording trips to Southern Africa. He began with street-music and immediately realised it was far more interesting than any ideas about it. Zulu guitar music is not only used as an accompaniment to long walking journeys, but as a means of making friends and working out social tensions: in what appears to be ritualised aggression, Zulu guitar players engage in a musical substitute for stick fighting. The two players will meet and one of them will say, 'You stab first.' The songs always include elaborate introductory flourishes and praise-poetry is recited at high speed over the guitar ostinato.

'Studies in Zulu History' began as an attempt to record the great Afrikaner festival at the church where King Dingaan killed the Boer leader, Piet Retief, a founder of Pietermaritzburg. On a day known as the Day of the Covenant a Boer massacre of the Zulus is remembered annually.

Kevin saw the faces of the congregation and got cold feet. It was midday, he wandered off into the veld and recorded the prehistoric sounds of insects, the heat rising and an occasional bird. He took the tape back to Europe and spent three years on and off in the Cologne studios making an electronic replica.

'Cover him with Grass' is derived from Basotho work-sounds in which old men split a log, children shout and women sing as they throw chips of stone while road-building.

'KwaZulu Summer Landscape' is an extended composition of natural sounds collected on a return trip.

These tape pieces serve as a curtain raiser to a long series of instrumental works which aim at reconciling African and European aesthetics. Islam tends to introduce new techniques to its converts, Christianity brings new objects. In the predominantly Christian South the musical techniques remain traditional, the instruments imported. Kevin chose to make an inverse assault on European music, bringing new techniques from the South and adapting existing instruments and forms: the harpsichord, the flute, the string quartet. He avoided exotica.

On returning from Africa he was bitterly disappointed to discover he was neither African nor European. Soon he realised that he was free, free to compose whatever he wanted. There is a Sufi saying, 'Freedom is absence of choice'. I believe this to be devotional music of the highest order. For me, Kevin is one of the more inventive composers since Stravinsky.

'The Songlines', his fourth string quartet, will be given its première by Kronos at the Lincoln Center in November

1988

HOWARD HODGKIN

Howard Hodgkin is an English painter whose brilliantly coloured and basically autobiographical pictures, done both with bravura and with anxiety, fall into none of the accepted categories of modern art.

He decided to become a painter at the age of seven and, by seventeen, had painted the one particular picture that set the seal on his later development. Now approaching fifty, he is a short, greying, big-boned man, often very red in the face, who can look positively seraphic, yet says he is afraid of looking ugly. His mouth can be tight, or sensual. You are captivated by his smile, or frozen by it. When walking down a street, he lets his arms swing loose and gives the impression of butting into a whirlwind. A brush with death, some years ago, has left him calmer, but more likely to swerve off on unexpected tangents. He longs for acclaim, and for oblivion. He is planning to live in beautiful rooms, yet seems far happier to be surrounded by builder's rubble. I have known him — and quarrelled with him — for twenty years. He is one of my best friends.

He comes from an upper-middle-class family of well-ordered minds and well-furnished houses. The Hodgkins are one of those puritanical, public-spirited dynasties that constitute, for Noel Annan, 'the intellectual aristocracy of England'. Among his eighteenth-century ancestors is the 'Father of Meteorology', who coined new names for clouds. A nineteenth-century Hodgkin discovered Hodgkin's disease (of the spleen and lymphatic glands); a twentieth-century cousin shared the Nobel Prize for Medicine. One Hodgkin was a famous grammarian; another wrote the standard history of the Anglo-Saxons. Among their relatives were the critic Roger Fry and the poet Robert Bridges. Howard's grandfather, Stanley Hodgkin, owned an engineering works that manufactured a pump called 'The Pulsometer'. His father was an obsessive collector of alpine plants who found, in his rock garden, a relief from the tedium of his job in Imperial Chemicals.

Such are the sources of his ambition and a certain taste for public honours. The rest is not quite so straightforward.

The experiences of his childhood seem to have given that ambition a rather unusual twist. He can remember, for example, floating in an enormous blue bath in a hotel in Cologne, and a picture of the Führer in the dining-room. He can remember a summer holiday in Carinthia around the time of the Anschluss, his German nanny flaunting a Nazi flag on her table, and the village boys who dumped her in the swimming-pool. He can remember, too, the day that Florence Hodgkin, his eccentric Irish grandmother, appeared in a black suit with a green hat, green artificial flowers, green blouse, green shoes, green umbrella, green bottles of champagne and a lot of green-wrapped presents in a green carrier bag. Black and green is still one of his favourite colour combinations and could – at a pinch – be his 'madeleine'. Only the other day he told me that the glossy green paint of his London flat made him feel 'secure' – and that the furniture was to be black.

Florence Hodgkin encouraged his childhood mania for collecting antiques; in 1938 she had already written a horoscope for the little boy born under the 'Royal Sign of Leo'. 'For Leos', she prophesied, 'colour is life.' She also predicted that her grandson would have a 'marvellous faculty for presenting facts in a new light', and would be 'immovable in his opinions'. The horoscope ended with a list of other Leos that included Julius Caesar, Napoleon, Mussolini, Alexander

71

the Great, Rembrandt, Henry Ford and Mae West.

In 1940 Howard was evacuated to the United States. He stayed at Long Island, in a Georgian house where the walls were covered with painted mock coromandel canvas, all very different to the formalised gloom of the Hodgkin houses in England. The sights of New York dazzled him and were registered, unforgettably, on his retina. His colour sense was Americanised. He went to Coney Island, and to the Museum of Modern Art where he trembled before the Matisses. At school he sang the 'Star-Spangled Banner' and 'America the Beautiful'. The other school kids were so beautiful they made him feel gauche and uncomfortable. When the war was over, and the time came to leave, America was still a Paradise, and England, quite definitely, the Fall.

He went to Eton, which he detested. Yet the result could have been much worse were it not for the art master, Wilfred Blunt, who encouraged him to paint 'imitation Fauves' and opened his eyes to the exotic, exquisite world of Rajput and Mughal miniatures. He seems to have understood, even then, that the Indian artists' sense of colour and composition offered a way out of the muddy impasse of most English painting. He dreamed of making a collection of Indian paintings for himself − and picked up one or two.

At fifteen, floundering in emotional turmoil, he prevailed on a psychiatrist to let him go back to Long Island. All that summer, under the influence of Vuillard, of Matisse, of Stuart Davis, of Egon Schiele and of erotic Indian miniatures − yet in a manner entirely his own − he painted the picture called *Memoirs*:

A woman − or rather a woman from the neck down − is seen reclining on a white sofa, dressed of course in black and green, with red-lacquered talons and a big diamond ring. The walls and carpet are red; the artist himself, wearing yellow trousers, and looking a bit like an adolescent Eric von Stroheim, has fixed his hallucinated stare (for this is an 'Artist and Model' composition in which the artist simply stares and memorises) on a point midway between the sitter's diamond and her décolletage.

To this theme — of figures in a room where something momentous or erotic may, or may not, happen — Howard has returned again and again. It's nice to think that, in a recent series of pictures, the artist no longer gawks at the model; instead something both momentous *and* erotic is actually going on — a happier change from the very 'black' lithographs of the seventies where the model appears to be confined to the room, ensnared within the hermetic interior.

After returning from America, he did not go back to Eton, but to Bryanston School, which has a better record for coping with 'artistic' cases. He lived with his house master, who was a friend of Auden: the art master was a pacifist and world authority on Victorian furniture. Howard spent his spare time rummaging in the antique shops and, one day, bought for five pounds a black bronze vase that came from the Golden Drawing Room at Carlton House. For a time he kept this treasure in his room with a length of purple velvet tucked up behind it. Then he decided to sell it and run away to Paris and be a painter.

He did not go to Paris. Instead, in a pair of white sandals and with a veneer of studied Bohemianism, he enrolled as a student at the Camberwell School of Art. One day, he summoned up the courage to show *Memoirs* to the Principal, who pronounced it 'a load of rubbish' — a painting so perverse he couldn't understand how it had come to be painted.

There followed a sullen, solitary battle. To the boy who had breathed the air of excellence in the Museum of Modern Art, the insularity and 'know-all' attitudes of the English were insufferable. His comforts, in London, were few. There was a Braque exhibition; he combed through Alfred Barr's book on Matisse; and there were rumours of a new school of painting in New York. The one memorable break was a visit to a house in the Highlands where Royal French furniture glittered in the northern sunlight.

On quitting Camberwell, he taught painting, first at Charterhouse School, and then at Lord Methuen's Academy at Corsham, where at least the surroundings were distinguished. He married, bought a house in London, and had two sons. He continued to paint, secretly and in anguish. His artist friends felt the force of his personality, but few had the faintest idea of what he was up to. Then, in 1959, he met a hypnotic personality named Cary Welch — a meeting which, he says, 'changed the course of my life'.

Cary Welch came from a well-to-do family from Buffalo, New York. Whilst at Harvard he conceived a passion for Indian and Persian miniatures. Against all advice he set about sinking a fair proportion of his inheritance buying them. The fact that this collection would drastically appreciate in value was incidental, and, at the time, far from certain: it was a copy-book case of not burying one's talents.

Welch and his wife came to live in London because, as a legacy of the Raj, the best public collections of Indian paintings were in England, and because you could still find paintings, cheaply, in private hands. Howard was overwhelmed by the onrush of Yankee enthusiasm and, perhaps, by a touch of envy for his new friend's entrepreneurial skills. First, he accepted all Cary's judgments; only later, as his confidence grew, did he discover that he liked a different kind of painting.

The upshot of the meeting was that Howard's hunting instincts were thoroughly aroused. He bought, sold and traded; he perfected the tactics of the bazaar; and for over ten years he channelled about half his creative energies into his collection.

Most painters collect works of art and some of them, like Degas, collect great works of art. Usually the collection serves the artist as an *aide-mémoire* and a confirmation of his own identity. Sometimes the artist's collection seems to appear of its own accord, simply because he has an eye, a bank account, a certain standing with the dealers, or something to swap with another artist friend. But in the case of Howard Hodgkin, none of this is true. I can think of no successful artist whose impulse to paint pictures is rivalled by an impulse to buy another kind of picture. His collection is an essential part of his life's work. Any retrospective exhibition of Howard's own paintings would, in my opinion, be incomplete without the Indian collection hanging beside them — though having once made a purchase, he has an equally strong impulse to hide it, to lend it, or at least to get it out of his sight.

After his first exhibitions at the Tooth Gallery, critics were quick to point out the formal similarities between the art of Mughal and Rajput India and his own. And they were right. But I have sometimes thought that Howard's pictures are a declaration of war against his Indian ones. He is obscure where they are explicit. He is mute where they tell a story. He fudges where they are finicky. His colours are deliberately jarring where theirs seek to soothe. Perhaps it's a case of renouncing the thing you love? Perhaps his 'walloped-down' pictures can be seen as an act of total renunciation.

I first made friends with Howard in the early Sixties; and happened to come in useful.

I knew a man in France, who knew a woman in Switzerland, who was the widow of a famous German scholar of Islamic art, who owned a great masterpiece of Indian painting. It was a page — perhaps the most beautiful page — of the Hamza-Nama, a colossal manuscript done for the Emperor Akbar around 1580. Howard lusted after it — the word is not too strong — and with a bit of juggling, he got it, though not before he had hocked off several lesser masterpieces.

At the time, I lived in a flat behind Hyde Park Corner which, he recalls, was the 'most dandyish interior I had ever seen'. I had recently come back from a desert journey in the Sudan and the sitting room had a monochromatic desert-like atmosphere and contained only two works of art — the arse of an archaic Greek marble *kouros*, and an early seventeenth-century Japanese screen. One evening, the Hodgkins and the

Welches came to dinner, and I remember Howard shambling around the room, fixing it in his memory with the stare I came to know so well.

The result of that dinner was a painting called *The Japanese Screen* in which the screen itself appears as a rectangle of pointillist dots, the Welches as a pair of gunturrets, while I am the acid green smear on the left, turning away in disgust, away from my guests, away from my possessions, away from the 'dandified' interior, and possibly back to the Sahara.

However, if my rooms astonished Howard, his house was a never-failing source of wonder to me. Already there were signs of that wilful vulgarity with which people of faultless taste protect themselves from faultless taste. But why, when he never tired of discussing the ultimate refinements of interior decoration, did he take such pains to make his own quarters look like a slum? Why the carefully cultivated damp-stains? Why the crumbling plaster, the peeling shreds of wallpaper and the back-breaking chairs? This was not an artist's loft. It was not a garret. It was a comfortable, middle-class London terrace house. Whatever the reason, it was not simply a matter of money.

I used to think that Howard kept his house 'untouched' for fear that any effort to improve it would detract from the energies he was pouring into his art and his collection. I have since come round to the idea that those austere rooms were more affected, more calculated and more dandified than anything I could dream of. It was his way of saying, 'This is my answer to my family and their brown furniture.' 'This is what England is really like.'

Around 1965, collectors began to buy Howard's pictures for real money and the Hodgkins bought a mill house in a very green Wiltshire valley. Again, you felt the builders would stay for ever, and when they finally did go, Howard spent hour after hour arranging and re-arranging the house to achieve the most tentative effect with the maximum amount of effort. The same is true of his paintings, which are built-up layer on layer of 'rubbings-out' — on Hemingway's principle that if you obliterate something it will always be there.

Around the same time, too, he found a new dealer in Kasmin, who insisted on, and paid for, his first trip to India. India became an emotional lifeline. Each winter he travelled all over the subcontinent, sopping up impressions — of empty hotel rooms, the beach at Mahabalipuram, the view from a railway carriage, the colour of cowdust in the evening, or the sight of an orange sari against a concrete balustrade — and storing them for the pictures he would paint, at home, in Wiltshire. The influence was now India herself, not the India of Indian painting. Then he almost died, of a tropical disease contracted there, and the enchantment palled a little. A picture entitled *Bombay Sunset*, painted in colours of mud, blood, and bile, perhaps shows that India was also his emotional cul-de-sac.

Meanwhile, the 'Hodgkin' side of his character had reasserted itself. He immersed himself in the art politics of England. He was appointed a Trustee of the Tate Gallery, then of the National Gallery, and was awarded the CBE. And then the story might, artistically, have ended, were it not for a chance encounter. The details of the encounter I leave to the imagination: the results were that Howard's painting took a sharp and unexpected swerve.

Gone were the portraits of forlorn married couples in rooms, to be replaced by a new kind of subject, and a new mood. In his most recent pictures, the sitters — though they still exist under layers of paint — are overwhelmed by dots, splotches, flashes and slabs of colour, recording situations or impressions that Howard, in his new persona, has witnessed. Some are simple enough: it doesn't require much imagination to see that the one called *Red Bermudas* is of a sunbather in Central Park. But who would guess that *Tea*, a panel over-splattered in scarlet, represents a seedy flat in Paddington where a male hustler is telling the story of his life? Howard has also returned to the 'Artist and Model' theme, in a series of

77

hand-coloured lithographs, revealing a new-found engagement with the erotic.

But Howard's pictures have always been, more or less, erotic — and the more erotic for being inexplicit. He seems incapable of starting a picture without an emotionally charged subject, though his next step is to make it obscure, or at least oblique. Yet is not all erotic art — as opposed to the merely pornographic — oblique? Descriptions of the sexual act are as boring as descriptions of landscape seen from the air — and as flat: whereas Flaubert's description of Emma Bovary's room in a *hotel de passe* in Rouen, before and after, but not *during* the sexual act, is surely the most erotic passage in modern literature.

1982

AT DINNER WITH
DIANA VREELAND

Her glass of neat vodka sat on the white damask table-cloth. Beyond the smear of lipstick, a twist of lemon floated among the ice-cubes. We were sitting side by side, on a banquette.

'What are you writing about, Bruce?'

'Wales, Diana.'

The lower lip shot forward. Her painted cheeks swivelled through an angle of ninety degrees.

'Whales!' she said. 'Blue whales! . . . Sperrrm whales! . . . THE WHITE WHALE!'

'No . . . no, Diana! Wales! Welsh Wales! The country to the west of England.'

'Oh! Wales. I *do* know Wales. Little grey houses . . . covered in roses . . . in the rain . . . '

1982

4

ENCOUNTERS

NADEZHDA MANDELSTAM:
A VISIT

It was snowing hard the afternoon I went to see Nadezhda Mandelstam. The snow melted off my coat and boots and made puddles on her kitchen floor. The kitchen smelled of kerosene and stale bread. On a table there were sticky purple rings, a vase full of begonias, and dried glasses left over from the lightness of a Russian summer.

A fat man in spectacles came out of the bedroom. He glared at me as he wound a grey scarf around his jowls, and then went out.

She called me in. She lay on her left side, on her bed, amid the rumpled sheets, resting her temple on a clenched fist. She greeted me without moving.

'What did you think of my doctor?' she sneered. 'I am sick.'

The doctor, I assume, was her KGB man.

The room was hot and cramped and strewn with clothes and books. Her hair was coarse, like lichen, and the light from the bedside lamp shone through it. White metal fastenings glittered among the brown stumps of her teeth. A cigarette stuck to her lower lip. Her nose was a weapon. You knew for certain she was one of the most powerful women in the world, and knew she knew it.

A friend in England advised me to take her three things: champagne, cheap thrillers and marmalade. She looked at the champagne and said, 'Bollinger!' without enthusiasm. She looked at the thrillers and said, '*Romans policiers!* Next time you come to Moscow you must bring me real TRASH!' But when I pulled out three jars of my mother's Seville orange marmalade, she stubbed out the cigarette and smiled.

'Thank you, my dear. Marmalade, it is my childhood.'

'Tell me, my dear . . . ' She waved me to a chair and, as she waved, one of her breasts tumbled out of her nightie. 'Tell me,' she shoved it back, 'are there any grand poets left in your country? I mean grand poets . . . of the stature of Joyce or Eliot?'

Auden was alive, in Oxford. Weakly, I suggested Auden.

'Auden is *not* what I would call a grand poet!'

'Yes,' I said. 'Most of the voices are silent.'

'And in prose?'

'Not much.'

'And in America? Are there poets?'

'Some.'

'Tell me, was Hemingway a grand novelist?'

'Not always,' I said. 'Not towards the end. But he's underrated now. The early short stories are wonderful.'

'But the wonderful American novelist is Faulkner. I am helping a young friend translate Faulkner into Russian. I must tell you, we are having difficulties.'

'And in Russia,' she growled, 'we have no grand writers left. Here also the voices are silent. We have Solzhenitsyn and even that is not so good. The trouble with Solzhenitsyn is this. When he thinks he is telling the truth, he tells the most terrible falsehoods. But when he thinks he is making a story from his imagination, then, sometimes, he catches the truth.'

'What about that story . . . ?' I faltered. 'I forget its name . . . the one where the old woman gets run over by a train?'

'You mean *Matryona's House*?'

'I do,' I said. 'Does that catch the truth?'

'It could never have happened in Russia!'

On the wall across from the bed there was a white canvas, hung askew. The painting was all white, white on white, a few white bottles on a blank white ground. I knew the work of the artist: a Ukrainian Jew, like herself.

'I see you've got a painting by Weissberg,' I said.

'Yes. And I wonder if you'd mind straightening it for me? I threw a book and hit it by mistake. A disgusting book by an Australian woman!'

I straightened the picture.

'Weissberg,' she said. 'He is our best painter. Perhaps that is all one can do today in Russia? Paint whiteness!'

1978

MADELEINE VIONNET

Madeleine Vionnet is an alert and mischievous old lady of ninety-six with eighty-six years of practical experience in the art of dressmaking. Her couture house on the Avenue Montaigne shut its doors in 1939, but at the mention of her name her former clients will sigh as if recalling the Golden Age. To historians of fashion she is a legend. They have acclaimed her 'The Architect of Couture': its only true creative genius. And when she announces flatly, 'I am the best dressmaker in the world and I *feel* it, too!' — there are valid reasons for believing her.

Her name never attracted the publicity — or the notoriety — of Chanel. She never pandered to the fashionable world and, I suspect, believed herself superior to it. She even maintained the word 'fashion' was meaningless to a true dressmaker. Yet she is probably the woman who, around 1900, rescued other women from the tyranny of the corset. She is certainly the inventor of the bias-cut, which transformed the course of modern dressmaking. And she insisted that women remain women when other couturiers would have their clients re-semble boys or machines.

The association of haute couture with the very rich makes it suspect for many people. But for Madame Vionnet, who once was penniless, couture is not a minor art. Like the dance it is an evanescent art, but a great one. She sees herself as an artist on the level of, say, Pavlova. She was single-minded in the pursuit of perfection, and even her exemplary common sense is tinged with a streak of fanaticism. The workmanship of her house was unrivalled. No one knew better how to drape a torso in the round. She would handle fabric as a master sculptor realises the possibilities latent in a marble block. Like a sculptor, too, she understood the subtle beauty of the female body in motion, and knew that graceful movements were enhanced by assymetry of cut. She wanted the body to show itself through the dress. The dress was to be a second or more seductive skin, which smiled when its wearer smiled. Madame Vionnet demanded of her clients that they be tall, have proper breasts and hips, and move easily. She could then match their beauty with her skill — and the result would be a partnership.

Today she lives in the Seizième Arrondissement, in a street top-heavy with apartment buildings from the Belle Epoque. The façade of her house is adorned with swags of fruit and metal balconies in the heaviest bourgeois taste. Once through the door, however, you enter a world of aluminium grilles, sand-blasted walls, mirror glass and sleek lacquer surfaces: an interior as clean-cut and unsentimental as Madame Vionnet herself.

'I have nothing old in my house. Everything is modern. I did it all myself.'

Like a Vionnet dress, this is spareness achieved expensively. When she moved here in 1929 the rooms were quickly purged of meaningless ornament. Even the sepia family photographs were ripped from their frames, sandwiched between sheets of plate-glass, and hung on walls that were otherwise free of pictures.

Squares of natural parchment line the salon. 'Each one a sheepskin!' she laughs. 'You see, I am a shepherdess.' The room is said to be the most exceptional art deco interior in Paris to have survived — with its owner — intact. There are fur-covered sofas, chromium chairs upholstered in white leather and tables of scarlet lacquer, the colour of Buddhist temples in Japan. The fireplace is of sheet copper, silvered. On it stands a photo of the Parthenon: a talismanic photo, for Madame Vionnet has always turned to Classical Greece for inspiration. Her portrait, resting on an easel, was painted by Jean Dunand, the 'lacquer master' of the 1920s. The face is made from a mosaic of the minutest chips of eggshell.

This refinement was the reward of a long struggle. Her father, Abel Vionnet, came from the Jura but earned his living at Aubervilliers on the outskirts of Paris. He was an octroi: that is to say, like the Douanier Rousseau, he was an internal customs officer who levied tolls on saleable goods as they passed along the highway. His wife deserted him: he and his daughter became inseparable.

The Vionnet family owned a farmhouse in the Jura 'with a stream where I could swim', but Madeleine did not see it until she was sixteen. She had been anaemic in Paris, and relatives suggested mountain air as a cure. 'But I was bored in the mountains. Papa had to come and fetch me again . . . ' Nevertheless, the Jura heritage has probably marked her character. The Jurassiens are a people apart. They have a fiercely independent turn of mind, and a history of rebellious and nonconformist attitudes. In the nineteenth century, the watchmakers of the Swiss Jura combined exquisite craftsmanship with practical Anarchism, and influenced all the great revolutionaries of the day. In Madeleine Vionnet the sense of excellence is there — and perhaps a touch of the anarchist.

The wife of one of Abel Vionnet's friends worked as a seamstress in a *maison de couture*, and at the age of ten Madeleine left school to join her. She got special dispensation to take the leaving exam a year early, and never wavered in her determination to succeed. She became ill but recovered. She married at eighteen, but divorced and her child died. She went to England — and she can still break into English at will — where she worked for Kate Reilly, who dressed the late-Victorian court in costumes of voluminous richness. She returned to Paris and was befriended by Madame Gerber, one of three sisters who ran the house of Callot Soeurs, which, with Worth and Jacques Doucet, formed the triumvirate that dominated fashion in France. Madame Gerber demanded the most exacting standards. Madame Vionnet confesses she owes all her later success to her, and keeps a photo of this forlorn-and-determined-looking woman constantly by her.

In 1900, ladies of fashion were still encased in a heavy armature, and would balance half an aviary on their heads. High-boned collars strangled them. Pointed shoes crippled them. The corsets that squeezed their waists into hour-glass shapes also snarled up their intestines and disturbed their health. But Isadora Duncan was dancing with bare feet, flapping breasts and trailing draperies . . .

'*Quelle artiste!*' says Madame Vionnet with an expansive gesture and backward shake of the head. '*Quelle grrrande artiste!*'

One couturier noticed a princess on a public bus. In a short time, fashionable ladies would burst from their prison.

Madeleine Vionnet was a leading liberationist. She claims the distinction of being the first dressmaker to discard the corset, while working for Jacques Doucet in 1907: 'I have never been able to tolerate corsets myself. Why should I have inflicted them on other women? *Le corset, c'est une chose orthopédique . . .* '

Certainly, she always believed that no woman can be beautiful if she is constricted. And from 1901 onwards she designed seductive peignoirs or tea-gowns: clothes to collapse in before the ordeal of dressing for dinner. Her models wore sandals, even went barefoot, and she plainly intended that women should adopt the *déshabillé* style in public as well.

Credit for suppressing the corset, however, usually goes to Paul Poiret, the designer who grafted the paraphernalia of *The Thousand and One Nights* onto everyday dress. Perhaps a misunderstanding of this crucial point of fashion history stems from Madame Vionnet's estimation of Poiret: 'Monsieur Poiret was not a *couturier*. He was a *costumier . . . très bien pour le théâtre!*'

With this neat dialectic distinction, she succeeds in equating his clothes with fancy dress.

Her own couture house opened in 1912. She shut it during the War, went to Rome, and returned to Paris at the close of hostilities. She induced Galeries Lafayette to back her, and in 1923 reopened in sumptuous premises on the Avenue Montaigne. The richest women in the world flocked to her: she never went to them.

'I was a dressmaker,' she says. 'I believed in my *métier*. I chose my friends for their brains, for their real worth and for no other reason. Monsieur Léger was a friend. Whenever he was tired of painting, he liked to come and watch me cut . . .

'No. I was never *mondaine*. I never dined in restaurants and, when I went to the theatre, I went alone. I have never cared to dress myself well. I was short . . . and I hate short women!'

Among the few clients she would consent to see was the Italian-born Duchesse de Gramont: 'Ah! She was a real model. Tall and lovely. When I was designing a dress, I had only to ask her to come and try it on . . . and I knew *exactly* where it was wrong!'

She seldom descended to the salon because 'if I saw a woman who was ugly or short or fat, I would show her the door! . . . *je dirai "Va-t-en!"'* Many of her clients were the wives of Cuban sugar millionaires: 'They were not intelligent, those Cubans! But they were properly made. They moved well, and you could do something with them.' Then Europeans began to plant beet; Cuban cane-sugar slumped, and the husbands objected to the bills.

'We planted beets,' the old lady chuckles. 'We lost the clients.'

Then there were the Argentines! At the mention of the word 'Argentine' — and the memory of Argentine women 'with undulating buttocks like carnivores', '. . . *avec leurs fesses ondoyantes des carnivores* . . .' — Madame Vionnet sinks her white head onto the pillow and, in a moment of unguarded reverie, sighs, 'They always said I loved women too much . . . !'

Perhaps the loveliest of the 'Argentines' was the Brazilian-born Madame Martinez de Hoz, who, after the Stock Market Crash, bought a share in the house of Vionnet and kept it going until Hitler's War.

'We were a village in those days, a town even . . . ' Vionnet used to employ 1,200 people in 21 ateliers. Her seamstresses worked in rooms that were a model for their day, airy and flooded with light: 'I remembered the horrible work conditions when I was a girl and I wanted ours to be the best . . . in that way you get the best work.' She stationed herself in a strategic position on the main floor: no one who moved across the room escaped her vigilant eye: 'We lost no valuable time . . . '

There was no time to be lost. The Maison Vionnet produced six hundred models a year, which is twice as many as Dior. Each dress was photographed for reasons of copyright: a practice hitherto unknown. Every label on a Vionnet dress bore the fingerprint of Madame herself. Illicit pirating of her designs distressed her, not for financial reasons, but because mass-production was a betrayal of her art. She needn't have worried. A Vionnet dress relied on the subtlest combination of fine workmanship and handling of cloth. It was, in practice, uncopiable.

She rarely designed models on paper, but created them in miniature on a small doll or mannequin eighty centimetres high. The doll is now one of the more famous props of French couture, but it mystified Abel Vionnet when his daughter brought it home in the evenings. She was a middle-aged woman, yet she persisted in dressing her doll. Had she failed to grow up?

She confesses she was to blame for his bewilderment: 'I dared not tell Papa the extent of my business. I was afraid he would pay us a visit, and make a public sermon on the evils of ambition.'

Once Madame Vionnet had evolved her style, she stuck to

it. When rival couturiers lifted skirts above the knee, she refused: 'To show the knee is *ordinaire* . . . *vulgaire* . . . !' She admired the fluid lines of Japanese costume and the severity of the Classical Greek tunic. Her most characteristic dress, to be seen in quantity at every race-meeting at Longchamps, was a shift of cream silk. But this Greek-inspired simplicity was manoeuvred to extremes of opulence. An evening gown of black velvet and white mink — her original combination — was the subject of one of Edward Steichen's best fashion photographs for *Vogue*.

A Vionnet dress looks nothing in the hand. It contains no pads, no artificial stiffening, and flops limply on its hanger. There are two hundred of them at the *Centre de Documentation de la Couture*, and they are something of a trial to the ladies who look after them. 'What can one do with it?' asks the curator with despairing eyes as she holds up a tube of flimsy white material — for she cannot work out how it was worn. She also tells me that Vionnet clients had the same difficulty, and used to telephone in panic when they couldn't understand how to put a dress on.

Not so Madame! She calls for the maid to take me upstairs, to the wardrobe where her favourite models are stored. We station a couturier's dummy beside her chair, and on it put a black evening dress with a design of sea-horses, in the style of Attic red-figure vase painting. Suddenly, the hands shoot forward and with a tug here, another tug there, the dress miraculously comes alive.

'I am a woman of the most extraordinary vitality,' Madame Vionnet assures me. 'I have never been bored for a second. I have never been envious of anyone or anything, and now I have achieved a certain tranquillity.' She is satisfied with her work, satisfied to sit in her salon and read a biography of Cardinal Richelieu.

'I could, of course, live in Rome,' she reflects, as if a move to Rome were a possibility. 'But I love my country and I wish to die here.'

She does tire easily and, towards the end of the interview, her conversation tailed off into staccato bursts. But she is still interested in the events of Paris fashion — and certainly knows what to dislike! '*Totalement déséquilibré!*' she snorts at a photo of a Courrèges dress in Vogue. Couture is the art for which she has lived, and she feels it is dying with her: 'It's very sad now . . . very reduced!'

Other dressmakers are divided into friends, foes, and those consigned to a limbo of indifference. She cherishes the memory of Balenciaga, '*Un ami . . . un vrai!*' On the subject of Christian Dior she was vague: 'He had a pretty name, but I did not know him.' And of Madame Chanel, who at one time must have galled her considerably, she had this to say: 'She was a woman of taste . . . Yes. One had to admit it. But she was a *modiste*. That is to say, my dear, she understood hats!'

On leaving her, I was worried that our photographer might disturb her tranquillity.

'No. He will not disturb me. I shall be very pleased to see him. *But* he cannot photograph my brain . . . !'

1973

MARIA REICHE: THE
RIDDLE OF THE PAMPA

Maria Reiche is a tall, almost skeletal, German mathematician and geographer who has spent about half her seventy-two years in the Peruvian desert surveying the archaeological monument known as the 'Nazca lines'. This astonishing curiosity lies on the Pan-American Highway some three hundred miles south-east of Lima and fifty miles inland from the coast, a flat waterless plain, lying high above two irrigated valleys, with the foothills of the Andean Cordillera backing up behind. This plain, the Pampa de Ingenio, is covered with a thin layer of sand and pebbles which has oxidised a warm brown colour on the surface. It has a texture rather like a meringue and overlies a bed of whitish alluvium. If you so much as tread on the Pampa you leave a white footprint that will last for centuries.

Nearly 2,000 years ago the local inhabitants realised they could use their pampa as a gigantic etching plate. And over the generations, they made what is surely the largest, and certainly one of the most beautiful, works of art in the world. The surface of the desert is furrowed with a web of straight lines, linking huge geometric forms — triangles, rectangles, spirals, meanders, whip-like zig-zags and superimposed trapezes — that look like the work of a very sensitive and very expensive abstract artist. There are lines as thin as a goat path, and as wide as airport runways. Some converge at a single point, others run on, five miles and more, straddling valleys and escarpments in their unswerving course. These surface drawings make little sense on the ground, and no aerial photographs do them justice. But from a light aircraft you can only gasp with amazement at their scale and the imagination of their makers.

As you bounce about the sky in the thermals that rise off the plain, you soon distinguish other figures. Apart from the geometric forms there is a zoo of animals and birds, looking rather like Steinberg drawings on an enormous scale. There is a whale. There are a guano-bird, a pelican, a humming bird, other unrecognisable birds and a frigate bird, with a distended sac under its bill. There is a dog. There is an Amazonian spider-monkey with a prehensile tail curving upwards in a spiral. There is a copy of a spider (of a species called *Ricinulei* that copulates with its hind leg). There is a tom-toddy figure with head and no body; a flower; a strange kind of seaweed; and a beast, half-bird and half-snake. There is also a lizard with its body shorn in two by the highway.

The lines on the Pampa de Ingenio were spotted in the late Twenties by the Aerial Survey of Peru. But for more than ten years the archaeologists were either ignorant of their existence or chose to ignore them. In 1939 Dr Paul Kosok of Long Island University was surveying Ancient Peru and followed up a rumour of ancient irrigation channels on the Pampa. He found the mysterious lines and was doubly astonished when the figures of birds and animals emerged from under his footprints. Kosok was not perplexed by the origin of the figures. Their style roughly coincided with those that decorated the pots of the local Nazca culture (even if the figures on the desert were finer and less folkish than the figures on the pots). But other questions troubled him. What was the point of this colossal creation when its makers, who did not have the aeroplane, could never have seen them properly? How could a people of simple peasants and warriors have mastered their superlative surveying technique without a knowledge of higher mathematics?

By chance Kosok timed his visit to coincide with the Winter Solstice, 21 June, the shortest day in the Southern Hemisphere. That evening at sunset he was crossing the Pampa where several lines ran in an east-west direction. He was delighted to find that the lower rim of the sun touched down at a point where one of the lines met the horizon. He decided that the line had been made for determining the date of the Winter Solstice. And he went on to speculate that all the lines and geometric forms were used as sightings to predict the risings and settings of the sun, moon and stars. The Nazca people, he said, had imprinted on the desert 'the largest astronomy book in the world'.

The Nazca Culture had been discovered in 1905 by the German Peruvianist Max Uhle. It was a smallish empire of warriors and peasant cultivators that flourished and declined between the second and eighth centuries of our era. The empire looked in two directions — across the Cordillera to the jungle, with its humming birds, its spider-monkeys and spiders; and to the sea coast, where white guano islands float on a heaving silvery sea. Nobody knows the real name of the Nazca people. First they were absorbed into the Inca and even earlier empires; then the Spaniards killed off the Indian population of these valleys and assured for them the anonymity of oblivion. One can but reconstruct their lives from the things they buried with their dead. And this is a rather hazardous business, since tomb-robbing is almost a national pastime and the robbers (the *huaceros*) have ransacked all but a few cemeteries. Seen from the air, the sides of the valleys are pockmarked with their holes.

On their patchwork of fields, irrigated by the annual run-off from the Andes, the people of Nazca grew the potato, the sweet potato, the avocado, the chile pepper, the lima bean, maize, manioc, pineapples, guavas and a multitude of little-known grains and fruit and vegetables. They had fishing boats and rafts which could only skim one of the world's best fishing grounds. For meat they ate llama and large quantities of guinea pig. They knitted and wove some of the most exquisite textiles the world has ever seen. They used every inch of the valley-floor for cultivation and stationed their houses, their temples and their cemeteries on the desert rim.

On the whole they seem to have been a cheerful and quite democratic people, well aware of the comic possibilities of life, and very unlike the character of their sinister northern neighbours, the Mochica. They did, however, share at least one of the Mochica's less pleasant customs — the cult of the severed head, preferably the head of a defeated enemy.

In trying to explain the existence of the Nazca observatory, Kosok outlined a theory of civilisation that has best been expounded by the German historian Kornelius Wittfogel. Wittfogel, himself a refugee from the politics of terror, saw an ominous continuum between the age of the Pyramids and the modern totalitarian state. In his scheme, the early empires of Peru, like those of Egypt and Mesopotamia, were 'hydraulic civilisations', that is, civilisations which owe their existence and their ideology to waterworks. He maintained that wherever you found large-scale irrigated agriculture, you found slave gangs and overseers. You found a population explosion and the emergence of a centralised state, with military dictators and foreign wars, whose purpose was to ensure a supply of cheap or free labour, and to purchase peace at home by sowing chaos abroad.

These early states saw the first paid informers, police methods, the systematic murder of rivals and savage inequality, with surpluses in the hands of the few and grinding poverty the lot of the masses. So important were the dates of the seasonal cycle — for planting, inundating and harvesting — that you found an outburst of astronomical calculation and astrological prediction. So important was it to keep the work-force in passive dependence, that this knowledge became the exclusive property of a caste of managerial bureaucrats, the futurologists of the ancient world. These were men morbidly wrapped-up in themselves and responsible to nothing but the system; they dwarfed the people with monumental architecture and threatened them with implacable sky gods.

Wittfogel was on the right lines but overstated his case. Archaeologists were able to contest his thesis by pointing out that the authoritarian state came into existence *before* the large-scale waterworks and not because of them. In other words, the dictators build the dams, not the dams the dictators. Perhaps more important is one feature that all states, early and late, have in common. To achieve cohesion they fix on a symbolic, ceremonial centre, which almost invariably carries celestial overtones, appealing to the inflexible order of Heaven to sanction authority on Earth. Stonehenge, the Temple of Heaven in Peking, Red Square, St Peter's, the Ka'aba at Mecca, the Versailles of the Sun King, or the Great Pyramid, to say nothing of the installations at Cape Kennedy, are a handful of examples only. The question here is whether the Pampa de Ingenio was the centre of such a state, and whether it was the creation of a managerial caste of priest bureaucrats. This was Kosok's question.

Maria Reiche came to Peru in 1932. She was a graduate of mathematics at Hamburg University, but, as a pacifist, she knew she had 'to get as far away from Germany as possible', and managed to earn a small living in Lima by teaching. Her mother had come from Hamburg, but her father was a judge in Saxony. In the first World War he was shot through the lung and invalided home. 'We used to ask him about the war, but he would not tell us. All the time he was thinking of his friends at the front. So he went back and this time he was shot dead. But if he *hadn't* died, I'd have been a little German bourgeois. I would *never* have escaped to the Pampa.' After seven years in Peru, she met Paul Kosok. He had just discovered the lines, but was returning to the United States. When he showed her the Pampa and suggested she put her knowledge of astronomy to practical use, she knew she had found her life's work.

For nearly forty years she has spent most of her time in the desert. She sleeps alone outside on a bed of stones, for there is virtually no rain. Her skin has burned and wrinkled in the way peculiar to those who live in arid places. She stands more than six feet tall. Despite her thinness, her legs are straight and muscular. 'One's legs are always *so* reliable.' Her fair hair has gone a streaky white, but her blue eyes are clear and lively, and her expression, which can at times be quite fierce, is usually one of girlish naïvety and enthusiasm for life. 'I feel things germinating inside me all the time. And at my age! But then I was very barren as a girl.' She plainly intends to live to be a hundred and says the people who live longest wear loose clothes. She eats very little; for a trip of several days she brought a packet of powdered milk, some cans of tuna fish, a block of quince paste and a bunch of bananas. She eats no meat, refusing even a bowl of consommé, though she managed a turtle steak in one restaurant.

In 1968 she published a small illustrated book about the Pampa called *Mystery on the Desert*. She had it printed for herself and arranged for its distribution. 'No editor is going to drink champagne from my skull.' The book attracted visitors from all over the world and, ever since, she and the Pampa have become something of a Peruvian institution. Most people in Lima still cannot bring themselves to take her seriously. To them she is the 'mad woman with the lines', a fanatical recluse, a regional curiosity that one should visit when driving south. Indeed, it *is* rather an odd sight, the old lady perched on top of an aluminium step-ladder, apparently gazing into nowhere, or measuring the desert with steel tapes.

I confess I half-expected to find her in the thrall of some mystical obsession. But instead she was one of the most hard-headed and least mystical people I have ever met. 'I do not care for the Bible,' she said. 'So much that is impenetrable. The world would be far better without it. If only we could abolish superstition!' She is a woman of sharp humour and stout common sense, and finds the idea of herself tramping about the desert faintly ridiculous. Her claims for the Pampa are modest, she does not trumpet vague or inadmissable theories. 'I have no theory,' she said coolly. 'I have the facts.' She is convinced that Kosok was right and that the Pampa is an astronomical instrument of sorts, but she does not underestimate the uncertainties. She believes the Pampa will only reveal itself when there is an accurate survey. This is the job she has set herself, an undertaking so vast that it will see her out. It is, however, a one-woman operation and I would not like to be the one who encroached on her territory. The Wennegren Foundation in New York once offered her the services of experts. 'But *I*, who have worked here for forty years, what *am* I if I am not an expert?'

She thinks that the method of transferring the figures to the ground was relatively simple. There was a standard unit of measure, based on the human body, probably the arm-span. This was transferred to a piece of string, and doubled and doubled ad infinitum, or halved and halved until it corresponded to the space between the knuckles. She hopes to isolate the exact standard length, like the Megalithic Yard which Professor Thom of Glasgow has found to underlie the placing of standing stones in Neolithic monuments in the British Isles. But she is coming to the depressing conclusion that the Nazca people employed slightly different standards. When plotting a figure on the desert they will have used a string with a peg at either end, one to scratch the surface, the other stuck in the ground. The outline of the spider, for example, is a succession of smoothly joined arcs of very different radii. I spent one morning with Maria demonstrating how it was done. 'One of those bearded people', she said, 'suggested I use aerial photographs. But I would *never* get the centre of the radii, so *what* is the point?' All morning, and into the blazing afternoon, she hopped about with her steel tapes, jumping from one line to the next, always on the white, and never on the brown surface of the Pampa. She could add up strings of decimals in her head, and, when these got too much for her, she scribbled them on the folds of her dress.

The Pampa is very vulnerable. For years Maria Reiche laboured to get people to recognise its importance. But now it is famous, the visitors are ruining it as fast as they can. Horses, cars, motor-bikes and dune-buggies have made their everlasting white tracks on the brown surface. Footprints have nearly blotted out the spider. Tourists and 'even the ignorant people from the museums' have added their own improvements to the figures. There are threats to criss-cross the Pampa with pylon lines and even to irrigate it. She has to watch this destruction with a quiet, fierce despair. 'It is terrible, *terrible*. One day I shall stand it no longer and I shall leave the Pampa.' She does not think she has enough official support, but the problems of protecting it are an official's nightmare. The Archaeological Service of Peru is hard-pressed enough. How can it cope with another site of a hundred thousand acres? The solution would be to declare it out of bounds, like a military zone, and she has something like this in mind. Meanwhile she will not distribute her book in Peru until she has official safeguards.

Another morning we went to look for a place where parallel lines rush across the floor of a dried watercourse and ride up to the mountains on the farther side. She woke me at four. She drank her milk, ate some bananas, and we started out over a lunar-like landscape, plantless but for the odd cactus, her great German legs striding out in front. About sunrise she turned to climb a scree. Some way up the escarpment, she slipped and began rolling down in a cloud of dust and stones. I hurried back to pick up the pieces, but found her sniggering with laughter at the bottom.

'I am *so* glad I learned how to ski when I was a child. Skiing teaches you how to fall.' I offered to carry her bags — an offer she had refused earlier — and, free of their weight, she climbed the hill, expecting to find the lines at the top. But when I caught up with her, sweating and out of breath, she said:

'Alas, we are on the wrong pampa!' We did not find the right pampa for another hour.

Maria Reiche has had a further dose of trouble, only this time from a rather cursory North American expedition that came to the Pampa, and went again, when she was not there. 'Expedition!' she snorted. 'With the Pan-American Highway running close by! This is *not* what *I* call an expedition.'

The unwanted visitor was Gerald Hawkins, the Anglo-American professor of astronomy from Boston, who made a name for himself in the early Sixties, when he announced he had 'decoded' Stonehenge and that it was a 'Neolithic Computer' for calculating equinoxes, solstices and eclipses. Hawkins irritated the 'professionals' at the time by his apparent failure to take awkward facts into account. In any case, having 'decoded' Stonehenge, he set about decoding other astronomically aligned monuments, including the Temple at Karnak in Egypt. Then he decided to take on the Pampa. He arrived one day with a team of surveyors and took what must have been a few rather hasty sightings. The 'expedition' even landed its Piper Cherokee on the surface of the Pampa. Hawkins returned to the United States with a set of aerial photographs, taken vertically by the Servicio Aerofotografico de Peru. He selected a number of lines and geometric forms, fed their alignments into his computer, fed also into the computer information of the movements of the sun, moon and constellations over 2,000 years and more, and announced, with a certain glow of satisfaction, that whereas a few lines *might* point to solstices and equinoxes, there were far too many that did not. 'The Sun-Moon-Stars theory', he wrote, 'has been killed by the computer.'

Maria Reiche is not the woman to accept this kind of thing submissively. After years of patient plotting and calculating, she is confident of her method and scorns the omniscience of the computer expert. Furthermore, she insists that working from aerial photographs must give extremely inaccurate results. 'This Hawkins spent very little time here. He could not have taken proper azimuths of the horizon. What kind of astronomy is that?'

Another visitor to the Pampa was Erich von Daniken, the Swiss fantast and author of two books, *Chariots of the Gods?* and *Gods From Outer Space*, which have sold 4,000,000 and 2,000,000 copies respectively. Von Daniken's thesis, which is not particularly original, is this: at some remote period, beings from Outer Space (the Gods) landed on Earth in flying saucers (their chariots), bringing with them a genetic engineering factory, in which they created, from inferior hominid material, *Homo sapiens*, possibly making the first woman in a retort. It comes as no surprise, in this rewriting of Genesis, to learn that the Pampa de Ingenio was a prehistoric airport, or space centre for gods. And in one shameless bit of cheating Von Daniken illustrates the leg-joint and claw of the big guano bird with a caption, 'Another of the strange markings on the Plain of Nazca. This is very reminiscent of aircraft parking areas in a modern airport.'

Maria Reiche knows how to cope with the saucer watchers. 'They are ignorant and uncultured people and they are usually in it for the money.' But another class of visitor totally mystifies her. The publication of her book coincided with the avant-garde phenomenon known as Earth Art. In the late Sixties artists in Europe and America reacted to the tyranny of the art gallery, and, with the ecological movement under way, felt it was time to return to the Earth that bore them. The New York artist Claes Oldenberg dug a 'grave-like pit' in Central Park. Walter de Maria drew parallel lines in chalk a mile long in the Mojave Desert, and then announced a project for a pair of walls a mile long. Artists were suddenly interested in every kind of prehistoric earthwork, in crop marks, in barrows, in the White Horses of Iron Age Britain, in the Spiral Mound in Ohio, and in the desert drawings of the Australian Aborigines, who ritually enacted the migrations of their ancestors by drawing them on the ground and dancing round them.

Even the collectors entered into the spirit of the movement.

Robert Scull commissioned the artist Michael Heizer (whose father was a pre-Columbian archaeologist) to dig a huge cut in the desert, and said, in a lecture at the Metropolitan Museum, that it was one of Man's deepest instincts to cut into the ground, and that, whatever his wife Ethel thought, part of the thrill of owning Heizer's piece was that it was stuck out in the desert and you couldn't have it shipped and auctioned at Parke-Bernet Galleries.

It was inevitable that the Earth artists should visit the Pampa. I particularly liked Maria Reiche's version of her encounter with a conceptual artist. 'I said to him, "What are you doing on the Pampa?" and he said, "I am an artist." "What kind of artist?" "I change the landscape." "Well, I hope you are not going to change *this* landscape." *What* can you do with such people? Nature is beautiful. The Pampa is beautiful, and *they* want to change it.'

Maria Reiche is not a recluse, and since she has become something of a cult figure, she basks in the publicity. 'I am Elizabeth Taylor in front of the camera.' Lufthansa, with its eye for a celebrity, now offers her tickets home. She appears at gatherings of the avant-garde in Germany, where she gets even more perplexed by the dense language of her admirers. Before we left Nazca she wanted to collect her mail from the post office. She came out staring at a card, printed with squares like graph paper. On it were ruled, in black ink, six plain rectangles divided down the centre. Above, a neat caption ran: A Series of Six Paintings each with a Central Vertical Division. It was, in fact, the prospectus from an art gallery in Düsseldorf, of an exhibition by a young English painter called Alan Charlton. 'I do not know what it is,' she said. 'I think they have not included the letter in the envelope. Perhaps it is for Government stamps?'

1975

KONSTANTIN MELNIKOV: ARCHITECT

In January 1973, on a morning of Stygian gloom, I called on Konstantin Melnikov, the architect, at his house on Krivo-arbatsky Lane in Moscow. I had already been in Moscow a couple of weeks trying to ferret out survivors from the heady days of the leftist art movement of the early Twenties. I had, for example, a wild-goose chase in search of an old gentleman, once a friend of Tatlin's, who owned a wing strut of the glider *Letatlin*. I even tried to find the man who, as a homeless student of the Vkhutemas School, had installed himself and his bedding *inside* the Constructivist street monument *The Red Wedge Invades the White Square*.

One evening, I went to supper with Vavara Rodchenko, the artist's daughter, in a studio flat that had also been the office of the magazine *LEF*. The shade of Mayakovsky, one of its editors, seemed to linger in the room. The bentwood chair you sat on was Mayakovsky's chair, the plate you ate off was *his* plate, and the fruit compotier was a present brought from Paris by a man who called himself 'the cloud in pants'. On the walls there hung a selection of Rodchenko's paintings — less fine, of course, and less mystical than those of Malevich, but making up for that with their dazzling display of vigour. In his daybooks, crammed with sketches, you could watch him anticipate and race through every style and variation of the post-war abstract movement in Europe and America. Small wonder, then, that by 1921 he had believed easel painting was dead, and when I asked his daughter whether she still possessed the three canvases he had shown at the exhibition 'The Last Picture Has Been Painted', she unrolled onto the floor three square monochrome canvases: one yellow, one red (and what a red!), and one blue. For all that, my visit to Mr Melnikov was the high point of the trip, since, by any standards, the house itself is one of the architectural wonders of the twentieth century.

The Arbat was once the aristocratic quarter of Moscow. It was largely rebuilt after the Napoleonic fire in 1812, and even today, in palaces of green or cream-coloured stucco, one or two of the old families linger on with their possessions. Melnikov's house – or rather pavilion in the French sense – is set well back from the street, a building both Futurist and Classical consisting of two interlocking cylinders, the rear one taller than the front and pierced with some sixty windows: identical elongated hexagons with Constructivist glazing bars. The cylinders are built of brick covered with stucco in the manner of Russian churches. In 1973 the stucco was a dull and flaking ochre, although recent photos show the building spruced up with a coat of whitewash. On the front façade above the architrave are the words KONSTANTIN MELNIKOV ARKHITEKTOR – his proud and lonely boast that true art can only be the creation of the individual, never that of the committee or group.

After I had entered the door on that dark January morning, I climbed the spiral staircase painted emerald green and came into the circular white salon where the architect himself, lying on a kind of Biedermeier chaise-longue, was having a grated apple for his elevenses. His son, Viktor Stepanovich, was grating the apple. The old man, he explained, could not take much solid food. He was very frail and disillusioned, and when he blinked his hooded eyes one had the sense of hopes abandoned and lost ambitions.

Viktor Stepanovich took me upstairs to the studio that on a

summer's day must have been one of the lightest and airiest rooms imaginable, but on this day of muddy clouds and snow flurries the atmosphere was one of liturgical solemnity. He was a painter. His canvases lay this way and that against the walls. He was also something of a mystic and mountain climber, and while we sat drinking vodka and cracking pine nuts, he showed me several pink Monet-like impressions of dawn in the Caucasus, which struck me as extraordinarily beautiful. When I asked if I could take some photographs of the house, he said, 'You must be quick!' For what I hadn't realised was that Anna Gavrilovna, the architect's wife, was hiding in the bedroom and thoroughly disapproved of having a Western visitor.

The house, as I said, was somewhat dilapidated. There were water stains on the walls; it was not particularly warm. Yet because Melnikov, for reasons of economy as well as aesthetics, had eschewed a slick, mechanical finish, and because he had stuck to the materials of his peasant boyhood — rough-cut planks and plain plaster — the effect was never shoddy but had an air of timeless vitality.

By the time we got downstairs, the old man was sorting through papers on his desk. By the window there was a plaster cast of a Venus: the yearning of a Russian for all things Mediterranean. He showed me photographs and drawings of projects — realised and unrealised — from his entire career.

Among them were the Makhorka Pavilion from the 1925 Moscow fair; the brilliant free-form arrangement of street stalls at the Sukharevka Market; the Paris pavilion of 1925; the Paris car park; the Leyland bus garage in Moscow; his various workers' clubs, which proved that he, like Le Corbusier, was a 'poet' of reinforced concrete; the plan for a monument to Christopher Columbus (to be erected in Santo Domingo); and, finally, a project for the Palace of the Soviets — half-pyramid, half-lotus — so wild in conception as to make the loonier architectural ramblings of Frank Lloyd Wright seem like so many little sandcastles.

Among the photographs from Paris, he showed me one of himself, a dandified figure standing on the staircase of the Soviet pavilion. Then, having pointed meticulously to the hatband of his Homburg, his cravat, and his spats, he asked me: 'What colour do you think they were?' 'Red,' I suggested. 'Red,' he nodded.

How a private family house — and not any old house but a symbolic coupled duet — came to be built in 1927 in the heart of Moscow, can only be explained within the framework of Melnikov's strange career. Fortunately there is now a first-rate guide in S. Frederick Starr's *Melnikov, Solo Architect in a Mass Society*, from which one can extract the bones of the story. Kostia Melnikov was a bright peasant lad whose father was a milkman. The family home, known as the Hay Lodge, was a cabin sixteen-foot-square in an outlying suburb of Moscow. 'Today,' he wrote in old age, 'looking back on my works, the source of my individuality is clearly visible . . . in the architecture of that building. Built of clay and straw, it looked like a foreigner in its own homeland . . . but all the magnificent carving of the surrounding houses yielded before it.'

The milkman Melnikov supplied a nearby academy where his young son was soon to be found rooting in the wastebaskets for scraps of paper to draw on. The family apprenticed him to an icon painter. His next job was in a firm of heating engineers whose proprietor, a second-generation Englishman, Vladimir Chaplin, recognised the boy's artistic talents and sent him to the prestigious Moscow School of Painting, Sculpture and Architecture.

This institution, Mayakovsky once said, was the 'only place where they took you without proof of your reliability'. It seems that Chaplin hoped his protégé would blossom into a painter of country scenes and was a bit chagrined when Melnikov changed tack from painting to architecture. The young man, however, was a wonderful architectural draughtsman. He designed schemes for grandiose neoclassical buildings. He married a plump, pretty sixteen-year-old girl from the middle classes, Anna Gavrilovna, and by the time the revolution came he had already built a car factory.

The savage winter of 1917–18 found the young Melnikovs half-starving, back with his family at the Hay Lodge. But gradually, as the nightmare of the Civil War receded, Melnikov — like Ladovsky or the Vesnin brothers — began to emerge as one of the most forceful architectural theorists of the renamed Vkhutemas School. His asymmetrical Makhorka Pavilion was a success among intellectuals and workers. At almost no notice, he designed the sarcophagus and glass cover for the embalmed corpse of Lenin and later would recall that one of the party hacks threatened to have him shot if he didn't get the work done on time. Then, in 1925, partly for his proven skill at operating within a minimal budget, he was awarded the commission to build the Soviet pavilion at the Paris Exposition Internationale des Arts Décoratifs.

With such outstanding exceptions as Le Corbusier's Pavillon de l'Esprit Nouveau, the exhibition was an exercise in opulent kitsch — the essence of Art Deco. Competing in vulgarity were a pavilion of Old Granada, a Ruhlmann and Patout pavilion, the Italian Fascist-Renaissance pavilion and the English pavilion — perhaps the silliest of all — in the Hollywood-Anglican style.

The Russians, in contrast, with their budget of only 15,000 roubles (at the time an equivalent of $7,650 U.S.) had no alternative but to build light. In fact, the whole structure, which sat on a site between the Grand Palais and the Seine, was made of the cheapest Russian timber, roughly shaped by peasant craftsmen, sent by train from Moscow, erected in next to no time, and painted red, grey, and white. Its plan, sliced with two staircases at the diagonal, was incredibly ingenious. Among the exhibits was a small version of Tatlin's tower — when the show was over this was left to the French Communist Party who promptly forgot about it. They failed to pay the storage charges of the warehouse and the tower sat unrecognised until it was chucked out and probably burned sometime in the early Sixties.

An English publication, put out by His Majesty's Stationery Office, had this to comment: 'The pavilion of Russia was of matchboard construction and was painted red . . . The exterior was largely of glass, and the whole looked like a dilapidated conservatory.' Others compared its aesthetic to that of the guillotine or said it was a 'stab in the back by the warriors of the Bolshevik Revolution'. But this did not prevent Melnikov from being the toast of the town, nor the great names of Modernism — Hoffmann, Le Corbusier, Perret, Mallet-Stevens — from admitting with great generosity that the Soviets had stolen the show. Le Corbusier took the young Russian under his wing and showed him all the Modern buildings worth seeing — among them his studio for Amédée Ozenfant — which may have put ideas into Melnikov's head about building a place of his own.

Melnikov was even the toast of White Russian émigrés who held a costume ball in his honour: guests came dressed as the 'new Constructivist architecture'. He went on holiday to Saint-Jean-de-Luz where, in answer to a commission from the Paris city fathers, he devised a scheme for a multi-storey car park for a thousand cars to be flung across the Seine like a bridge and supported by colossal Atlas-like caryatids on either side. The commission, needless to say, fell through.

Meanwhile, Melnikov's friend Rodchenko, who had come with his project for a workers' reading room, far from revelling in the high jinks, detested Paris and all it stood for. 'The cult of women,' he wrote home, 'like the cult of worm-infested cheese or oysters, has reached a point where to be fashionable is to be ugly.'

Melnikov, in later years, said he was terribly tempted to stay in France, yet his peasant instincts seem to have called him back. He boarded the train for Moscow, where he soon found he had stirred up a hornet's nest of jealousy in the Vkhutemas School. The denunciations followed but, buoyed up by an apparently limitless faith in his own genius, he decided to press on regardless. He built an extraordinary depot for the Leyland buses which the Soviets had bought from England. Then, in 1927, he set about building his house.

He seems to have hoodwinked Nikolai Bukharin, the party official who put the site at his disposal, into thinking that the design would have immediate relevance to the problem of mass public housing. But, as he himself confessed, the time had come he felt to be both architect and archi-millionaire.

Given the fertility of his imagination and his keen ability to grasp some feature and use it for his own ends, it is hard, if not impossible, to pinpoint Melnikov's sources. He is known, as a student, to have studied the utopian projects of Boullée and Ledoux, both of whom designed cylindrical buildings. He is thought to have admired the interlocking cylinders of grain elevators in the American Midwest, which were published by Le Corbusier in his *L'Esprit Nouveau*. He examined the structure of certain Muscovite churches. And as for the honeycomb construction, whereby windows can be added or subtracted without affecting the weight load, it reminds me of the cylindrical brick tomb-towers of Islamic Central Asia. There was, it is well known, a strong Islamic influence on early Soviet architecture.

I would also like to think that on one of his summer drives around Paris someone drove him to the parish of Chambourcy to see the Désert de Retz, a building that was being 'discovered' around that time by Colette, among others.

The Désert, a colossal truncated Doric column with a stack of oval and round rooms piled up around a spiral staircase, was designed and built by an eccentric Anglomane and friend of Boullée, the Chevalier de Monville. It is surely the most imaginative building of the eighteenth century still standing. yet, although classed as a national monument since 1941, the French government in its wisdom allowed it to fall into ruin. The windows of the drum are oval and rectangular, but there is something about their arrangement which seems very close to the spirit of Melnikov's house. At the time I didn't have the wit to ask him.

Melnikov himself, in answer to the self-imposed question 'What is it that prevents genius from manifesting itself in architecture?' wrote that his lack of money was converted into an 'immense richness of the imagination'. His sense of autonomy had swept away all sense of caution, and the practical economies forced him to risk as much, relatively speaking, as was risked by Brunelleschi when building the dome of the Florence cathedral.

I never got a chance to go into the bedroom because Anna Gavrilovna was hiding there. I suspect, however, that the altar-like beds had been done away with as well as the uniform yellow-green colour of the walls, which Melnikov — who had certain theories about colour and sleeping patterns — associated with restful sleep.

Scattered all over the house were bits of bourgeois furniture, neoclassical chairs, or an Art Nouveau carpet — in fact, throughout there was an atmosphere of antimacassar and samovar at odds with the original spirit. Viktor Stepanovich told me that during the years of the Stalinist 'night' his mother had salvaged whatever she could from her old family home.

Melnikov, mercifully, did not have to share the fate — of cattle trucks to Siberia — which befell a Mandelstam, a Babel, or a Meyerhold. Yet gradually the vultures closed in. First his colleagues denounced him as a Formalist. Then, at a meeting of the Soviet architectural establishment, about eight hundred hands shot up in support of a motion that would prevent him from practising his profession.

The death knell of visionary architecture in Russia had already been sounded when Lenin's commissioner for enlightenment, Anatoly Lunacharsky, announced, 'The people also have a right to colonnades.' It did, admittedly, take time for the spread of that deadly megalomaniac style known as Sovnovrok (New Soviet Rococo), which was bound to be anathema to Melnikov. For forty years he simply sat at home doing nothing. Occasionally there was talk of his rehabilitation, but nothing really came of it, so that by the time of my visit the house, for all its vestiges of vitality, had become a sombre and gloomy private palace — as sombre as Prokofiev's 1942 Sonata.

When I bade the old man goodbye, he smiled a smile of wistful melancholy and, raising one hand, drew in the air a graph of his blighted career. If one could have recorded it accurately on paper, it might have looked something like this:

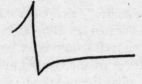

1988

ANDRÉ MALRAUX

The career of André Malraux has startled, entertained and sometimes alarmed the French. As archaeologist, writer of revolutionary novels, compulsive traveller and talker, war hero, philosopher of art and Gaullist minister, he is their only living first-class adventurer. At 73 he is a national institution, but an institution of a most unpredictable kind. They consult him as an oracle; and if his replies bewilder, none will deny him one of the most original minds of our time. Furthermore, Malraux has an opportunist sense of timing, he has witnessed and influenced great events in modern history. He alone can tell you that Stalin considered *Robinson Crusoe* 'the first Social-ist novel', *and* that Mao Tse-tung's hand is 'pink as if it had been boiled', *and* that Trotsky's white skin and haunted eyes made him look like a Sumerian alabaster idol. He is also one of that select company who won the confidence of General de Gaulle.

The bones of his story are those of a talented young aesthete who transformed himself into a great man. At twenty-two, already suffocating in the false euphoria of post-war Paris, he mounted an amateur expedition to discover Khmer ruins in Cambodia, but the colonial authorities arrested him for making off with some sculptures half-lost in the jungle. The spite of his prosecutors, and his forced stay in Phnom Penh, alerted him to the offensiveness of colonial rule; and once he had evaded the prison sentence, he started an anti-colonial newspaper, *L'Indochine Enchainée*, in Saigon.

Some rather nebulous activities in or around the 1925 Communist uprising in Canton earned him the reputation of a Red activist. He returned to France with a passion for the Orient and created an entirely new kind of revolutionary novel. The best known, *La Condition Humaine* (Man's Fate), recounts in a bewildering sequence of episodes the later Shanghai rebellion against Chiang Kai-shek in 1927. The heroes, most of whom reflect facets of Malraux's character, scheme, spatter with blood, pit themselves against impossible odds and usually die in the process. Malraux himself emerges as a high-minded atheist, a fighter for social justice, haunted by death, yet denying the hope of immortality. His subject is Man, his tragic fate and heroic defiance in the face of extinction.

The Malraux of the Thirties was the anti-Fascist and hero of the Left, with the black forelock over his eyes, the nervous tic, the frown and cigarette and finger pointing wrathfully. His flair for personal publicity never deserted him; haranguing meetings of the *Front Populaire*; dashing with Gide to Berlin to plead for the Bulgarian Communists falsely accused of lighting the *Reichstag* fire; or irritating a conference of Marxist writers in Moscow with his liberal opinions. Malraux may have been a fellow-traveller, but never held a party card. He continued to travel, to move in fashionable circles, and hold down a post with the Paris publishing house of Gallimard, where he had charge of the art publications.

In his next incarnation he led a Republican bomber squadron in the Spanish Civil War with the honorary rank of colonel. Legend has it that Malraux wheedled some ancient pursuit planes out of the sympathetic, but politically neutral, French Government of Léon Blum. He flew on sixty-five bombing raids and sometimes even piloted himself (without a pilot's licence). At Medellin in the autumn of 1937 the Malraux squadron halted a Fascist column advancing on Madrid; later, at the battle of Teruel, German Heinkels forced it out of the air. Malraux — to the relief of the Air Minister,

Cisneros — left Spain on a fund-raising tour of the United States, and, without speaking English, agonised American ladies with descriptions of nurses removing bandages from wounds without anaesthetics. The ladies paid for anaesthetics.

His detractors unflatteringly compared him to Lord Byron and laughed at his 'artistic' flying jacket. But he emerges as the most effective foreign writer in a war of foreign writers; more effective, for example, than Hemingway. He crystallised these exploits into a novel, *L'Espoir* (Days of Hope), and a film of the same name. Before he had been a tourist on the fringe of revolution, now he courted death, mastered his fear of fear and survived, exchanging a cold cerebral world for *la fraternité virile*. He is one of the few writers clear-headed enough to describe the almost sexual arousal of men in battle. Spain changed him, perhaps from a potential suicide, into a survivor. His early heroes die of bullets, gangrene, tropical fever or by their own hand. Later, geared by a mysterious hope, they survive air crashes, poison gas, or tank traps. Spain also opened his eyes to the methods and aims of Soviet Marxism.

With France mobilised in 1940 he signed up as a private in a tank regiment. The career of T.E. Lawrence had fascinated him for years and critics have seen a conscious imitation of Aircraftsman Shaw. Malraux was captured by the Germans but escaped to the Free Zone and spent the early war writing; only to reappear in 1944 as a stylish *maquisard* with the pseudonym of Colonel Berger. Fighting in the red sandstone hills of the Corrèze, the old internationalist became a patriot. He fell into an ambush, and was wounded and captured by the Germans as he drew their fire from his English Resistance colleagues. For this he received the DSO. The Gestapo hauled him before a firing squad but did not fire, reserving him for interrogation. The same thing, he is proud to say, happened to Dostoyevsky. At the end of the war he resurfaced as commander of the quixotic Alsace-Lorraine Brigade under General de Lattre de Tassigny, and helped prevent a Nazi reoccupation of Strasbourg.

Malraux's rediscovery of France prepared the intellectual ground for his friendship with General de Gaulle. One rumour has it that, on meeting Malraux in 1945, the General said: 'At last I have seen a man!' Malraux became Minister of Information in the first post-war government. He master-minded the nationalistic propaganda of de Gaulle's *Rassemble-ment du Peuple Français* in 1946–47. After 1958 he was Minister for Cultural Affairs, when he had Paris scrubbed clean, and made his celebrated visits to Kennedy, Nasser, Nehru and Mao Tse-tung. His alliance with the General astonished all opinions, Right and Left, and probably themselves. But the two had a great deal in common.

Both were intellectuals *and* adventurers with a taste for military glory, even if Malraux's was on a small scale. They were fascinated by the exercise of power and by the role of the archetypal hero who saves his country; both also shared the idea of national renewal through catastrophe. They delighted in the French language; hyperbole was their natural form of expression. They were estranged from the values of their class, and despised politicians and industrialists. Without attempting to enter their world, they sympathised with the plight of workers trapped by twentieth-century machine civilisation. But they saw through the simple-mindedness of exaggerating the class struggle at the expense of national unity, believing that social justice is best obtained in a nation that knows its own ground. Malraux once asked Jean-Paul Sartre: 'The proletariat? What is the proletariat?'

They knew as fact that nations will usually act nationalistic-ally and were unimpressed by specious internationalism. They were alive to the dangers of Stalin well before Church-ill's 'Iron Curtain' speech at Fulton, Missouri. Malraux scorned the 'extreme masochism of the Left' and said he saw no point in becoming more Russian and less French. The *Rassemblement* aimed at attracting the poor because the poor were patriots. But de Gaulle's and Malraux's appeals to French grandeur went straight over the workers' heads. Instead it was the *grande petite bourgeoisie*, often for venal reasons, who flocked to the Gaullist cause and gave the movement its self-contradictory character. Malraux remained precariously on the Left of the Gaullist Party and often felt compromised by it. But the General always valued his 'flashing imagination' and was at least partly conditioned by him to the idea of decolonisation.

What makes Malraux a great figure is not necessarily his verbal performance or his writings. His life is the masterpiece. He has lived out the fears and hopes of the West in the twentieth century and has survived. He advances a prophetic insight, that Man (alone, now that the gods have gone) will outlive the threat of his extinction; and that great men, with all their faults, will continue to exist.

This said, one must confess to difficulties. Malraux inhabits the Mythical Present. He deliberately confuses the event with the archetypal situation. Alexander the Great, Saint-Just, Dostoyevsky, Michelangelo or Nietzsche are his intellectual companions and he moves among them on familiar terms. Legendary figures take substance; works of art come alive; modern people dissolve into myth. Mao Tse-tung, 'the great bronze emperor' of the *Antimémoires*, is somehow inter-changeable with the gleaming statue of an ancient Meso-potamian priest-king. Nor does Malraux believe in false modesty. He opens his memoir of de Gaulle, *Les Chênes qu'on Abat* (Fallen Oaks), with the observation that creative geniuses (such as himself) have never left records of their conversations with men of History — Voltaire with Frederick the Great or Michelangelo with Pope Julius II — and leaves the impression that, whereas the great man belongs to History, the great artist belongs to Eternity.

Then there is the problem of style. His presence mesmerises his listeners. They feel physically charged by his voice as it alternates from staccato outbursts to slushy whispers; then they find themselves flailing for sense. He taxes his reader's intelligence to the limit. Images, sensations, exhortations, philosophic reflections and startling analogies are telescoped one over the other. Glittering insights are followed, as if in repentance, by ponderous explanations which do not really explain. The 'difficulties' of Malraux once drew from Cocteau the wicked quip: 'Have you ever heard of a human reading *La Condition Humaine*?' In translation the writing suffers a sea-change. The highly-charged rhetoric, which is glorious in French, is unacceptable in English.

Malraux's breathless career has left lesser spirits far behind – and irritated. French literary circles have poured their energies into exposing its contradictions, but there remains a dimension which eludes them. Experts greeted his writings on the philosophy of art as amateurish, even if as astute a critic as Edmund Wilson valued them among the great books of the century. One art historian, Georges Duthuit, excelled himself by refuting Malraux's *The Imaginary Museum* with his own three-volume work, *The Unimaginable Museum*. Without daring to call him a coward, Sartre dismisses Malraux's exploits in Spain as 'heroic parasitism'.

His private life is not for dissection. It is scarred by the suicide of a father, and a wife, two brothers and two sons killed. Yet he arouses suspicion that he has bottled up unpleasant secrets. His divorced first wife Clara took it upon herself to lay him bare as a fantast, but the effect of her memoirs is so infuriating that they increase him and diminish her. The fact is that men of action have a habit of consigning past loves and indiscretions to oblivion in the hope of better things to come. Malraux has a formidable memory, but he updates his recollection of the past to conform with his view of the present. By temperament he was never a note-taker or diarist, as his autobiography *Antimémoires* proves.

Malraux is alone. He can have no followers. He never allowed himself the luxury of a final political or religious creed, and is too restless for the discipline of academic life. He is unclassifiable, which in a world of -isms and -ologies is also unforgivable. His knowledge advances on a global front. The technique is that of the intellectual guerrilla. When the going is clear, he blinds his opponent with brilliance and detonates charges under his nose. Confronted by superior opinion, he gives ground, but, gliding off at an oblique angle, lures him into the marsh of semi-ignorance before the final attack. One threat he holds over his detractors; he may at any minute agree with them.

I first met Malraux two years ago at the house of his American friends Clement and Jessie Wood. At one point in the conversation he turned his green eyes on me and said: 'And Genghis Khan? How would you have stopped him?' Silence. Recently I had the opportunity of spending an afternoon with him and asked if he would talk about Britain; about General de Gaulle's attitude to Britain; and about the mental blockage between Britain and France.

We met at Verrières-les-Buissons, the family house of the Vilmorins, who are the great horticulturalists of France. Louise de Vilmorin was his companion for the last three years of her life. Her *salon* overlooks a planting of rare conifers, blue-grey and dark green in the winter light, with a cluster of white birch trunks gleaming beyond. Among her sofas and chairs, covered in blue and white cotton, and the Chinese porcelain stools and the animals of gilt, lacquer and pearl-shell, Malraux has spread his own territory, scattering his sculptures and paintings round the room. Then there are his drawings of cats, the cats he used to doodle through the long speeches of Gaullist ministers in session.

Malraux was wearing a light brown jacket with lapels like butterfly wings. He never relaxes in conversation, but strains forward on the edge of his chair. He listens to questions with intense concentration, sometimes resting his forefingers vertically on his cheekbones, before bursting into words and gestures. From under the melancholic mask he occasionally allows a glimpse of his highly developed sense of the ridiculous.

'First,' he replied to my preamble, 'what I think about

England is far from what most of the French think. They are mostly anti-English and I am extremely pro-English.

'And I will tell you why. Our whole civilisation is threatened by its most serious crisis since the fall of Rome. As the young have discovered, the secret divinity of the twentieth century is Science. But Science is incapable of forming character. The more people talk of human sciences, the less effect human sciences have on man. You know as well as I do that psychoanalysis has never made a man. And the formation of man is the most pressing problem facing humanity. England, to my eyes, is about the last country to have *une grande création de l'homme.*'

I almost interrupted. It was the first week in January. From across the Channel the English, far from creating anyone, seemed intent on ripping each other apart.

'There have been two countries, and astonishingly, two only, which have coined a word to designate the exemplary man. *Attention!* I am not speaking of the aristocrat. You have the Spanish *caballero* and the English gentleman; and England and Spain are both colonial countries. Since then there has been one other exemplary type — the Bolshevik. It doesn't matter if it was true; the important fact is that the archetype occupies the collective conscience of the nation. The only country that did it better before *you* was Rome. Rome created a type of man to hold the world in check for five centuries. After him came the knight, but the knight was never a national figure, whereas the Englishman was English and the Roman was Roman. From Rome to England there were no nationalists. There were remarkable men, but they were never nationalists. And that to my mind is the capital importance of England.

'A thing I find tiresome about the French is that their view of England is extremely Victorian. I do not think of England as necessarily Victorian or necessarily Imperialist. But the England of Drake is (*is* not *was*) a very great country. In her greatest moment she had no empire.

'And when you ask me what I think of England, I'll say you have one great problem . . . '

The voice assumed a tone of exhortation. His problems are always moral problems; believing that if moral problems are set right, economic ones look after themselves.

'The essential problem is: Will England find a way to recreate the English type? A new incarnation it will have to be, because the Victorian gentleman had nothing to do with the gentleman of Drake. The English character was strong enough; all the same it varied with the centuries. Will you rediscover yourselves?'

'I think,' I said, 'you're suggesting we revert to type. At heart we are an island of buccaneers and pirates.'

'*Et joyeux!* Tell me,' he said, smiling, 'when did the English stop talking about Merry England?'

We could not decide. Chaucer, we said, was real Merry England. Drake was still Merry England. But the Puritans were melancholic, not merry. And Merry England certainly didn't survive the Industrial Revolution.

The next topic was the British Empire; how it was an aberrant episode in our history; and how we may even have borrowed the idea of Imperialism from the Indian Empire of the Moguls.

'You must not run down the Mogul Empire,' he said and then rapidly outlined how Akbar the Great was the first Muslim ruler to break the Islamic anathema and encourage portraits of himself (because any likeness must show the essential beauty of the soul); how this potent symbol proved him a universalist in the manner of the French Revolution; how, therefore, like Napoleon he was, and how unlike Queen Victoria; and how this explained why the Muslims made a great civilisation in India and the British never did, comparing the Mogul cities like Agra, Delhi and Lahore with the Anglo-Indian Bombay, Calcutta and Madras, which he described as 'transplanted British building suffocated by *bidonvilles*'.

I asked him about T.E. Lawrence. In Lawrence's career and

personality Malraux seems to have recognised elements that coincided with his own. He once nearly completed a biography of Lawrence, *Le Défi de l'Absolu*, but the war prevented its publication.

'I was interested in the questions his life proposed. I was never exactly influenced by Lawrence. Because if you put Lawrence into modern dress, what was he? Technically, a resistance fighter parachuted into Arabia. Just as you parachuted English officers into France in the last war and we fought along with them, so the War Department in Cairo parachuted officers into the desert. There were no aeroplanes, but technically it was the same thing.

'No, the person who interests me is the Lawrence who raises the fundamental question, the meaning of life itself. Before him there were any number of great spirits who questioned life, but always in the name of some superior power . . . like the Crusader who put his life in the hands of Christ. But the case of Lawrence is unique. Here was a man who questioned life, but did not know in what name he questioned life. And he was not ashamed by it. *Lawrence, en grandiose, c'est mai '68.*'

Malraux once described Lawrence as the 'first liberal hero of the West', seeing in him the prophet of decolonisation. In retrospect he believes the most significant fact of the century to be Britain's abandonment of India and one of its most courageous acts the Labour Government's decision to leave in 1947. Once British India, 'a symbol of immense importance', had gone, any idea of *Algérie Française* was stillborn. Lawrence was 'an astonishing prophet in the historical perspective', defending what Britain did 30 years later, and an extremely poor prophet of *realpolitik* in that he did not see that the future ruler of Arabia was Ibn Saud.

I turned the discussion to de Gaulle. Rumour has it that Malraux lost his interest in Lawrence once he had discovered the General. Most Englishmen, I had explained, disliked de Gaulle. They saw in him a relentless Anglophobe. We had sheltered him in the war; Churchill had in fact made his career and later he showed nothing but ingratitude. (De Gaulle, as French Under-Secretary for Defence, flew to London on 17 June, 1940. Legally he had mutinied. The next day he made his famous broadcast over the BBC. In London he moved rather diffidently at first, even writing to General Weygand, the French Commander-in-Chief, inviting him to England to lead the Free French.) Did he, on meeting Churchill, I asked, see the possibility of becoming de Gaulle as he later was? Did he lose his modesty in the face of Churchill?

'I believe it. I believe it. But take care! You are surely right. On condition that you are not *too* right. He will not have said to himself the evening of his meeting with Churchill: "Now it is I." I don't think that at all. I think it was . . . like the sun's curve. At first he will have said to himself: "Perhaps it is unnecessary to call Weygand?" And then he will have said: "If there were no Weygand?" And then: "That is just as well. Sir Churchill is a great statesman and one can have confidence in him. If Weygand comes he will only make intrigues." And in the end he thought exactly as you say. Remember to put a fog over the affair. Because it cannot have been clear to him at the beginning however much it became clear later.'

Was there, I persisted, a real meeting of minds? They were, after all, both outsiders. Could this be the reason that both chose to incarnate the soul of their country?

He deflected this one by suggesting I put in my portrait of de Gaulle something which was rarely discussed, the General's ambivalence. 'When one speaks of de Gaulle's admiration for England it is true. When one speaks of his hostility and irritation it is true. But the real truth lies between the two. You must not forget the man's age. When de Gaulle was twenty the British Empire was the greatest reality in the world. It was not a question of sympathy. America was of small consequence. As a young officer in the First War, he thought, as did everyone else, the moment England enters the war, Germany will be lost. Now, when he arrived in London in 1940, he well knew that British power was not what it was, but he continued to have the impression of its power. So when Churchill said to him, "Between Roosevelt and you, I will always choose Roosevelt" (Roosevelt constantly tried to get rid of de Gaulle), everyone thought he was furious because that meant: "I will not choose you." It was not that at all. He was stupefied! Because for the first time he heard the voice of England saying: "I am no longer the first power in the world." And from that moment England meant something quite different to him.'

De Gaulle once wrote: 'When all is said England is an island; France the cape of a continent; America another world.' Was his refusal to let Britain into the Common Market his oblique way of protecting us from the continental adventures we so little understand? 'It was not so pure,' Malraux said.

'It was his excessively strong feeling of England's destiny. [The French *destin* seems to be stronger than the English, and implies 'historical fate'.] England's destiny was not the Common Market. He used to say: "If England enters the Common Market, England will be lost. And if England is lost, it is not attractive for us, Continentals, to have her in the Common Market." For the General, you must remember, was passionately concerned with destiny.

'*There* was a man who arrived in his little plane and became one of the most important men in Europe. If he didn't believe in destiny, who could? He found an England, pressed to the point of extinction, but rescued in inventing Churchill, who pulled her out of Hell to save her. For him there was an English destiny and a French destiny and any reasonable French policy was to be founded on the British destiny, as he, de Gaulle, conceived it. He wanted to spare England and the Common Market. He wanted a *parallel* England, but with guarantees she did not become an American agent. [This may refer to de Gaulle's objection that Britain had access to American technology whereas France did not.] But he did not want to block the British.'

And most people in England would agree with him, I said. He then talked of another complicating factor, the General's attitude to France. When very young de Gaulle had formed his 'certain idea about France'. He had a contract with her as a lover with his bride. (He once said to Churchill: 'If I am not France, what am I doing in your office?') 'But the only other country he thought of as a person was England. He never thought of Germany in the same light.'

He had wanted to preserve France from Americanisation?

'I have rather mixed feelings about that. One side of the General's character was *antimachiniste*. At Colombey he used to go and chat with the wood-cutters. The wood-cutters for him were the Middle Ages. But he would never visit the locksmiths.'

However, de Gaulle had seen, he said, the need for a European federation to block the American industrial attack. He never believed in a politically federated Six, merely a convenient alliance. In this alliance he chose Adenauer, but then 'like all great political figures, he had more than one iron in the fire. A German one. And a British one. They were both serious. The others no.'

What had drawn him and de Gaulle together? Did both intuitively realise that political actions of today and the great myths of the past somehow coincided?

'Every historical figure who possesses that strange dimension one calls "poetic" rediscovers mythical elements in himself . . . I don't in any way take myself for a man of History, the General, yes. He began life at twenty with the thought: "How can I serve France as St Bernard served Christ?" St Bernard made Clairvaux [the first abbey of the Cistercian Order near Colombey-les-Deux-Eglises]. And the General — he could of course have been killed in 1918, but his vocation was very similar. You used to have the same spirit in England. I always find very beautiful the piece of paper they found on the frozen corpse of Scott: "I have done this to show what an Englishman can do." The man was dead, so it was good. If he'd written it in a *bistro*, it would be nothing.'

He then discussed how all the great heroes of history have had to perform a similar set of actions before being acclaimed as heroes. But there were two very different types. 'There is the positive hero and the negative hero, and the two do not mix. The negative hero usually has far greater poetic power. Lawrence and Ché Guevara were negative heroes. Alexander the Great was a positive hero. De Gaulle, all things considered, was a positive hero; he certainly lacked the masochism of a Lawrence. But the negative hero is a victim. If Guevara today were President of Bolivia it would never have worked. A hero like that requires the crucifixion.

'But to return to the General, it was wonderful that he did what he did at the age of fifty and with so few means . . . unlike Caesar or Alexander who had immense resources. This struck me forcibly when I was talking to Mao Tse-tung. At one moment in our conversation I saw he understood General de Gaulle far better than the French. And for all Mao knew France could be in Sicily! When I asked him: "Why do you attach such importance to General de Gaulle?" he replied simply: "Because he is a man like me. He saved his country." *C'est bizarre*. Mao knew very well the General wasn't a Communist. But he recognised the transcendent side . . . the hero who saves his country.

'The bond between the General and myself probably lay in what one can call the Irrational. The others followed him for tangible reasons. [There was a faintly hostile tone as he talked of *les autres*, and I thought of the tax-scandals and racketeering that have stuck to the word Gaullism.] But there was in the General a quality that went above their heads, something he only shared with me.'

Was he tempted by the idea of monarchy? They sometimes say that de Gaulle was a king without a kingdom. As a young expert in tank warfare he had once hovered around the monarchist party. My suggestion produced an appalled shake of the head.

'He thought there would be no succession, for what he had done reposed on the Irrational. All the same he attached immense importance to legitimacy. But *his* legitimacy was June 18. He came to realise that no one else could have done it. If his Constitution was good, it would probably work. But that was not the same as his legitimacy.

'He had one quality that was not monarchic at all, but one we admire in all great men who make constitutional experiments. Take the example of Julius Caesar in his role of dictator ... de Gaulle was a little like him. If you use the word "dictator" in the Roman sense, then he was a dictator; in the modern Fascist sense, no.

'The General had another dimension. He believed that certain events implicate rights and certain duties. He had, of course, read Roman history. And in ancient Rome, what was a dictator? It was power given to one of the consuls under dramatic circumstances. The dictatorship was not usurped. It was given by the Senate. In the First War Clemenceau, as *Président du Conseil*, enjoyed far greater powers than the other members as long as the war lasted. But the General also believed, a little religiously, that, in dramatic circumstances, legitimacy comes from the hand of God. That is how he saw June 18 ...'

Then what did he make of the *évènements* of May 1968?

'That most people saw it in an absurd manner. There was an infectious world rebellion of youth ... in Holland, France, Japan, Germany, etc. He was well aware of it. Far more important there was in France the political problem of the trade unions. And there was an accidental encounter of the two. The unions profited from the student chaos, but they were not united, as the unions proved by refusing to co-operate with the students. The two phenomena were inevitable, the meeting not.'

But he felt his authority weakened by May 1968? 'Yes, yes,' he said, 'he did. At one point he thought: "It will be better if I go. Either the country will recover ... or else the Deluge."'

Malraux gave a press conference at the time in which he said: 'The General is bitter as a man whose wife has deceived him with a servant.' Now he continued: 'I asked him in retirement, "When do you think you will return?" and he replied, "Always." I am sure it was the truth. But I am also sure the contrary was the truth. Because a man with a destiny like that never knows. You only have to look at the correspondence of Napoleon. Technically the Hundred Days was sheer folly. But if you think of Napoleon as a little artillery lieutenant who became Emperor of the West, then he could always have won a battle. It reminds me *en comique* of Joseph-ine Baker, who said: "It's far easier to become a star again than become one."'

And Quebec? On 27 June, 1967, on a state visit to Canada, de Gaulle stood on a balcony and shouted: '*Vive le Quebec Libre.*' The Cabinet of Lester Pearson announced that this was 'unacceptable', and the General, cutting his visit short, flew to Paris at once. Surely Quebec was a mistake?

'But he had a passion for it! The situation was unique enough. The bomb attacks were beginning. They gave one the feeling there would be a great drama in Quebec. In fact there was none and the Canadians arranged it among themselves. But the General was taken in by those who wanted help from us.'

Malraux's loyalty to the General does not blind him to his faults. He used to exclaim: 'Now there is his exaggerating!' at de Gaulle's latest anti-American outburst. But he will always defend him, as a tutor will defend a difficult but brilliant student. Indeed he will defend all his old friends. Amid the recriminations of liberated Paris, he was a faultless executor to his friend, the writer Drieu la Rochelle, who collaborated with the Germans and shot himself. As minister he would always help out of trouble an old battle companion of the International Brigade.

His political career had its great moments — the foreign visits, the procession round the gold coffin of Tutankhamen exhibited at the Petit Palais, the spectacle of Paris emerging from its layer of grime, or his funeral oration for his friend Braque. (In his study hangs 'the Braque by which all Braques must be judged' — a seashore with fishing boats, reduced nearly to nothingness as if by a Japanese Zen master.) Yet his higher aims as minister failed. His brief was the 'expansion and *rayonnement* of French culture'. Perhaps he was too little of a cultural chauvinist to put this message across? Perhaps his own ideas were too elevated for ordinary people to grasp? He believes that all art is a defiance of man's fate, and that through art a nation rids itself of its demons. He has a real hatred of the mediocre. And he must have suffered from the hatred he aroused, as a Gaullist, among the artistic Left and to find his *Maisons de la Culture* smeared with their graffiti.

And the very idea of a Ministry of Culture has something totalitarian about it. Didn't he feel compromised?

'In France all art exists on the margins of society. I could not have survived in the Ministry of Foreign Affairs. One good thing about this country is that there exists an old respect (which you do not have in England) for the thinkers whose influence bore fruit in the Revolution, Voltaire, Rousseau, etc. . . . Their influence gave a legitimacy to all art that was marginal.'

English art, I said, is at its best when it is really English and its great artists, like Palmer or Blake, are lonely eccentrics. Whereas in France foreigners often set the pace. 'Think of Picasso . . .'

'Ah, but that is the Soul of England!' He had seen an opening and was advancing towards it as towards a gap in the defences. 'England is never as great as when she is alone. And France is never France when she fights for herself. The real France is the France of the Crusades or the Revolution. When the French fight for mankind they are wonderful. When they fight for themselves, they are nothing.'

I mentioned Anatoly Lunacharsky, Lenin's Cultural Commissioner and prototype for all Ministers of Culture. At once he conjured up an anecdote of Lunacharsky censoring Eisenstein's film *October*. 'There is art; there is cinema. But . . . snip . . . snip . . . there are also politics.'

He continued: 'The Bolsheviks were sadly misinformed about art. But they had been exiled in the same *bistros* as the Cubist painters. Lenin returned to Russia with the idea that, after all, Cubism was the natural expression of the proletariat, and that is funny enough. It didn't last long, but gave the Russian avant-garde breathing space to develop. It vanished once Lenin was dead; for Stalin there was no such thing as cubism . . . But in Lunacharsky you have the mixture of an old émigré who drank *café-crème* at La Rotonde with Chagall and who ordered theatre sets from him, and a Bolshevik minister with the responsibilities of a minister. From day to day he had a bridge ahead and a bridge behind, and then he died.' He was not simply discussing Lunacharsky, but airing the difficulties of any intellectual trapped by the realities of power.

When it comes to the Russians, Malraux's sense of the ridiculous breaks loose. At my first meeting he told the following anecdote of how he and de Gaulle took Khrushchev to the Salle des Glaces at Versailles.

De Gaulle (tapping one foot on the parquet floor): 'This is the famous *parquet de Versailles*.'

Khrushchev (bending down): 'We have exactly the same at the Hermitage in Leningrad, but ours is made with ebony.'

De Gaulle to Malraux: 'This man is beginning to bore me.'

Then there is the story of de Gaulle's visit to Stalin after the Yalta Conference. Stalin had a special showing of a film of Russian soldiers slaughtering Nazis. As each German fell, Stalin squeezed the General's knee till it was bruised. 'Finally,' he said, 'I had to take my leg away.'

Malraux described Solzhenitsyn as a nineteenth-century Tolstoyan novelist who had ignored the advances of Pasternak or Babel. He repeated the story of Gide's visit to Stalin to enquire about the role of the homosexual in Soviet society, and how a frantic Kremlin staff prevented the visit; Gide would have been deported to France, but they to Siberia. He also recalled with affection Sir Isaiah Berlin, surely for verbal dexterity Malraux's most distinguished rival. 'He shares with me the same comic recollections of Russia. We were there at the same time and moved in the same circles. Even as late as 1934 when the purges were beginning, Russian intellectuals lived in a *milieu extravagant*. It was like Montparnasse in the First War. It had a quality that was utterly Shakespearian.'

He continued with a description of writers' cafés in Republican Madrid, with George Orwell as a *garçon timide*, and how Hemingway bought his first smoking jacket to attend his (Malraux's) fund-raising lecture in New York. 'I did not know him well. Later I saw him occasionally in France. But the last time I had the impression that the malady had already begun.' The two cordially loathed each other. Hemingway thought 'Camarade Malraux' a poseur and Malraux thought Hemingway a fake tough. Earlier I had asked him about the American. '*Hemingway, c'est un fou qui a la folie de simplicité.*'

Changing the subject I asked how it was that black African peoples had fewer complexes about their French colonial past than their English-speaking counterparts?

'For us this is the heritage of the French Revolution. The blacks were made citizens of France by the Convention of 1792. And the result is bizarre enough. Because a Senegalese can say to half my friends: "But I was French before you." An enormous number of Parisians have parents from Alsace, Nice, etc., which only joined France in the nineteenth century. But Senghor [poet and President of Senegal] could say, if he wanted to, "I have been French since 1792." The Convention emancipated the colonies. Afterwards Napoleon imposed the old conditions because of Joséphine, but the idea of emancipation lingered on.'

How did Malraux see a life of action? 'There is a type of man who requires action for its own sake as a painter requires paint and canvas. But, take care! Many of the greatest men of history, especially those involved in *la grande politique*, have not seen much direct action. It is a matter of individual temperament. You cannot categorise it. Napoleon was bellicose enough. Alexander also, but Caesar much less, and Richelieu not at all. And Richelieu was one of the greatest French men of action. He lifted France from a third-rate power and left it the first country in Europe.'

This is not what I meant. After all Malraux had seen plenty of direct action before concluding that 'adventure no longer exists except in the hearts of governments'. What did his own actions mean to him?

'In France intellectuals are usually incapable of opening an umbrella. When an intellectual bothers to become an orator or fight for his country, that is already something. Let us say, I have a happy mixture of intelligence and physical courage, one which I proved from day to day in Spain. It is an accident, a happy accident, but none the less an accident and a banal one! The classic French intellectual is the *homme de bibliothèque*, the writer in his library, a tradition that begins with Voltaire — and is in fact untrue because Voltaire took extremely strong political positions. But the reputation of the man in the library took hold. There is one figure whom you are too young to remember, but who played a role of immense importance — Anatole France. Anatole France was a gigantic talent. He had a state funeral. But Anatole France was not only an *homme de bibliothèque*; his heroes were *hommes de bibliothèque*.'

'But you escaped from the library?'

'When . . . you return from Asia and you find all your companions on the *Nouvelle Revue Française* writing novels about homosexuality and *attaching immense importance to it*, you are tempted to say, "There are other things. The Tomb of the Unknown Pederast under the Arc de Triomphe is a little much."'

Malraux has no objection to revolutionaries as such, only to hot-air revolutionaries, a class he calls the 'sensitive souls of the Café Flore'. His attitude to revolution is 'Go to Bolivia or stay in the Café Flore.' He admires Régis Debray and recently lunched with him. It was a great success even if Madame Debray found the proceedings a little undialectic. Two years ago visitors to Verrières were amazed to find his study turned into a command headquarters and Malraux himself poring over maps of East Bengal. Mrs Gandhi, to his evident irritation, did not want her father's old friend on the battlefield, and he did not visit Bangladesh until after independence.

'But if India had not entered the arena, I could have done something very serious. I wanted to take about six hundred officers to Bengal. In France there are any number of retired army officers, not particularly young, but not excessively old. And they are very bored and very ready to march. With six hundred officers above the rank of captain we could have had an officer training school to turn out 2,000 Bengali officers in six months. All their officers had been Pakistanis, and we could have done a great service.'

And how did he find Mujibur Rahman? 'Europeans make the mistake of thinking he's a kind of Gandhi or Nehru . . . Mujibur has a charismatic action. When he tours the country, he thinks everything is wonderful because they receive him everywhere in a magisterial way. He creates a passionate atmosphere. "Bangladesh will overcome!" etc. But that is far from certain. He is a pure man, I don't doubt. There is no corruption in him, but there is corruption in the state and their difficulties are gigantic. But I, for one, am not too pessimistic. When in our time you do not have a totalitarian government, the action of the individual at a local level is strong enough to create an organisation. It is not the Central Government of India that makes India. And the progress of India since independence, *formidable!*'

And what of the prospects for an adventurer today? He did not think the word had much sense. A faint possibility, perhaps, in Central Asia (after all the Soviet Union is the last Imperial Empire to have survived). 'But,' he said sadly, 'there are blocks of flats in Samarkand.' We ended the conversation

on Afghanistan, with its pale green rivers and Buddhist monasteries, where eagles wheel over the deodar forests and
tribesmen carry copper battle-axes and wreathe vine leaves
round their heads as they did in the time of Alexander.

'And Tibet,' he said, 'there is always Tibet. . . '

1974

WERNER HERZOG IN GHANA

In January 1971, I paid my first visit to the West African country known then and from time immemorial as Dahomey, and in particular to the decayed slaving-towns on the coast — Ouidah, Porto Novo, Grand Popo — which in their heyday exported more slaves to the Americans than did any other part of the continent. The towns are referred to collectively as Little Brazil — a legacy of generations of mulattos and manumitted blacks who 'returned' to Africa in the nineteenth century and set themselves up in the slave business.

At Ouidah the two sights of the town are the Python Temple and Sigbomey, the Brazilian *casa grande* built by the slaver millionaire Dom Francisco Felix de Souza. He had come to the Slave Coast sometime after 1800 as lieutenant of the Portuguese fort, and after staging a palace revolution in which he deposed one king of Dahomey for another, he set about reorganising the Dahomean army — with its corps of Amazon warriors — as the most efficient military machine in Africa.

As a reward for his services, Ghezo, the new king, awarded de Souza the title of *chacha*, or viceroy, of Ouidah and a monopoly over the sale of slaves, which had recently been declared illegal by the British government.

De Souza owned a fleet of slave-ships, some with the new

Bermudan rig, which beat faster to windward than the frigates of the West Africa Squadron. Prince de Joinville, a son of Louis Philippe, came to call and described fantastic displays of opulence — silver services, gaming saloons, billiard saloons — and the *chacha* himself wandering about distractedly in a dirty caftan. Toward the end of his life, however, the slaver fell foul of his friend the king, was ruined by his Brazilian partners, and was abandoned by his brood of mulatto sons. He died a madman, and on Ghezo's orders, was buried in a barrel of rum, together with a beheaded boy and girl, under his Goanese four-poster bed.

The bed is still there. At its foot there was a statue of Saint Francis of Assisi — the slaver's namesake — while on the bed table stood a silver elephant, the family emblem, and a half-empty bottle of Gordon's gin in case the old man woke up thirsty. An old black woman showed me round, a de Souza herself, who expatiated in halting French on the days when her ancestors had been rich, famous, and white. When she pulled aside the bed sheets, she revealed, instead of a mattress, a mound of fetish material: blood, feathers, palm oil, and metal images of Dagbé the Holy Python.

Here plainly was a story worth telling, but when I came back seven years later, Dahomey had changed its name to the People's Republic of Benin. The 'thought' of Kim Il Sung was all the rage and, to my amazement, I found myself one morning arrested as a mercenary, stripped to my underpants, and forced to stand against a wall in the searing sun while vultures wheeled overhead and the crowd outside the barracks chanted '*Mort aux mercenaires!*' A platoon practised arms-drill behind my back, and the soldier guarding me cooed melodiously, '*Ils vont vous tuer, massacrer même!*'

After this interruption I lost the stamina to pursue my researches, though I had acquired ripe material for a novel. Since it was impossible to fathom the alien mentality of my characters, my only hope was to advance the narrative in a sequence of cinematographic images, and here I was strongly influenced by the films of Werner Herzog. I remember saying, 'If this were ever made into a movie, only Herzog could do it.' But that was a pipe dream. The novel, *The Viceroy of Ouidah*, appeared in 1980, to the bemusement of reviewers, some of whom found its cruelties and baroque prose unstomachable.

About three years later I was travelling in the Australian outback, and on returning to the motel one day in Alice Springs, I found a note saying that Herzog was looking for me. Someone had given him one of my books when he was making *Fitzcarraldo* in the Amazon. He wondered if I'd be interested in helping with the script of a new film about the Aboriginals, *Where the Green Ants Dream*.

He was at Melbourne airport to meet my plane, an ascetic figure in threadbare fatigue pants and a sweat-shirt that exposed the laughing-skull tattoo on his shoulder. Within a couple of minutes our conversation had taken off in various abstruse directions.

It happened that he and I were tackling the same subject, the relation of Aboriginals to their land. He had his ideas. I had mine. I felt that to mix them would only add to the general confusion. I did, however, find him a dog-eared copy of *The Viceroy of Ouidah*. He said, 'This is a text I like. One day we will make it into a movie.' The line he liked best was given to me by the eight-year-old Grégoire de Souza, who, contemplating a trail of white ants that led into an unplugged refrigerator, said, '*Le frigo existe.*'

I saw Werner once or twice after that. And he would phone me from fishing trips in Northumberland, where his brother-in-law was an Anglican parson. He was, I discovered, a compendium of contradictions: immensely tough yet vulnerable, affectionate and remote, austere and sensual, not particularly well-adjusted to the strains of everyday life but functioning efficiently under extreme conditions.

He was also the only person with whom I could have a one-to-one conversation on what I would call the sacramental aspect of walking. He and I share a belief that walking is not simply therapeutic for oneself but is a poetic activity that can cure the world of its ills. He sums up his position in a stern pronouncement: 'Walking is virtue, tourism deadly sin.' A striking example of this philosophy was his winter pilgrimage to see Lotte Eisner.

Lotte Eisner, film critic and associate of Fritz Lang in Berlin, had emigrated in the early 1930s to Paris, where she helped found the Cinémathèque. Much later, after seeing Werner's *Signs of Life*, she wrote to Lang in California, 'I have seen the work of a wonderful young German film-maker.' To which he replied, 'No. It is impossible.'

She was soon to become a guiding spirit of the new German cinema, giving young directors the benefit of her immense experience and, because she was Jewish, helping to re-establish continuity with a great tradition of film-making that had been shattered under Hitler.

Werner, I'm told, was her favourite. And in 1974, when he heard she was dying, he set out walking, through ice and snow, from Munich to Paris, confident that somehow he could walk away her sickness. By the time he reached her apartment she had recovered and went on to live another ten years.

As for filming *The Viceroy*, quite unexpectedly I had a call from a New York agent offering to buy an option on the rights. The man had the grace to say the book was not hot property, and the sum he mentioned was derisively small. I called up Werner, who without a flicker of hesitation said, 'I'll buy the rights' — and did so.

I thought no more of it. The difficulties of filming in West Africa seemed insuperable. I then picked up an impossibly rare disease in Western China, yet rumours reached my hospital bed that the project was under way. Klaus Kinski would play the part of Dom Francisco, the slaver. The title would be changed to *Cobra Verde* (the book is peppered with references to snakes and snake worship). The first half of the film would be shot in Colombia, not in Brazil. Ouidah would be Fort

Elmina on the coast of Ghana, and the up-country palace of the Dahomean kings would be the mud-brick complex that Werner was having built in a grassland dotted with baobabs in the north of the country, near Tamale.

I first saw the palace on a Tuesday, as my plane came in to land. It could have existed since the Iron Age but had, in fact, been finished on Saturday. Werner's girlfriend, Christina, saw us dip our wings and came to fetch me from the airstrip.

Breakfasting in the shade. The cameras are turning and the king of Dahomey (played by a real king) is carried from his palace in a litter. His courtiers surround him, yelling their heads off. Most of them hold the *asin*, which are animal-headed standards covered in gold leaf. The king himself is smothered in gold jewellery, much of it real, and wears an imposing gilded crown. All the actors wear robes of yellow, orange, or tawny brown, which, set against the mud wall, gives an effect of sombre and glittering richness.

The king flexes his biceps and flicks his fly whisk. Chintz umbrellas float like jellyfish above his head.

'It's too much for me,' says the set doctor, who is Portuguese. 'I can't believe it. Really it's too *much*.'

Other film-directors, faced with the problem of recreating a nineteenth-century African court, would have put it in the hands of the set and costume designers and ended up with a fake. Werner, by hiring a *real* court and not changing a thing except the odd Taiwanese watch, more than makes up for lack of historical accuracy by establishing an authenticity of tone.

Dust-stained, wearing broken plastic sandals and a wet hand-kerchief tied around his forehead, Werner sprints about from the camera to the actors and back. He bumps into the fetish priest, an androgynous figure pirouetting round and round in white crinoline. He apologises and sets the man spinning once more.

I'm amazed by the old-fashioned Germanic courtliness with which he handles his African cast. Without a hint of condescension he takes a woman by the arm, as if he were escorting her to a ball, and shows her how to walk through the Great Gate. The others follow. For the next shot he says, 'Ladies, you now have the privilege of giving us the best screams.' Or to the king: 'Nana, would you please lean back so we can see your very royal face.'

On the tie-beams of the Great Gate stand the hunters: real hunters, members of a hunting tribe in the North. Their trousers are sewn from strips of indigo cotton, their jerkins covered with gris-gris. They wear quivers full of arrows, and civet skins dangle from their belts. Their basketwork helmets are equipped with buffalo horns, which, silhouetted against the sky, make them look like the guardians of Valhalla.

Werner cannot resist the old Wagnerian touch. He renamed two Brazilian girls in the script Valkyria and Wandeleide, and when I tax him that the music of Wagner could not have reached Brazil in the early 1800s, he laughs.

When he first suggested I come to Ghana, I was too weak to climb stairs and said, 'Do you want a corpse on your hands?' Later I decided I'd be fit to travel, with one proviso: if I brought a wheelchair, someone would push me around. The answer came back: 'A wheelchair will get you nowhere in terrain where I am shooting. I will give you four hammockeers and a sunshade bearer.' Now that invitation, even if one had been dying, was irresistible.

The king, His Highness Nana Agyefi Kwame II, Omanhene of Nsein, is a man of magnificent presence and a slightly extended upper lip. When Werner first floated the idea of using a real king instead of an actor, his Ghanaian colleagues said it was unthinkable. But Nana, like most kings, was obviously longing to play in a movie. The snag was how he, a good king, could assume the role of a bad king and be deposed. Yet he comes across as a far more convincing character than the cardboard tyrant of my book, as a man who knows he is doomed and faces his fate with equanimity. While his women get ready to strangle him, he says with all the weariness in the world, 'I will go now and get some sleep.'

The courtyard wall is lined with skulls, and the lintels and steps are paved with skulls. 'How', I asked Werner at lunch, 'did you get away with all those skulls? What did the villagers think?'

'Oh, they liked them. They built with enthusiasm.'

The trouble with making the skulls out of plaster instead of plastic is that they tend to get chipped and have to be repainted with a thin layer of mud and water. This mixture is known as swish, and the 'swish boy' — who has skin and hair of a uniform golden brown — carries a sheaf of paintbrushes stuck in his curls, steps about gingerly, and paints out the whitish scars.

A huge crowd has assembled on the fringe of the set: villagers, townspeople, Peace Corps workers. The problem is to keep them quiet while shooting, since, as always in Africa, a lively trade goes on. Women sell fritters and boys sell lurid-coloured sweets. One young man is peddling a substance in plastic packets. This, I assume, must be ganja but turns out to be false teeth.

The ladies of the court are forever slipping off between scenes to change into something fresh.

Werner asks, 'Do they understand nothing of continuity?'

The Viceroy of Ouidah has a complicated time structure and ends with the *chacha*'s daughter on her deathbed remembering the death of her father over a hundred years earlier. This seemed impossible to incorporate in the film, and Werner was puzzled how to end it until Kinski took the matter from his hands.

The week before my arrival, at Elmina, there was a scene in which Kinski had to haul a canoe down the beach. Along this coast there are two lines of breakers, with a strip of white water in between. Beyond the second line there are sharks, but swimming is always dangerous because of the undertow. A freak breaker caught him unawares and thumped him onto the beach. Suddenly conscious that he was playing the final scene, Kinski allowed himself to be dragged back into the waves and rolled back, time after time, onto the sand.

In retelling the story, Werner seems almost overcome with gratitude (there were some bad scenes later in Colombia, for which gratitude would not be appropriate). 'This wonderful human creature,' he says. Or 'This exceptional human being. I tried to consider the film without Kinski. It was impossible. It was inevitable he should play it.'

Kinski — he himself would be the first to admit it — is not easy. He leaves a trail of smouldering resentment wherever he goes. The love-hate feud between him and Werner — which has taken on legendary proportions in film gossip — is a bit overdrawn.

But they do make a noise in public.

When not wanted on the set, Kinski retires to his bungalow, sleeps, reads, cooks, and repels everyone — except Werner — who knocks on his door.

In the afternoon, Kinski arrives at the palace: a sexagenarian adolescent all in white with a mane of yellow hair. Not exactly my idea of a Brazilian slaver, but let that pass. The scene he has to play is one in which, smeared with black make-up and trussed like a pig for the spit, he must crouch and endure the insults of the king: 'Why have you sent 350,000 warships to my shores?' 'Why did you kill my greyhound?'

I overhear Kinski wisecracking with the set photographer and introduce myself. The arctic eyes swivel round: 'Oh, you're the one who wrote the book? I liked that book. I'm sorry we had to change it, but I think we're doing something very rhythmical here.'

He changes into a blue Napoleonic officer's coat — genuine but moth-eaten — trimmed with silver braid.

'Maybe', he turns to me, 'the film will help the book.'

'Maybe.'

I go and sit with the continuity girl.

'He seems in a very good mood,' I say.

'That is because he has made everyone very angry.'

One of Kinski's quirks is that he insists on demonstrating how each shot should be framed. This caused a dreadful scene with the original cameraman, who left Elmina in a huff. A replacement, Viktor Ruzicka, came out at a moment's notice from Prague. An imperturbably cheerful man, he knows precisely how to handle the star, when to be indulgent and when to be firm.

'Hey, Viktor,' Kinski shouts, 'do they still have toilet paper in Czechoslovakia? Polanski told me that in Warsaw . . . '

'Of course we have toilet paper.'

'Okay?' Werner interrupts. 'Shall we shoot it now?'

'That's what we're here for,' says Kinski.

The make-up man comes and dabs more black on his face. Werner, meanwhile, is organising the crowd.

'Now everyone look at the white man!' he calls.

'Black and white,' says Kinski.

Thursday morning. Nothing is happening. Nana is late for his deposition scene. Perhaps he doesn't want to be deposed after all? But finally he appears, striding across the courtyard in an orange-and-purple *kenti* cloth. He inclines his head to me and says, 'Good morning, Englishman!' He had been checking that his courtiers were all safely on the bus.

A second king, Nana of Elmina, also plays a part in the film and has turned up here unannounced to see how things are going. I suspect he wants to do another act. He is nattily turned out in a crimson robe sewn with purple satin ribbon. Together we watch the deposition scene. He complains of fever.

At Elmina the screenplay called for him to abase himself before Dom Francisco and to fan him. Since Nana had never fanned anyone in his life, this was quite a psychological blow.

'I am totally confused,' he said. 'But I will do it for the purpose of the fillum.'

He has also read *The Viceroy of Ouidah*.

'Well, sir,' he says to me, 'you have written a very round-about book.'

'You live in England?' Kinski asks.

'Not much.'

'I don't even want to change planes in England.'

A man with about forty dogs on leashes has been sighted on the outskirts of the village. All the dogs walk proudly ahead of him. The man travels around the villages buying up dogs. He then sells them in the North, where dog is eaten.

The houses of the village are built of mud with conical roofs of thatch. One of the shutters is chalked with the words SIMPLE BOY.

Viktor orders it to be shut. From within comes the quacking of a muscovy duck.

Picorna is a virus that attacks men and animals, and as you drive into Tamale, there is a notice that reads FEELING THE

HEAT? COME TO THE PICORNA ENTERTAINMENT CENTRE FOR A NICE COLD BEER.

Nearby is another, less frequented bar: AYATOLLAH DRINKS BAR NO CREDIT GIVEN.

What the eye sees, the hand reaches out for. In Ghana the largest unit of currency is worth about a dollar. To make simple payments, you have to run around with a shopping bag full of banknotes. The girl in charge of cash is dismayed by the ever-swelling numbers of open hands.

Nana of Elmina, never at a loss for a pious homily, has this to say: 'It's like pig breeding. Some pigs are greedy feeders. Some are nice pigs. You never can tell.'

The orders for the day include the following: 'Attention — 250 Amazons arrive from Accra by night; prepare accommodation at the army barracks.'

The Amazons (Werner called them *Amazones*) are nice girls from Accra with names like Eunice, Beatrice, Patience, Primrose, Maud, and Rhoda. At Elmina there were 700 of them, trained in machete drill by a lion-faced Italian stunt director, Benito Stafanelli. They behaved very badly. They outraged the villagers by singing songs of fantastic obscenity. They went on strike for more money and nearly staged a riot.

At 8.30 in the morning their buses arrive at the palace. We hear shrieks and yells on the far side of the wall.

'The situation may get out of hand,' says Werner in a sombre voice. 'Someone will have to pray for us.'

The Amazons saunter across the yard and then go off to change, or rather strip, into their Amazon costume: a yellow cache-sex, breasts smeared with whiting, and for a helmet a scarlet gourd dotted with cowrie shells. They carry machetes, shields, and spears. The spears have their tips bent over, but one could still take your eye out.

Waiting — as always happens on a film set — for something to happen, I sit with the girls and overhear snatches of conversation.

'Take off your brassière, Jemimah!'

'How can you take up with that coward?'

'Yeah, but what can you do? He is a human being.'

'He is only walking by himself. He has no wife.'

'Women in Europe do not *do* that, Rhoda!'

The day is unbearably hot — about 113° F, 45° C — and the Amazons are wilting fast. They have been called on to make a spectacular charge on the palace. We sit in the portico and watch the rehearsal. Suddenly the girls are hurtling toward us, spears waving, with Werner barefoot in the lead. 'Come on, girls!' he shouts. 'Faster! Faster!'

We have supper in a white-painted bungalow known as the Casino, and we are drinking our umpteenth beer of the evening when the Amazons arrive. There has been some dispute about their pay. They have already been paid more than their contract, but that does not make them happy. Egged on by Kinski — who declares, 'I'm for the girls!' — they surround the Casino and raise a fearful din. We draw the curtains, but the wind blows them open. Faces appear through the louvres: 'You will die.' 'You think you can stuff a black woman. You'll see.'

Werner paces the room in a state of extreme agitation. Usually he puts all such transactions in the hands of subordinates, and now they've bungled it. The Portuguese doctor quite loses his head. 'I'm an African!' he shouts (he was born in Mozambique). 'I know how serious this shit is.' Then when he has calmed down a little, he adds sententiously, 'When in Rome, do as the Romans.'

Outside, the Amazons kick and shove the building, which under their combined weight could collapse. One suspects, however, that they are not really trying. But they do burst in. Glasses fly. A girl gets kicked, and the man who did the kicking turns red and white with rage. Not so Werner, who towers above the assembly and announces, 'My sense of justice tells me —' at which the kicker screams, 'You mean your sense of stupidity!'

There is some ugly talk of bringing in the army. Instead, Werner — a monument of sanity in a cast of nervous breakdowns — slips out through a side door and confronts the girls. At the sound of his habitual cry — 'Girls! Girls!' — the rumpus simmers down. He and their spokeswoman, Salome, immediately reach a compromise. Laughing happily, the girls go back to their buses.

Werner comes back in, exhausted, and says to me, 'That was only an arabesque.'

Next day. Sunday. A day of rest. The door of the Casino is covered with red mud footprints. Another drama is unfolding at the military barracks.

As part of her equipment, each Amazon has been given a foam-rubber mattress, but the soldiers, having shared the mattresses all night, make off with them in the morning.

'It's disgusting,' Kinski tells Werner. 'Do something.'

Werner and I drive to the barracks, a collection of rickety wooden buildings, where he must again defuse the situation. Eagerly the girls cluster around him. With a hierophantic gesture, he cries, 'Girls! Girls! I love you.' A squeaky voice pipes back, 'And we love you, too!'

He apologises, sorrowfully, for the scene last night. He apologises for the stolen mattresses. 'If I could take justice from my rib, I would give it to you.' Alas, there is nothing to be done.

Next, the Amazons' bus drivers, claiming that the mattress crisis has delayed them, insist on an extra day's pay.

'Let's get out of here,' says Werner. 'Quick!'

Tuesday. There is one more scene to be shot in Africa, a night scene in which the future King Ghezo rescues the Brazilian from prison. I would like to stay, but the plane for London leaves Accra tonight. Besides, I am needed to relay messages to Munich: on the logistics of getting the crew plus a ton of equipment from Tamala to Bogotá via Madrid.

A few weeks later on another plane I sit next to a New York lawyer whose client, a big Hollywood name, once chickened out of one of Werner's films.

'Herzog?' the man said. 'Don't go on a trip with him.'
'But I have.'

1988

5
RUSSIA

GEORGE COSTAKIS:
THE STORY OF AN
ART COLLECTOR IN THE
SOVIET UNION

George Costakis is the leading private art collector in the Soviet Union. And his is no ordinary collection, but one of compelling interest to all who would understand the art of this century. For twenty-six years he has conducted his private archaeological excavation — and this is what it has required — to unearth the Leftist art movement which burst on Russia in the years around the Revolution. Russia's revolution is the outstanding intellectual event of the century, and her painters, sculptors and architects rose to the occasion. During the First War the centre of artistic gravity shifted from Paris to Moscow and Leningrad where it remained for a few turbulent years.

'I will make myself black trousers of the velvet of my voice,' sang its most conspicuous spokesman, the poet Vladimir Mayakovsky. Young women shivered with pleasure at the voice of the man who called himself 'the cloud in pants'. Characteristically it took a Russian émigré, Serge Diaghilev, to galvanise the fading talents of Western Europe into a show of activity. But by his exile he divorced himself from the source of his inspiration. The Russian soil is a powerful mother and few of her artists survive the trauma of parting.

Those with strong will power stayed. The uniqueness of the Russian situation encouraged in them an almost Messianic belief in the power of art to transform the world. And because the most extreme apostles of modernism had opened their arms to the Bolsheviks, they were able to press their claims. Admittedly they fought each other (with fists) and divided into schismatic groups, each broadcasting its manifestos which read like the anathemas of the medieval church. They called themselves misleading names — Constructivists, Productivists, Objectivists, Suprematists — which often reflect personal vendettas rather than any real ideological split. As a whole, however, the work of the Leftists has a freshness and confidence, which towers over the smartness, the hysteria and the aridity of much European art of the Twenties.

When the full history of the Russian movement comes to be written — and to some extent we must thank Costakis that it can be written — it will probably emerge as the most significant of all. Whatever we think, later generations will look on the twentieth century as the century of abstract painting. Two Russians, Kasimir Malevich and Vassily Kandinsky, are its pioneers, and to understand the movement properly we must place it first in its original Slavic context.

For a few euphoric years the avant-garde flourished, but its anarchic philosophy appeared to contradict the crucial tenets of Soviet Marxism. It attracted official disapproval; was formally sat on; and the paintings disappeared under beds or into the vaults of museums. When Costakis began, Leftist art was quite forgotten. Outside the Soviet Union it attracted a few disparaging comments. Inside it did not arouse a flicker of interest. In 1947 an art critic could denounce Cezanne's dishonest 'indifference to subject matter' and complain that his fruit and flowers 'lack aroma and texture'. In those days the non-figurative artist was a pariah.

Costakis was the 'mad Greek who buys hideous pictures'. He spent fifteen years in the cold and if, over the past ten, his apartment has become an object of pilgrimage, it gives him very obvious satisfaction. In his twenties Costakis bought tapestries, silver and Dutch landscape painting. '. . . Kalf . . . Berchem . . . this kind of thing. Then little by little they all looked to me like one colour. I had twenty paintings on the wall and it was like one painting.' He cannot single out any one event of childhood that inclined him towards works of art, but imagines the ceremonial of the Orthodox Church may have affected him. 'But this is not the real reason. All my life I wanted to write a book . . . or make an aeroplane . . . or invent some industrial miracle. *I had to do something*. And I told myself, "If I continue to collect old paintings, I will do *nothing*. Even if one day I will find a Rembrandt, people will say 'He was lucky' and that is all."' Then, in the dark days after the war, someone offered him three brightly coloured paintings of the lost avant-garde. 'They were signals to me. I did not care what it was . . . but nobody knew what anything was in those days.'

The three paintings signalled to Costakis the existence of a world he had never suspected. Whenever free from his duties at the Canadian Embassy he hunted for 'lost' pictures 'thrown around all the corners of Moscow and Leningrad'. The hunt led to old people who imagined time had passed them by. Some were broken by events and delighted to have even a token of recognition. He rescued canvases that were rolled up or covered with dust. He met Tatlin before he died, 'the great fool', who designed the *Monument to the Third International*, and lived alone with some hens and a balalaika. He befriended Stepanova, the widow of the comprehensive genius Alexander Rodchenko. He tracked down the friends of the great Malevich. He bought works by the émigrés Kandinsky and Chagall; by Lissitzky, the master typographer, and Gustav Klutsis, the Constructivist designer; by Liubov Popova, the 'strongest painter of her generation' ('When she was fighting for art, she was a man; but in bed she was a woman'); and by Ivan Kliun, whose cosmic abstractions anticipate Rothko. With persistence he traced obscure artists who had signed the early manifestos, finding in them qualities their contemporaries had overlooked. And as he accumulated, he pieced together the story of their ideologies, alliances, fantastic projects, squabbles and love affairs; for revolutionary freedom was synonymous with free love.

Costakis was never rich, but he paid every rouble he could afford, sometimes offering two or three times the price asked. (I was told this independently.) The next acquisition was always a real struggle. Some years ago he saved up the money for a car, and his wife was ecstatic about the prospect of picnics in the country. A few days later a Chagall arrived and the car returned mysteriously to the garage for repairs. He asked her, 'Which do you prefer, the Chagall or the car?' to which she replied, 'I like the Chagall but . . . ' The Chagall stayed on the wall and the car stayed in the garage.

Costakis's family stayed in Russia through the Revolution and Civil War. His father came from the Ionian island of Zacynthos and had tobacco interests in Southern Russia. His mother, now in her advanced nineties, lives in a dacha outside Moscow and recently discovered amid general surprise that she could speak fluent English after fifty years of not speaking it. Her son is a complex, very likable man of sixty-one, with solid black eyebrows, quizzical eyes and a diffident but disarming smile, belied in photographs. 'Photographers make me look like a crook.' He is resourceful, yet innocent to the point of unworldliness at the same time. In a good mood he is almost uncontrollably buoyant; when agitated he plays the guitar and sings Russian folksongs in a dark melancholy voice.

He and his irrepressibly cheerful Russian wife live in an apartment at the top of a new white tile and concrete block on the Prospekt Vernadskogo in a far-flung extension of the city. From its windows you overlook an anonymous landscape of tall buildings, spaced far apart and exposed to the wind that whistles in from the forest. In February the snow lay thick. Only the odd tree and black fur-hatted figures, threading along thin muddy paths, punctuated the white space between the buildings.

On his own territory Costakis becomes one of the great personalities of Moscow. He has placarded the walls with pictures, and pinned unframed canvases to doors. Vibrant colours and elemental forms of paintings dance around the walls; the exuberance of the artists themselves seems to linger in the apartment. Too often a visit to a famous art collection entails a display of sterile exhibitionism on the part of the owner; but Costakis infects all comers with his enthusiasm. Some art historians have been less generous with him. With the calculated meanness of scholars they have picked his brains and failed to acknowledge their source.

The rooms vary between the neatness of a museum and the amiable chaos of family life. There are samovars and painted Russian peasant boxes, a collection of icons, Congo fetishes, Chinese tea-kettles and Eskimo carvings from the Siberian Arctic. Occasionally Costakis's son comes home on leave from the Soviet Army. His daughters arrive at all hours with husbands and boyfriends expecting to be fed. It is also home for two large affectionate dogs, a Borzoi and a Kerry Blue Terrier. And as Russia's unofficial Museum of Modern Art it attracts the expert and curious from all countries. The visitors' book begins with an autographed line by Stravinsky and continues with a string of familiar names. The deferential comments of museum directors from East and West underline the collection's uniqueness. A famous Soviet actor writes: 'One of the best and most alive museums in the world. I am not drunk.'

The existence of the Costakis collection introduces an unfamiliar aspect of life in the Soviet Union. In Western imagination the Marxist State is the declared enemy of private property; and some might suppose that a valuable private art collection merely reveals the inconsistency of Marxism. This is not so. Nothing in the Soviet legal code prevents a man owning pictures any more than it prevents him owning a pair of boots. Nor can one suggest, by way of explanation, that Costakis uses his Greek citizenship to enjoy special rights and immunities. He does not.

There are plenty of private collections in the Soviet Union today and prices are rising. An entry in Costakis's visitors' book which reads, 'An example to all of us Russian collectors of avant-garde art', tells us he has competition. But two awkward facts remain; that abstract art was banned by 1932; that it has failed to resurface on the walls of museums. The Ministry of Culture, however, is showing signs of a more indulgent attitude. Rumours are in the air of a Soviet Museum of Modern Art. Costakis, who is tender-hearted towards the country of his adoption and will not have her slandered, sees in this a vindication of his life's work. He cannot afford to give them outright, but one day he would like to see his pictures in that museum.

The reasons for the ban are far from clear. Western opinions on the subject have long entertained a consoling fiction, that Party bureaucrats failed to understand Leftist art, therefore hated it and branded it as subversive. Its disappearance is used as an excuse for pious assertions on the need for artistic freedom and for exposing 'official' Soviet art to ridicule. These have not been helpful. I do not mean to suggest that Leftist artists were not horribly wronged in the late Thirties. But the idea that their art was banned through ignorance is a trite explanation which belittles its significance.

In the opinion of its makers, the Bolshevik Revolution had set man free. The proletariat had won — was, in theory, dictator, and had the right to decide what was, or was not, proletarian art. Marx had hoped that once the worker had free time he would 'among other things, paint'. But for all his genius, he was not visually inclined and did not suggest *what* the worker should paint. Nor did his theory allow for the visual awareness of the Russians, nor for the Russian painter's status as prophet and teacher. No government can afford to ignore him; and this is a fact not appreciated in the West, where a revolutionary art is defused by the patronage of the rich. One of Lenin's secretaries records how people were led before Repin's painting *The Barge-haulers on the Volga* in the Tretyakov Gallery in Moscow and converted to revolution by its message against injustice. Now all good Bolsheviks believed that art belonged to the people. But by October 1917 there are two contradictory opinions on the form the new art should take.

In one camp were the Futurists. (I use the word Futurist in the widest sense.) As the old order tottered, they had conducted a war of nerves against middle-class morality and taste. They saw themselves as a wrecking-party which would unhinge the future from the past. Their painters saw in French Cubism a preliminary shattering of images beloved by the bourgeois. The philosopher Berdyaev said Picasso was the last of the Stone Age Men. Their poets had an 'insurmountable hatred for the language existing before them'. They drained poetry of its meaning and insisted on the primacy of pure sound. 'Words are but ghosts hiding the alphabet's strings.' They published their manifestos — 'Go to the Devil' — 'The Thunder Boiling Cup' — 'A Slap to Public Taste' — on the cheapest paper, 'the colour of a fainted louse'. Mayakovsky and David Burliuk, the self-appointed storm-troopers of Futurism, paraded around St Petersburg in alogical fancy dress; crowds wondered if they were clowns or savages or fakirs or Americans. Mayakovsky once advised his audience to 'carry their fat carcasses home'.

But the Futurists usually came from 'good' families, and their posturing was of the essence of middle-class revolt. The Bolsheviks were tougher, more serious and their view of art different. The populist composer Mussorgsky had once said that artists must 'not get to know the people, but *be admitted to their brotherhood*'. If serious, the artist must merge in with the masses and do nothing to affront the taste of the common man. That taste was bound to be traditional. And the pragmatic Lenin saw the need for an art which would broadcast the Revolution in simple, traditional images.

Lenin was the son of a provincial director of schools, and historians have often noticed the firm, pedagogic manner with which he handled his colleagues. Edmund Wilson even called him 'The Great Headmaster'. Certainly his concept of *partiinost*, or sacrificial party spirit, reminds one of loyalty demanded for the schoolteam. His tastes were old-fashioned and austere. He knew that Marx's moral and historical interpretation of history was right. He knew his own interpretation of Marx was right. And he also knew that if he waited for capitalism to collapse he would wait indefinitely.

On this crucial point there are two distinct trends in Marx's thought. One encourages the worker to rise and batter his oppressors. The other says capitalism will evaporate in the quickness of time and in accordance with the laws of history. Marx's open legacy crystallised into the quarrel between the Bolsheviks and the Mensheviks. Lenin, as Bolshevik leader, appointed himself the active agent of history, who would accelerate its inevitable process by force. The Mensheviks dreaded force, preferring a gradual change to Socialism, through educating the workers.

Among the Bolsheviks themselves there was a similar split. A challenge to Lenin's authority came from an ambitious Marxist called Alexander Malinovsky, who had changed his name to Bogdanov, which means 'Son of God' (God in this case being the 'People'). He founded a rather nebulous institution called *Proletcult* which, he said, was 'a laboratory for proletarian culture', and had set up a colony in exile on Capri which Lenin had visited and loathed. Bogdanov countered Lenin's demand for unity by calling for 'Three Ways to Socialism – Political, Economic and Cultural'; in particular he insisted on the independence of cultural matters from the government. The Futurists preferred the independence of Bogdanov's *Proletcult* to Lenin's centralisation. From the start they were in the wrong camp.

Years of committee meetings in exile (those of the Second International were held in Tottenham Court Road) had convinced Lenin that liberal intellectuals were weak-kneed and ineffectual. Unity, unity at all costs obsessed him, and he saw 'no special basis for different directions in art'. Anything that reminded him of idealist philosophy he distrusted, and he would chide his colleagues for 'coquetting with religion'. Maxim Gorky might exclaim, 'Almighty, Immortal People, Thou art my God!' but Lenin never. If he was a dreamer, he was, in H.G. Wells's verdict, 'a dreamer in technology'. His saying 'Communism is Electrification plus Soviets' expresses his faith in the machine as saviour and agent of Socialism.

Marx had warned against the delusions of abstract thought, and Lenin probably thought the same of abstract art. At first he thought it harmless, but tolerance gave way to irritation. He disliked the street monuments which left spectators gasping for sense. And when some artists 'cancelled out' the trees of the capitalist period in the Alexandrovsky Gardens outside the Kremlin by painting them in bright colours that wouldn't come off, Lenin and Krupskaya were very cross. In a dry memorandum of October 1920 Lenin wrote: 'No creation of a new proletarian culture, but the development of the best models of existing culture . . . ' Marxism does not despise the achievements of the past.

Certainly the new masters of Russia preserved its treasures. Once the Winter Palace was stormed, the inventory of its contents began and looters were shot. Anatoly Lunacharsky, Lenin's first Commissioner for Education, had once made his listeners cry as he evoked the wonders of old in the Naples Museum. In November 1917 he made himself cry at news of the destruction of the Kremlin and St Basil's, and resigned from the Revolutionary Committee. 'I cannot stand it. I cannot stand the monstrous destruction of beauty and tradition.' He reinstated himself two days later when he heard the news was false.

In contrast, a mood of iconoclastic fervour swept the Leftists. They couldn't have cared less what happened to the Kremlin. Marinetti had once called it 'an absurd thing'; for all they were concerned it could burn. Malevich hoped all towns and villages would be destroyed every fifty years and said he'd feel more sorry about a screw breaking off than the destruction of St Basil's. The avant-garde hadn't counted on the Bolshevik uprising, but they were the only group of artists in Russia to welcome it. Calling themselves Leftists, they clamoured for complete monopoly in the arts.

They behaved with customary lack of caution but superhuman energy. Mayakovsky's slogan 'The streets our brushes, the squares our palettes' flushed artists out into the open. They decorated the Agit-Prop trains which toured the country, staged mass spectacles, placarded old palaces with monumental posters, bundled Tsarist monuments into parcels of throbbing red cloth, played a symphony on factory sirens, evolved a new typography to broadcast the new message and said they were breaking down the divisions between art and engineering, or between painting and music: the latter is not difficult in a country where colours have equivalents in sound; reindeer bells tinkle red and for one poet the noise of the 1905 Revolution was mauve.

The ideas of the artists conflicted. At one extreme was Kandinsky, who for some years had been painting the private landscapes of his mind. He believed in painting as a healing ritual to cure mental anguish and wean men from materialism. 'Painting', he wrote, 'shall free me from my fears.' But men like Tatlin and Rodchenko insisted that materialism was the only value that counted. All the artists, however, agreed to hate the image. The art of the new man must suppress all representation of man. Malevich, an eloquent if erratic propagandist, thundered against the Venus de Milo ('not a woman but a parody') and against the 'rubbish-filled pool of Academic art' with its female hams, depraved cupids and congealed legacy from Greece. His tone is that of Isaiah on the subject of idols and I think the comparison apt. For beneath the Russians' obvious devotion to human images lurks an impulse to smash them to bits. The ugly riches of late Tsardom, it is true, were an open invitation to the wreckers, but iconoclasm in Russia has a longer history.

As 'Third Rome' and guardian of an orthodoxy denied by the renegade West, Russia inherited from Byzantium her peculiar attitude towards the image. The statue of an emperor or icon of a saint proved the legitimacy of a political or religious idea. The saying 'He who delights in the Emperor's statue delights in the Emperor' applies as well to Justinian as to Tsar Nicholas II. Authoritarian societies love images because they reinforce the chain of command at all levels of the hierarchy. But an abstract art of pure form and colour, if it is serious and not merely decorative, mocks the pretensions of secular power because it transcends the limits of this world and attempts to penetrate a hidden world of universal law.

Anarchic peoples, like desert nomads, hate and destroy images, and a similar image-breaking streak runs through Russian history. The apparent endlessness of the country encourages the search for inner freedom, and Revolutionary Russia seethed with levelling movements — with mystics of all kinds, the *Brodiagi* or perpetual pilgrims, flagellants, Adventists, people in search of the Seventh Dimension and the famous *Molokany*, or Milk Drinkers, who influenced Tolstoy.

Malevich was touched by mystical yearnings. In his hands the non-objective canvas became an icon of anarchy and inner freedom: this is what made it dangerous to Marxist material-ism. Of his painting *Black Square* he said he had felt 'black nights within' and a 'timidity bordering on fear', but as he decided to break with reality and abandon the image: 'a blissful sensation of being drawn into a "desert" where nothing is real but feeling, and feeling became the substance of my life'. Now this is not the language of a good Marxist, but of Meister Eckhart — or, for that matter, of Mohammed. Malevich's *Black Square*, his 'absolute symbol of modernity', is the equivalent in painting of the black-draped Ka'aba at

Mecca, the shrine in a valley of sterile soil where all men are equal before God. And if this seems far-fetched, I quote the judgment of Andrei Burov, an architect who left the Constructivist Movement: 'There was a strong Muslim influence and orthodox Mohammedanism at that; by way of decoration only clocks and letters were allowed.'

With militant enthusiasm the artists of the Left set about demolishing class barriers and imposing the art of equality on the people. They then asked the Government to suppress the Society of Easel Painters and abolish all traditional forms of painting. The very fact of the Revolution demanded a complete break with the Academic tradition, which was alien and Western. The cry went out to jettison the relics of the past to prevent the new man being 'weighed down like an overloaded camel'. In Bogdanov's opinion, the art of the past was not a treasury but an arsenal of weapons against the former age. 'We will smash the old world wildly,' announced Mayakovsky, who then suggested everything from Adam to Mayakovsky be consigned to the dustbin.

> A White Army Officer
> when you catch him
> you beat him
> and what about Raphael
> it's time to make museum
> walls a target
> let the mouths of big guns
> shoot the old rags of the past!

To many officials, the Leftists were to the 'left of common sense'.

What had caused the hysteria? One suspects they were overcompensating for not having fought alongside the Bolsheviks. But more important, the mystique of the machine seems to have gone to their heads. As John Reed, an American Communist, wrote: 'The devout Russian people no longer needed priests to pray them into heaven. On earth they were building a kingdom more bright than any heaven had to offer . . . ' That kingdom was the kingdom of the machine. The backwardness of Russian industry before the First War is, I am told, often underestimated. The machine-age came late to Russia, but when it did, it came with startling abruptness. The growth-rate was phenomenal. Industrial units were few, but were the largest in the world, and Texas oilmen would visit Baku to witness the latest techniques of oil-extraction. With the Revolution, the means of production had devolved on the workers themselves and in their hands the man-made machine would transform humanity. Such was the hope. 'We are masters of the machine,' said Mayakovsky, 'therefore we need not fear it.' The machine was going to introduce true Socialism. Experts said it would take six months.

Now Lenin's mechanical materialism was tempered by his sense of the practical. The Leftists did not know his restraint. Most of them hated nature, or pretended to. Man had a Promethean mission to hack up the earth and fashion it to his taste. The position of mountains and other inconvenient geographic features was 'far from final'. Malevich, whose mysticism was aroused by machinery, called for man to 'seize the world of nature, and build a new world belonging to himself'. Other artists described themselves as 'Saints in the Church of the Machine'. In Vsevolod Meyerhold's 'biomechanical' theatre the actors suppressed any life-like emotion and behaved as though they were stage-machinery. Pavlov's dogs salivated mechanically to stimuli. The concept of the house as a 'machine for living' probably originates in Russia and not with Le Corbusier. There was an infatuation with an imaginary America with calls to 'Chicago-ise the soul' and 'do our work like a chronometer!' to 'desoul' art and reduce painting to the scientific application of colour.

Once they had 'desouled' painting, painters could dispose with it altogether. The monochrome canvas, in effect, declared its extinction as an art form. Malevich exhibited his

White on White canvases, which were his ultimate expression of non-objective bliss. Tatlin painted a plain pink board. At an exhibition at the Vkhutemas School in 1921 called 'The Last Picture Has Been Painted', Alexander Rodchenko showed three plain canvases in the primary colours. His sketchbooks which lead up to the 'suicide of painting' still belong to his daughter in Moscow and reveal him as a conceptual genius on the level of Marcel Duchamp. In two years he tried out and discarded almost every experiment the New York abstract painters tried in the Fifties and Sixties before reaching the present impasse.

But in 1920 the Russian avant-garde was undismayed by the impasse. A useful art and architecture of iron, glass and concrete would, in one opinion, replace the old culture of wood, 'itself a bourgeois counter-revolutionary material'. The man-made thing became the object of a minor cult, the factory a shrine to the dignity of labour. Tatlin designed stoves and casseroles, though one cynical observer noticed that if all artists went into the factories they would be reduced to designing labels. Nevertheless, when today we talk of the dehumanising effects of the machine, it's strange to hear Malevich's adulation of the 'big city's metallic culture, the culture of the new humanised nature'.

And the kingdom of the machine was not confined to earth. Air travel had also gone to their heads. In 1892 Konstantin Tsiolkovsky, who taught physics and mathematics at a girls' school in Ryazan province, had said: 'This planet is the cradle of the human mind, but one cannot spend one's life in a cradle.' So, being a genius, the Father of the Russian Space Programme invented the first wind-tunnel and outlined the principle of the reactor rocket. A less-talented visionary, who had the grace to call himself Kreisky 'the Extreme', pioneered the concept of stellar engineering. 'We shall arrange the stars in rows . . . We shall erect upon the canals of Mars the Palace of World Freedom.'

Tatlin's projected iron and glass *Monument to the Third*

International, which was to have spanned the Neva, appealed to the yearning for the infinite. Its spiral form (which certainly has Islamic ancestry) combines the idea of cyclic renewal with limitless upward progression. Later 'the great fool' retreated up the tower of the Novodyeviche Monastery to design an articulated glider called *Letatlin*, but it never flew. One critic described Malevich's *White on White* as a 'rocket sent by the human spirit into non-existence'. The artist then passed from easel painting to a search for perfect architectural form, and made a series of plaster models. The fact that he called them *Planetes* suggests he intended his buildings to orbit.

Bad living-conditions inflate the life of the fantastic. Berthold Lubetkin, the architect, who was a student at the Vkhutemas School, recalled for me the winter of 1918. He shared a room with sixteen other students behind the Metropol Hotel in Moscow. They ate hyacinths from window boxes; slept between the joists wrapped in newspaper because they had burned the floorboards, had no blankets and no source of warmth other than a flat iron which they heated in the porter's stove. A fellow student called Kalesnikov was unable to find a room and bored a hole in Lissitzky's street monument *The Red Wedge Invades the White Square*, where he installed himself for the winter. The same Kalesnikov submitted to the school a project (recalling conceptual art of 1794 or a story by Borges) for converting the earth into its own terrestrial globe by attaching a steel arc from pole to pole, on which the artist could hop off for a day and a night.

This brand of proletarian thought might, at a pinch, get through to the industrial worker — albeit with negative results. But there was no room for the peasant, the wronged peasant chained to the black soil and the seasons of ice and mud and sunflowers and dust. The Leftists preferred not to think about the peasant, and hoped that his condition was transitory. There was, it was true, a strain in Russian intellectual life which regretted the passing of old Russia and idolised the peasant, from afar, as the incarnation of Russian virtue. But this peasant-consciousness had become tainted with middle-class longing for the primitive. Peasant smocks had arrived in the literary salons of St Petersburg, peasant themes and peasant colours in the Diaghilev Ballet. The painter Mikhail Larionov evoked peasant lechery, yet continued to wear wing collars. There was, however, one real poet of the earth, Serge Esenin, a blonde innocent who awoke the tenderest emotions in both sexes. But he failed to master the contradiction of his roots and assumed Bohemianism (which included marriage to Isadora Duncan). He destroyed himself with drink, then cut his wrists.

The Leftists may have ignored the peasant. Lenin and the Party did not. Peasants accounted for eighty per cent of the population. Without their help the country would now starve. And in 1921 the government, prostrated by Civil War, granted an unknown freedom of action to the peasant in the New Economic Policy. Lenin believed that peasant solidarity was the course of true Russian Communism. 'We are, in a sense, pupils of the peasant,' he once said. Now the peasant might be illiterate, but his visual acuity was exceptional. For centuries he had 'read' the Bible story on the iconostasis of his church; he had 'read' folk-tales and news on woodcuts, called *lubok*, which he pinned up in his cottage; and now he wanted to 'read' the message of Revolution and the discomfort of his old tormentors.

Today we recognise the artists and architects of the Left as great original geniuses. We marvel at early Soviet photomontage posters by Rodchenko or Lissitzky, which pack on to a sheet of paper all the enthusiasm of the Red Revolution. But their original message did not get home to its intended audience, the whole people of Russia. They did not pass this tricky barrier of communication. By their own admission they decided what the people should want, not what it did want. And, it must be said, the people wanted to possess the monumental architecture, opulent decoration, and gilt-framed pictures with which the old rulers of Russia had encrusted their lives. Lunacharsky was correct when he said: 'The People too have a right to colonnades.'

The Society of Easel Painters revived itself and vigorously denied that the last picture had been painted. Architects began again to load buildings with ornaments. And the dispute between the 'formalists' and the 'realists' degenerated from an acceptable dialogue to mud-slinging and worse. Tatlin, speaking for the Constructivists, used to say: 'The material is the carrier of a work's content'; that is, an object of arresting form in steel and glass could express the vitality of the machine-age. The 'realists' would say, this is nonsense: it will convey messages only to people who are first primed to receive them. So why bother? The one way an artist can encourage workers in a steel factory or in the harvest field is to paint their heroic struggle realistically; and the only way to beat the camera at this game is to make the figures more heroic-looking than they really are. Such was the rationale of the Socialist Realist Style which replaced the abstraction of the Left.

In any case, 'urban life enriched by a sense of speed' rapidly disenchanted the Leftists. They began to see the machine as an enemy. Mayakovsky — the gentle giant with fountain-pens in his top pocket to prove his modernity — visited America, said it was fine for machines but not for men, and granted amnesty to Rembrandt before putting a bullet through his brain. With his death in 1930 it was obvious that the Leftist Movement had failed. The Party did squash it. But it also died of fatigue.

1973

THE VOLGA

On the MV *Maxim Gorky*, a cruise-boat belonging to Intourist, I spent ten September days sailing smoothly down the Volga; through the Volga–Don Canal, and on down the Don to Rostov. The days were clear and the nights were cold. All the other passengers were Germans. Some had been Panzer officers who had wasted their youth in Siberian labour camps, and were revisiting the scene of lost battles. Others had been pilots whose planes had failed to crash. Then there were the war widows — moist-eyed women clinging to the remains of prettiness, who forty-one years earlier had waved and waved as the trains drew out for the Russian front — and who now, when you asked why they had come to the Volga, would bow their heads and say, '*Mein Mann ist tot in Stalingrad.*'

Also on board was the Prussian Junker, Von F — a proud ex-aviator with the planed-off skull of Bismarck and a stump of an arm on which he balanced his Leica. His fate, in peacetime, was to be a water-engineer; and he would be up at dawn, pacing the deck in a dark green loden coat, gazing bleakly at the locks through which we passed. His views on the technical achievements of the Soviet Union were summed up in the words 'East minus West equals Zero'. He had fought for the Fascists in Spain. Yet nothing could be more agreeable, on our rare walks ashore, than to pace through the steppe grass beside this stringy and optimistic man, while he aired his encyclopaedic knowledge of Russia, or the migration of barbarian hordes. From time to time he would point to a bump on the horizon and say, 'Tumulus!' — and once, when we had come to a slight depression in the middle of a level plain, he stopped and said, conspiratorially, 'I believe this is a fortification from the Second World War.'

Every morning, at eight precisely, a peremptory voice would sound over the loudspeaker, '*Meine Damen und Herren* . . . ' and announce the events of the day. These began with a programme of gymnastics on the sun-deck — which, to my knowledge, no one attended. Then there might be a lecture on the turbulent and revolutionary history of the Volga region. Or a visit to a riverside town. Or to one of the hydroelectric schemes which have turned this Mother-of-all-the-Rivers into a chain of sluggish inland seas the colour of molasses.

We went aboard the *Maxim Gorky*, after dark, at Kazan. The ship's band was playing a medley of melancholy Russian favourites. A woman in peasant costume offered us the customary bread and salt; and the captain, whose deep blue eyes were set in a face composed of horizontals, went about squeezing everyone's hand. The river port lay on a reach of the Kazanka river, a short distance from the Admiralty, where Catherine the Great once landed from her state galley — after almost being drowned. Beyond a mole we could see the lights of tugboats towing barges up the Volga. After supper, a paddlesteamer with a raking funnel tied up in the berth ahead. Her cabins were freshly varnished, and there were swagged lace curtains in her saloon.

I asked the captain how old such a vessel was.

'Eighty years,' he said. 'Perhaps even one hundred.'

She was the ordinary passenger boat from Moscow to Astrakhan on the Volga Delta — a journey which took ten days. The stopover at Kazan lasted half an hour. Then a boy slipped her mooring rope from the bollard; her paddles frothed the water, and she eased back into the night — a survivor of the Ancien Régime, reminding one of the stiff-black-skirted ladies sometimes to be seen manoeuvring through the foyer of the Moscow Conservatoire.

Chekhov took a Volga cruise for his honeymoon in 1901. His wife was Olga Knipper, the actress for whom he wrote *The Cherry Orchard*. He was, however, already suffering from consumption, and his doctors had ordered a 'koumiss cure'. Koumiss is fermented mare's milk, the staple of all steppe nomads and remedy for every kind of sickness. The 'noble mare-milkers' appear in literature as early as the *Iliad*, and it was nice to think of Chekhov — on his paddlesteamer — scribbling notes for a new short story, and sipping a drink known to Homer.

Kazan is the capital of the Tartar Autonomous Republic, and lies about five hundred miles due east of Moscow at a point where the Volga, after meandering through the cities of northern Muscovy, takes a right-angled bend towards the Caspian. There are two Kazans. One is the Russian city, with its kremlin and cathedrals, founded in 1553 by Ivan the Terrible after a victory which finally rid Russia of the so-called 'Tartar-yoke'. The other Kazan, punctuated here and there by minarets, is the Muslim town to which the Tartars were banished, and where they have remained. Tartars number nearly half the population, speak Tartar as their first language, and are the descendents of Batu's Horde.

For the purpose of Russian history, the words Tartar and Mongol are synonymous. The Tartar horsemen who appeared on the fringe of Europe in the thirteenth century were thought to be the legions of Gog and Magog, sent by the Antichrist to announce the End of the World. As such, they generated the same kind of fear as the hydrogen bomb. Russia bore the brunt of their attack. In fact, so long as the Tartar empire survived, the Russian Grand Dukes were sub-vassals of the Great Khan in Peking — and this, together with a folk memory of whistling arrows, piles of skulls, and every kind of humiliation, may account for a certain paranoia the Russians have always shown towards the slant-eyed peoples of Inner Asia.

The Volga is the nomadic frontier of Modern Europe, just as the Rhine-and-Danube was the barbarian frontier of the Roman empire. Once Ivan crossed the Volga, he set Russia on her course of eastward expansion, which would roll on and on until the Tsar's colonists met the Americans at Russian river in northern California.

I went ashore before breakfast. Hydrofoils skimmed by and, in the flowerbed beside the boat terminal, a solitary mongrel sat chewing verbena. Through a mishmash of telegraph wires I caught site of the Peter-and-Paul Cathedral which, at this hazy hour of the morning, resembled the pagoda of an imaginary Cathay. The terminal building was deserted; but in the square behind, sweepers were sweeping the night's fall of leaves; the stench of cheap gasoline hung in your nostrils; and a woman in a scarf of aniline roses was unshuttering the front of her kvass bar — in front of which a queue had formed.

Kvass is a beer brewed from rye flour, but I did not want it for breakfast. I wanted koumiss, and had been told I could get it. 'Koumiss, *nyet*!' the woman said. Was there anywhere, I persisted, that did sell koumiss? 'Koumiss, *nyet*!' she repeated. 'Koumiss, *nyet*!' bellowed a Tartar in a black hat and black padded jacket. He had been standing behind me.

Plainly, the mares weren't giving milk at this season, and plainly I should have known it. So I went back to the quay where another, northbound steamer had docked. Families with bundles were shuffling up the gang-plank. Soldiers in top-boots were striding about as if they had saddles between their legs. Then a slender young man stepped ashore carrying a single stalk of pampas grass.

At eleven we went into town. Across the street from the university, the bus pulled up in front of a reckless adventure in stucco, its façade encumbered with naked figures, and its windows painted with peacocks and peonies. This, the guide confessed, had been the house of a millionaire. It was now a technical bookshop.

By contrast, apart from the odd hammer and sickle, there was nothing in the sombre, neoclassical university building to distinguish it from any minor college in the American Midwest. Students strolled about with satchels, or sunned themselves in a small memorial garden. The entrance hall, however, was lined with pictures of sad-faced academics, and we were made to wear grey felt overshoes in case we damaged the parquet flooring.

Upstairs we were shown the lecture room where Lenin studied law before being booted out for taking part in a student strike — a room of bare benches, a blackboard, a white-tiled stove, and green shades around the gas lights.

In his Kazan days, of course, Lenin had not yet assumed the name of that other, Siberian, river, the Lena. He was Vladimir Ilyich Ulyanov — a boy with red hair and an excessively determined lower lip, who, with his mother and sisters, had come here from his native Simbirsk. Only a year before, his elder brother Alexander had been executed in St Petersburg for making a bomb to kill the Tsar. The Ulyanovs' house is a cosy timber building, painted treacly brown, and situated in a hilly suburb once known as 'Russian Switzerland'. On hearing of his brother's death, young Vladimir is supposed to have said, icily: 'That means we shall have to find another way.' And in the half-basement, you are shown a scullery, hardly more than a cubby-hole, where, feet up on the stove, he first dipped into *Das Kapital*.

Another student was Count Leo Tolstoy. He was at the university for five-and-a-half years in the 1840s, studying Oriental languages, law, history and philosophy. Already, at the age of eighteen, he was keeping a diary of his thoughts and 'Rules of Life': 'Keep away from women' . . . 'Kill desire by work' . . . But, in the end, he decided his professors had nothing to teach him, and ordered the coachman to drive to Yasnaya Polyana. 'Men of genius', he wrote only twelve years later, 'are incapable of studying when they are young, because they unconsciously feel that they must learn everything differently from the mass.'

On leaving the Ulyanov house, the Germans went back to the *Maxim Gorky* for lunch. I gave them the slip and went to the Maxim Gorky Museum, a whitewashed building on a corner, next to a playground with cardboard figures of athletes. Across the street, people with wooden shovels were pitching a pile of potatoes into a cellar. Inside, two motherly women brooded over an immense display of photographs and memorabilia associated with this now almost deified novelist. His desk was awash with knick-knacks; and along with his suits, there was a pair of Samoyed reindeer-skin leggings.

Gorky — Alexei Maximovich Peshkov as he was then — came here as a blushing boy from Nizhni Novgorod (now Gorky) in 1884. He, too, had hoped to enter the university, but the authorities turned him down as being too young, ignorant and poor. Instead, he had to educate himself in tawdry lodgings, in flophouses, in a brothel, on the wharves along the river, or in the cellar of the bakery where he earned himself a wage. These were his *Universities* — the title of the second volume of his autobiography. His friends were amateur revolutionaries and professional tramps. At the end of one winter, he shot himself — but the bullet pierced his lung and not his heart. The river called him, to the South; to the freer air of the Cossack steppe; to what, later, he called his 'Sky-Blue Life'. He left Kazan by boat: 'The ice on the Volga had only just broken up. From upstream floated porous grey ice-floes, bobbing up and down in the muddy water. The boat overtook them, scraping against her sides and shattering into sharp crystalline flakes ... The sun was blinding ...' For three years he lived as a hobo. Then he published his first short story in a Tiflis newspaper. A map in the museum charted the zigzag course of his wanderings — and then we looked at the photographs: the successful young 'peasant' author, in an embroidered shirt, reading to a gathering of bourgeois intellectuals; the villa in Capri, dated 1908; or with his new friend, now definitively known as Lenin, who would insist on going to the beach in a bowler. Then New York; then another villa, in Taormina; and then back to Moscow in the Twenties. The last pictures, taken in his hideous art nouveau house on Kachalova Street just before his death (by poisoning?) in 1936, show a kind old man at the end of his tether.

The streets of Kazan bore the imprint of a vanished mercantile vitality. Yards once stacked with barrels of fish-oil or bitumen now lay overgrown with burdocks and thistles. Yet the little log houses, with their net curtains, their samovars, their currant bushes, their African violets in the window, and the streams of blue woodsmoke spiralling from their tin chimneys — all reaffirmed the dignity of the individual and the resilience of peasant Russia. Somewhere on these streets was the 'house of comfort' where Tolstoy lost his virginity; and where, once the act was over, he sat on the whore's bed and broke down and blubbed like a baby. This is the subject of his story *A Holy Night*.

Strolling into the yard behind a church, I found a nun feeding bread to her pigeons. Another nun was watering the geraniums. They smiled and asked me to come for the service, tomorrow. I smiled back, and said I should not be in Kazan. Later we all tried to lunch at the Kazan Restaurant, but only got as far as its grandiloquent gilded entrance. '*Nyet!*' said the black-tied waiter. He was expecting a delegation. So instead we had cabbage soup and fried eggs in a noisy white-tiled café, presided over by a powerful Tartar woman, who couldn't stop laughing. Her head was wrapped in the kind of white cloth superstructure you sometimes see in Persian miniatures.

The lanes of Tartar-town were muddy but, on some of the houses, the door and shutters were a lovely shade of blue. By the door of the mosque sat an old pair of shoes. The interior was dingy, and the evening sunlight, squeezing through a coloured-glass window, made blotches of red on the carpet. An old man in an astrakhan cap was kneeling to Mecca, to say his prayers. On top of the minaret, a golden crescent glinted over this, the northernmost extension of Islam, on the latitude of Edinburgh.

After dark, at a Friendship Meeting, I saw a slender Tartar girl craning her neck to watch the foreigners. She had glossy black hair, rosy cheeks, and slanting grey-green eyes. The dancing seemed to excite her, but a look of horror passed over her face when the Germans played musical chairs.

The *Maxim Gorky* sailed through the night, down the Kuybyshev Reservoir and past the mouth of the Kama river. By dawn, we were approaching Ulyanovsk. On the way we must have passed the ancient city of Bolgar where, in the tenth century, an Arab traveller called Ibn Fadlan awoke one morning to see some sleek ships at anchor in the river. These were the Vikings. 'Never', he wrote, 'had I seen a people of more perfect physique. They were tall as date-palms, and reddish in colour. They wear neither coats nor mantle, but each man carries a cape which covers one half of his body, leaving one hand free. Their swords are Frankish in pattern, broad, flat and fluted. Each man has tattooed upon him trees, figures and the like, from the fingers to the neck.' At the approach of winter, one of the Viking chieftains died, and his companions decided to bury him, in a ship mound, on the bank of the river. Such is Ibn Fadlan's descriptions: the ship carved with dragons, four posts of birch; the frost-blackened body sewn up in its clothes; a faithful dog sacrificed, and then the man's horses. Finally, the slave woman, who was to be buried as well, made love to each of the companions. 'Tell your master,' they said, 'I did this out of love for him.' On the Friday afternoon, the companions held her up three times over the ship's rail. 'Look!' she cried out. 'I see my master in Paradise, and Paradise is beautiful and green, and with him are the men and young boys. He calls me. Let me join him!' — whereupon an old She-Giant, the hag they called the 'Angel of Death', took the woman's bracelets from her wrists. The companions drowned her cries by beating on their shields. Six men made love to her again; and as she lay back exhausted, the 'Angel of Death' slipped a cord around her neck, and a dagger between her ribs.

Approaching Ulyanovsk, the cliffs along the Volga were dotted with summerhouses, each set in its orchard of tart green apples and painted a different, bright, peasant colour. Ulyanovsk is Lenin's home town — which, until it was renamed in 1924, was the sleepy provincial capital of Simbirsk. People used to call it 'The Place of the Winds'. The bus zigzagged uphill from the waterfront and came to a wide street lined with poplars and timber houses. This was Ulitza Moskovskaya where the school inspector Ilya Nikolaevich Ulyanov lived with his severe and beautiful wife, Maria Alexandrovna Blank. She was a devout Lutheran of Volga-German descent; and in her orderly house — with its bent-wood chairs, its painted floors, antimacassars, flounced net curtains, piano, wallpaper of daisies, and map of Russia on the dining-room wall — you felt the puritanical, not to say pedagogic, atmosphere of Lenin's own quarters in the Moscow Kremlin.

Edmund Wilson, who came here in 1935 to take notes for his book *To the Finland Station*, wrote that there was little to remind the traveller he'd ever set foot outside Concord or Boston. A few doors up, I had seen a shuttered Lutheran church. The place reminded me, rather, of Ohio.

Photos of the school inspector showed a pleasant, open-faced man with a bald dome, side-whiskers and the elevated cheekbones of his Astrakhan Tartar forebears. Alexander, by contrast, took after his mother — a moody-looking boy, with a shock of black hair, flaring nostrils and a fall-away chin. But in the lip of young Vladimir you got a taste of the Earth-Shaker . . .

Threading through the cramped bedrooms, the guide pointed to the children's paper boats, their hoop, the nurse's sewing machine, and a drawing, by Lenin's sister, of Dutch windmills — windmills, perhaps, of the Volga-Dutch colony downstream. All the cot-frames had spotless, white, plumped-up pillows. In Alexander's room we saw his chemistry test-tubes, and the gold medal he pawned in St Petersburg to buy the nitric acid for the bomb. He was, at the time, studying marine isopods at the School of Biology.

The Ulyanovs were a literary family and, as she gestured to the bookcases, with its sets of Goethe and Heine, Zola and Victor Hugo, the guide said that Maria Alexandrovna had spoken nine languages — 'including German', she added, smiling at the Germans.

'She *was* German,' I said.

The guide froze and said, 'NO!' in English.

'And up the road,' I said, 'that's her Lutheran church.'

The guide shook her head and murmured, '*Nyet!*' — and the German ladies turned on me, and frowned. Obviously, from either standpoint, I had uttered a heresy.

In 1887, when Vladimir Ulyanov was in the seventh grade, the headmaster of the Simbirsk *gimnaziye* was Fedor Kerensky, whose son, another Alexander, would grow up to be an emotional young lawyer with a mission to save his country — 'that ass Kerensky', who removed the Tsar, and was in turn removed by Lenin. In the classroom where Lenin studied there was a black desk with a bunch of crimson asters on it. At least once in his or her school career, every pupil has the right to sit at *that* desk.

Downstairs in the entrance hung a huge canvas of Lenin, in his student's greatcoat, contemplating the break-up of the Volga ice. The image of Russia as a river or a slow-moving ship is one that occurs again and again in her music, literature and painting. 'The Song of the Volga Boatmen' inspired perhaps the most politically effective picture of the nineteenth century — Ilya Repin's *Barge-Haulers on the Volga* — which shows a gang of peasants heaving a ship against the current. The laden ship is returning from a mysterious eastern land, whence will come a saviour to redeem a suffering people.

After lunch, I strolled about The Crown — the old aristo-cratic quarter of Simbirsk, now shaved of its mansions and churches and replaced by acres and acres of Karl Marx Garden, tarmac, and the offices of the local Soviet. At the edge of the tarmac, I crossed a bridge of rickety timbers and ambled downhill through the Park Druzby Narodov — a wilderness of decaying summerhouses and gardens gone to seed. Thistles choked the path, and the leaves of the brambles were red. There was a smell of potato tops burning on a bonfire. Below, the river dissolved into the haze. I peered through a scrap-metal fence and saw an old man pottering round his cabbages in the last of the summer sunshine.

On the waterfront I went aboard one of the shore stations, a kind of house-boat, painted the ice-floe green of the Winter Palace, where in Tsarist days travellers would eat, rest, or have a brief affair between steamers in one of the cabins upstairs. On a bench by the boarded-up kiosk, a man without fingers was munching a bun. He eyed me suspiciously, having heard that there were Germans about. When I said I was English, the metallic teeth lit up and he started explaining how many Germans he'd shot in the war: 'Boom! Da! . . . Boom! Da! . . . Boom! Da! . . . ' — slicing the sky with his fingerless fists and getting so excited I was afraid he'd forget I wasn't German, and I'd end up in the oil slick. I said goodbye and he pressed a fist into my outstretched hand.

One of the Intourist guides was an agitated young man who spoke perfect French and wore a white shirt printed with Cossack sabres. He said that few sturgeon were caught nowa-days in this part of the river: for caviare one had to go to Astrakhan. For some reason he knew all about Lenin's visit to London for the Second International, and even about Lenin's English friends, Edward and Constance Garnett. I said I had known their son David, a small boy at the time, who used to keep in his wallet Lenin's bus ticket from Tottenham Court Road to their house in Putney. '*Mais c'est une relique précieuse,*' he said.

The rum merchant at our table on the *Maxim Gorky* would wait, frantic with concentration, in the hope of ambushing all the butter pats. Sometimes, if he saw us faltering over the main course, he would raise his fork in the air, say, 'Please?' and prong the lumps of pork from our plates. He had fought at the battle of Stalingrad. Out of a company of 133, he was one of seven survivors. He shared his cabin with a school-master, an impetuous ballroom dancer, perennially bronzed, whose transplant of hair seedlings resembled a young rice paddy. He had been the observer on a Stuka. He had, at one time or other, bombed several of the places on our route, and was returning in the spirit of *Kameradschaft*.

Not far from Kuybyshev, we moored alongside a fuelling barge around ten o'clock. There were gas flares along the horizon. The night was warm. On the barge's deck a young man, in gumboots and shirt open to his navel, sat sprawled on a chair while an old woman who could have been his grandmother tugged at the rubber fuel pipe, then screwed in the nozzle. The barge itself was a Constructivist masterpiece, cobbled together by dockyard welders and painted grey and red. In the stern, some babies' nappies were hanging out to dry on the same clothes-line as half a dozen carp. And what a life went on below! No sooner had we tied up than a party of girls swarmed out of the cabin, invaded the *Maxim Gorky*, and began to dance. One of our crew, a boy with a neat sandy moustache, had rigged up a tape-recorder on the aft deck; and they were all soon jigging away to some rather offbeat disco music. The boy was terribly concerned to give the girls a good time; kept ordering people to dance with each other; and, with perfect manners and not a hint of condescension, made a point of dancing with the ugliest of the bunch. She was, it must be said, vast. For twenty minutes she revolved on her axis, slowly, like a stone statue on a pedestal, while he capered round and round, laughing, singing and kicking. Then the fuel pipe woman shouted; the girls poured back over the rail; everyone waved, and we slunk back into the night.

In my cabin I had a copy of *War and Peace*. I turned to Chapter Twenty and reread the account of old Count Rostov dancing the 'Daniel Cooper' with Marya Dmitrievna: (*le terrible dragon*): 'The count danced well and knew it. But his partner could not and did not want to dance well. Her enormous figure stood erect, her powerful arms hanging down (she had handed her reticule to the countess), and only her stern but handsome face really joined in the dance . . . '

Wrapped in his loden, Von F was up at sunrise to inspect the three locks that mark the end of the Kuybyshev Reservoir. 'Remarkable,' he said, alluding to the six hundred kilometres of inland sea that backs up nearly all the way to Gorky. 'But,' he waved at the walls of the lock-basin, 'this concrete is cracked.'

It was freezing cold. The sun was a ball on the horizon. The last lock-gates parted and we advanced into a path of golden light. Beyond, the Volga had shrunk to the proportions of a river. On the west bank were a sandy beach and a line of poplars: on the east, a string of fishermen's shanties and boats hauled clear of the water. We rounded a bend and saw the Zhiguli hills, the only hills hereabouts, once the refuge of bandits and revolutionaries. Their slopes were clothed in birch and pine, and their names: the Brave Man's Tumulus, the Maiden's Mountain, the Twin Brothers . . .

From Zhiguli island we then drove to Togliatti, the largest automobile factory of the Soviet Union. Togliatti is named after the former head of the Italian Communist Party; yet the factory owes its existence to the leading Italian capitalist of his generation, Giovanni Agnelli. Agnelli, I was once told, sat out most of one Moscow winter, in the Metropol Hotel, watching executives from every great car corporation come and go — and, eventually, by his presence, winning the contract for Fiat.

An expanse of glass and concrete stretched away over a

naked plain. But the aim of our rather arduous bus journey was not to visit the factory but to establish where, on the horizon, it ended. Once this point was reached we turned back. Meanwhile, the guide bombarded us with statistics. The average winter temperature was −18° C. Cars streamed off the production line at an average of 2,500 a day. The average age of the workers was twenty-seven. The average number of marriages was 5,000 a year. Almost every couple had an apartment and a car, and there were very few divorces.

In a car park by the Volga we came across a wedding couple. The bride was in white, the bridegroom in a red sash. They seemed shy and embarrassed; and the Germans, having at last found something human in Togliatti, proceeded to treat them as an exhibit in the zoo. Pressed to the balustrade by amateur photographers, the pair edged away towards their car. They had thrown red roses into the scummy water, and one of these had snagged on a rock.

When I woke the next morning the trees were gone and we were sailing through the steppe — a lion-coloured country of stubble and withered grass. There were fiery bushes in the ravines, but not a cow or a cottage, only a line of telegraph wires. I sat on deck, turning the pages of Pushkin's *Journey to Erzerum*: 'The transition from Europe to Asia is more percept-ible with every hour; the forests disappear; the hills level out; the grass grows thicker . . . you see birds unknown in Euro-pean forests; eagles perch on the hillocks that line the main road, as if on guard, staring disdainfully at the traveller. Over the pastures herds of indomitable mares wander proudly . . . '

For reasons of Soviet security the locks were unmarked on the map of the Volga that had been pinned to the ship's notice-board. As a result, the reservoirs and rivers resembled a string of sausages. Again and again, the tour leader warned against taking photos, and spoke of armed guards and other bogey-men who would pounce on anyone seen flashing a camera. The lock before Balakovo was a particularly impress-ive specimen with a road-and-rail bridge running over it, and a gigantic orange mosaic — of a Hermes-like figure, presumably representing 'Communication'. Von F was itching to sneak a shot, and had his camera hidden up his sleeve. Yet apart from the women who worked the machinery, the lock looked deserted except for a gang of spindly boys who catapulted pebbles that bounced on to our sky-blue deck.

It was a Sunday. The sun was shining: picnickers waved from the bank, and wheezy launches chugged up and down the river, loaded to the gunwhale with trippers. At three, we went ashore at Djevuschkin Ostrov, Maiden's Island, where a Khan of the Golden Horde once kept his harem. Before that, however, the island had been the home of Amazons. The Amazons had the practice of making love to their male prisoners, and then killing them. Sometimes, the prisoners put up a fight, but one young man agreed, willingly, to be killed — if they would grant him one favour in return. 'Yes,' they said. 'I must be killed by the ugliest among you,' he said — and, of course, got off the island. The story was told by Svetlana, an Intourist girl with a wonderful curling lip and green come-hither eyes.

I struck inland along a path that led through stands of red-stemmed nettles. The wormwood gave off a bitter smell underfoot. Aspens rustled, and the willows blew white in the breeze. The young willow shoots were covered with bloom, like the bloom on purple grapes. A pair of ducks flew off a weedy pond. Then there were more willows, and more water, and then the blue distance and sky. Crossing a patch of bog, I thought, 'This is the moment in a Turgenev sketch when the narrator and his dog are crossing a patch of bog, and a woodcock flies up at their feet.' I took a step or two forward — and up flew the woodcock! There should also have been, if this *were* a Turgenev sketch, the distant sound of singing and, after that, the sight of an apple-cheeked peasant girl hurrying to a tryst with her lover. I walked another hundred yards or so, and heard first the singing and then saw a white peasant headscarf through the trees. I approached, but the woman went on blackberrying. She was not young. She had hennaed hair and false teeth. I offered her the mushrooms I'd collected, and she said, '*Nyet!*'

Back at the boat station, another Winter Palace in miniature, the guardian had caught a small, sad-faced sturgeon, and our deckhands were tremendously excited at the prospect of fish stew. One carried a cauldron, another a knife and, while the cauldron was boiling, the fishermen and an officer played billiards in the lower-deck saloon. Osip Mandelstam says, 'The hard-headed knocking together of billiard balls is just as pleasant to men as the clicking of ivory knitting needles to women.' I, for one, could think of worse places to be holed up in — a routine of Russian novels, fishing, chess, and billiards — interrupted by an occasional visit from the *Maxim Gorky* to remind one that this was 1982, not 1882.

Monday, 27 September, was a blustery morning that began with a lecture on the inland waterways of the Soviet Union. Two nights earlier, I had seen a small sailing yacht beating upstream. If only one could get permission, how adventurous it would be to sail from the Black to the White Sea! In Kazan, which we had left only four days earlier at the height of an Indian summer, it was now four degrees below.

Next day, we stayed on the boat. From time to time a smudge of smokestacks and apartment blocks moved across the horizon. One of the towns was Marxstadt, formerly Baronsk, and capital of the Soviet Republic of the Volga Germans. 'And where are those Germans now?' asked a lady from Bonn, her neck reddening with indignation as she gazed at the thin line of shore. 'Gone,' I said. 'Dead!' she said. 'Or in Central Asia. That is what I heard.' Later in the afternoon we cruised close inshore along cliffs whose strata were striped in layers of black and white. Over the loudspeaker, a deep bass voice sang the song of the Cossack rebel Stenka Razin. We saw a flock of black and white sheep on a bare hill. Suddenly, in the middle of nowhere, there was a MiG fighter perched on a pedestal.

Stepan (or Stenka) Razin, the son of a landowner on the Lower Don, believed that the Cossack custom of sharing plunder should form the basis of all government. He believed that these levelling practices should be applied to the Tsardom of Russia itself. The Tsar, at the time, happened to be Peter the Great. At Astrakhan, Razin captured a Persian princess who became his mistress and whom he dumped in the Volga to thank her, the river, for the gold and jewels she had given him. At Tsaritsyn, he murdered the governor, one Turgenev, possibly a forebear of the novelist. Abandoned by his followers, he was defeated at Simbirsk and beheaded in Moscow. In Soviet hagiography he is a 'proto-communist'.

We arrived at dawn at Volgograd. The city once known as Stalingrad is a city of stucco and marble where Soviet veterans are forever photographing one another in front of war memorials. Rebuilt in the 'Third Roman' style of the Forties and Fifties, it rises in layers along the European bank of the Volga; and from the flight of monumental steps leading down to the port, you can look back, past a pair of Doric propylaea, past another Doric temple which serves as an ice-cream shop, across some sandy islands, to a scrubby Asiatic waste with the promise of deserts beyond.

At ten, to the sound of spine-tingling music, we, the passengers of the *Maxim Gorky*, assembled in Fallen Heroes Square as a delegation of penitent Germans to add a basket of gladioli and carnations to the heaps of red flowers already piled up that morning around the Eternal Flame. On the side of the red granite obelisk were reflected the Christmas trees of the garden, and the façade of the Intourist Hotel, built on the site of Field-Marshal Paulus's bunker. A squad of cadets came forward at a slow march, the boys in khaki, the girls in white plastic sandals with white tulle pompoms behind their ears. Everyone stood to attention. The rum merchant and the schoolmaster, both survivors of the battle, performed the ceremony. Their cheeks were wet with tears; and the war widows, who, for days, had been bracing themselves for this ordeal, tightened their fingers round their handbags, sniffed into handkerchiefs, or simply looked lost and miserable.

Suddenly, there was a minor uproar. Behind us was a party of ex-soldiers from the Soviet 62nd Army, who had come from the Asiatic Republics. Their guide was showing them a photo of Paulus's surrender; and they, hearing German spoken nearby, seeing the 'enemy' inadvertently trampling on a grass verge, and thinking this some kind of sacrilege, began to murmur among themselves. Then a bull-faced man shoved forward and told them to clear off. The ladies, looking now more miserable than ever, shifted hastily back on to the concrete path. '*Most* interesting,' said Von F, as he swept past on his way to the bus.

Once the war was over, someone suggested leaving the ruins of Stalingrad *as they were* — a perpetual memorial to the defeat of Fascism. But Stalin took exception to the idea that 'his' city should remain a pile of rubble, and ordered it to be rebuilt the way it was, and more so. He did, however, leave one ruin intact — a shell-shattered mill-building on the down-ward slope to the river. Now marooned in acres of concrete plaza, the mill lies between a model bayonet, some two hundred feet high and still in scaffolding, and a structure the shape and size of a cooling-tower where visitors (by previous appointment) can view a mosaic panorama of the battle. I stood on the plaza and felt I could almost chuck a stone into the river — yet, despite Hitler's hysterical screaming, despite the tanks and planes and men, the Germans could never reach it. The Russians fought to the slogan, 'There is no place for us behind!' It was probably as simple as that.

All around were elderly men and women, some missing an arm or a leg, and all aglow with medals in the sunshine. Then I caught sight of Von F, striding furiously around a selection of Soviet armaments lined up on display. 'No thanks to the Americans!' he said, lowering his voice. 'It was American tanks, not these, that saved them . . . and, of course, Paulus!'

'How?'

'Good Prussian soldier!' he said. 'Continued to obey orders . . . even when those orders were mad!'

In an earlier discussion, I asked Von F why Hitler hadn't gone straight for Moscow in the summer of '41. 'Fault of Mussolini,' he answered flatly. 'The invasion of Russia was planned for the spring. Then Mussolini made a mess in Greece and Germany had to help. It was too late in the year for Moscow. Hitler refused to make the mistake of Napoleon in 1812.'

Mamayev Kurgan is a hill in a northern suburb where the Tartar Khan Mamay once pitched his royal yurt and where, to celebrate the twenty-fifth anniversary of Stalingrad, the Soviets have built a monumental complex to the Fallen Dead. During the battle, whoever held the hill held Stalingrad; and though the Germans took the water-tower on the summit, Marshal Zhukhov's men hung on to the eastern flank. When they cleared the site, an average of 825 bullets and bits of shrapnel were found on each square metre. Leonid Brezhnev opened Mamayev Kurgan with the words, 'Stones have longer lives than people . . . ' The monuments, however, were made of ferro-concrete — and Von F, as an expert on ferro-concrete, didn't rate their chances of longevity all that high.

The first thing we saw from the bus was the gigantic statue of The Motherland, striding into the haze and waving a sword instead of the Tricolour — for, plainly, she owes her inspiration to Delacroix's *Liberty Leading the People*. From Lenin Avenue we then set off for the hilltop — but what an obstacle course lay in between! Like pilgrims to, say, Rome or Mecca or Benares, visitors to Mamayev Kurgan are obliged to progress round a sequence of shrines — Fallen Heroes Square, the Hall of Valour and many more — before arriving at the feet of *The Motherland*. And there are no short cuts! 'Kurgan' is a Turko-Tartar word meaning 'hill', 'mound' or 'grave' — and Mamayev Kurgan, with its grave, its temples and the 'sacred way', reminded me of the great temple complexes of ancient Asia. In this same steppe region a Turkic tribe, known as the Polovsty, used to set stone statues over their burial kurgans — and these, known as *kameneye babas*, served as a memorial for the dead, and a warning to tomb robbers.

I could hardly help feeling that *The Motherland* represented Asia, warning the West never to try and cross the Volga, never to set foot in the heartland. The atmosphere was eerie, and religious: all too easy to scoff at; but the crowds, with their rapt and reverential expressions, were no scoffing matter. I followed a lame old woman into the Pantheon. Her down-at-heel shoes had been slit at the toes to relieve the pressure on her bunions. She shuffled forward, in a raincoat, on the arm of a younger companion. She had tried to make herself a little festive by wearing a red scarf shot with tinsel. Her cheeks were caked with white powder, and streaming with tears. As she crossed the Court of Sorrows, her raincoat flapped open — to show a white blouse covered in medals.

At three, in the city planetarium, we watched a film of the battle, put together from German and Soviet newsreels (and adorned with cosmic overtones). The film was supposed to be violently anti-German, and the Germans had been warned not to attend if they felt squeamish. It could have been much worse. It never once stooped to mockery or satire; and in the heart-rending shots of wounded German prisoners, you felt that the film-makers, at least, were not glorifying the Soviet victory, rather showing the utter futility of war. That night, as we headed for the Volga-Don Canal, I sat at the bar beside one of the Panzer officers who sadly contemplated a double Georgian brandy and said: 'For us Germans this has been a hard day.'

The journey was ending. It was a sunny, silvery morning as we sailed into Rostov-on-Don. In the shallows a team of fishermen were drawing in a seine net. An old man sunned himself in an inflatable rubber dinghy. Tugboats tooted, and a crane unloaded crates from an ocean-going ship. There were old brick warehouses on the waterfront; and, behind, the city rising in terraces to the onion-domed cathedral on the hill. Along the esplanade, beds of soviet-coloured salvias were waiting to be nipped by the first autumn frost. The ship's band played 'Shortenin' Bread' as we docked. Meanwhile, onshore, a troupe of Cossack dancers, none older than twelve, had tumbled out of a bus and were putting on a rival entertainment. Two boys held up a banner which said 'Friendship' in any number of languages from Latvian to Portuguese; and the girls, like drum-majorettes in their shakos and scarlet jackets, flicked their legs about amid the flurrying leaves. A hundred yards away there was a statue of Maxim Gorky.

Rostov was a city of shady, tree-lined avenues shamelessly given over to private commerce. Policemen and police-women sauntered round the street markets with an air of amused condescension while Armenians haggled with Russians, Cossacks haggled with Armenians, and wallets bulged with roubles as the piles of aubergines, persimmons and secondhand furniture, little by little, diminished. An old babushka gave me a bunch of bergamot and I went away sniffing it.

Someone pointed to a slit-eyed woman with a shopping bag and asked, 'What are all these North Vietnamese doing here?' 'They're not Vietnamese,' I said. 'They're Kalmucks. They're the locals.' The Kalmucks live across the river in their own republic. They were the last Mongolian people to ride over into Europe and they settled there. Even now, they are Lamaists. One Kalmuck boy looked very racy, with a sweep of shiny black hair, and a monkey chained to the pillion of his motor-bike.

I went to the museum and caught a whiff of goat's grease floating off the churns and ladles in a reconstructed Cossack cottage. In the section devoted to 1812 hung a portrait of V.F. Orlov Denisov, the regimental commander whom Tolstoy fictionalised, with a lisp, in *War and Peace*. There was also an English print, entitled 'Foxy Napoleon — Tally Ho!' and the following verse:

> Hark, I hear the cry Cossack
> They have got the scent of me
> I must take to my heels at once
> They are close to my brush.

After dark on our last night in Russia, I strolled downhill, through the old merchants' quarters, and saw a crystal chandelier alight in an upstairs room. The walls were covered with faded red plush and there was a gilt-framed canvas, of mountains and a river. I stood under a street lamp, and tried to imagine the tenant of the room. On the pavement, little girls in white socks were playing hopscotch. Two sailors, their caps thrust back on their heads, came out of a shooting-alley and sat down on the kerb to share their last cigarette. Then an old lady, in a grey headscarf, came to the window. She looked at me. I waved. She smiled, waved back, and drew the curtain.

At the foot of the steps I passed Maxim Gorky, staring from his pedestal, across the gently flowing Don, towards the plains of Asia.

1984

6

CHINA

HEAVENLY HORSES

The Emperor Wu-ti (145–87 BC) was the most spectacular horse-rustler in history. He craved the possession of a few mares and stallions which belonged to an obscure ruler at the end of the known world, and in getting them he nearly engineered the collapse of China.

Of all the Sovereigns who claimed the Mandate of Heaven, Wu-ti was among the least modest. Other emperors would settle into a round of colourful ritual and harmless pleasures. Whatever they did was known to be perfect, in that their most insignificant actions mirrored the unchanging movements of the heavenly bodies. The ideal emperor, they said, should divorce himself from practical affairs and 'ride on the perfection of his counsellors'.

But Wu-ti knew at heart the dangers of taking advice from eunuchs, magicians and members of the old families. He was a monopolist. He believed it his right to order the everyday existence of all of sixty million subjects, to tax the rich out of existence and divert all money towards himself. Since, by the fact of his divinity, he controlled the seasons, his moods of love and hate merely reflected changes in the weather. When he castrated his Grand Historian, for venturing to put in a word for a disgraced general, it was no more significant, morally, than a hoar-frost.

He was, however, an improvement on his predecessor, Shih-Huang-ti, the Great Unifier. He did not hound the intelligentsia and burn their books. He preferred to manipulate his subjects, not slaughter them. And like all self-possessed people he was prey to doubt. Why should the Yellow River want to burst its man-made dykes? 'You're breaking the laws of nature,' he shouted at the flood, but the flood raged on. How upsetting, too, when magicians turned out to be frauds! One adventurer dressed himself up in a feathered costume, pretended he was only half-mortal, and the wretch couldn't even turn cinnabar to gold.

Increasingly the Emperor pondered the uncertainties of death. Were there Immortals? Where were they? Was there an Afterlife? Or a yawning blank? He travelled up and down the Empire in search of the answer. He sacrificed on mountain-tops. He followed up rumours of an immortal footprint. Sometimes the omens were favourable. One year they caught a unicorn, which was encouraging. Then the fungus of immortality sprouted inside the Imperial Apartments, which was better. But why didn't the Immortals eat up the dried meat and jujubes he set for them on a special terrace? And how the court flatterers lied: first they told him to imitate the exploits of the Yellow Emperor who had been lifted, with his retinue, up to Heaven on a whiskered dragon. They then said, 'This is the grave of the Yellow Emperor,' which it couldn't be. Then, realising their mistake, they said, 'This is the grave of his coat and hat.' Immortality was a very, very confusing topic. As he grew more confused and mistrustful, he concluded that the answer lay in the Far West — with the Heavenly Horses of the King of Ferghana.

As the Chinese people had multiplied, their field systems had crept over the face of China like a skin rash. In the south there were rice paddies, in the north, millet; and as Chinese rainfall was irregular, farmers always had to irrigate their crops. In a mountain village the headman would delegate a cheerful work-party to dam the local stream. But down on the plains, stopping the Yellow River in spate required an authority more versed in the art of repression.

Chinese civilisation, like that of Egypt, rose from the banks of great rivers. Under the ritual, the Emperor was Chief Water Authority; his government a machine for the control of corvée labour; his granaries the National Bank which could starve as well as feed. Imperial decrees used to begin 'The World is based on Agriculture'; for the settled world — the only conceivable world — depended on fettering millions to the land and forcing on them a back-breaking routine of work on fields or dykes. Hence the horror of the officials when the machine broke down. Hence their dismay as they thought of the nomads on the northern frontiers. Hence their Great Wall — not so much a defence to keep outsiders out as a fence to keep their own people in.

An ocean of grass extends westwards from Manchuria to the Hungarian Plain. Over its undulating horizons, mounted nomads moved their flocks on a restless search for food. In winter they sheltered under the lee of mountains from the *buran* or white wind of winter; in the spring they relaxed when the flowers lacquered the ground. They were squat men, glued from childhood to their horses, their faces as red as their leather boots. The elements, which hardened them, produced an inflexible attitude of mind. Perpetual movement was their creed, not simply to avert the bad consequences of sitting still, but as an end in itself. In their eyes man was a born migrant, settlement the perversion of degenerates, and cutting the soil to grow crops, murder. They had no use for ceremony. Their migration was their seasonal ritual, their music the howling of mastiffs, clanging of bells, and pattering of feet. But they did have an idea, terrifying in its simplicity, of an All-Powerful Something in a Bright Blue Sky. They called on it to justify all their actions.

In the reign of Wu-ti, the nomads who hovered over the northern frontiers of China were the Hsiung-nu, who were to reappear as the Huns four centuries later when they ripped the Roman Empire apart. Living in felt tents or covered wagons they reduced their possessions to bare essentials, channelling their appetite for finery into brilliant clothes, patchworks of dyed skins and an art of metal ornaments that writhed with snapping monsters. In camp the rich lived as the poor, drank the same fermented mare's milk and ate the same lamb. Wealth could be measured only in terms of livestock, and the lack of stored goods blurred social differences. In any case wealth in animals was precarious. One late snowstorm or a bad drought could reduce a rich man to penury; and this gnawing unease made him cast envious eyes on sitting targets in China. The steppe might appear limitless, but there was never enough grass to go round. Tribes were unstable within their territories and the nomad world was racked with raids and counter-raids.

To a sovereign as spirited as Wu-ti it was intolerable to have a frontier boiling with these kidnappers and extortionists. Without provocation their mounted horsemen would spill over the Wall, swoop on farmsteads 'like flocks of crows', spatter the countryside with blood, truss up their loot and disappear into fogs. But he refused to be blackmailed into sending them provisions and silks (the Huns even had the nerve to call it tribute). If they wanted the luxuries of civilisation, they'd have to come and beg for them, prostrate themselves and become citizens. However, it was useless to argue with their ruler, the Shan-yu. Morally, he lived in another world. The only way of controlling the menace was a mixture of deceit and force. And as the Huns wore wolf-masks and armour with reptilian leather scales, it was preferable to think of them not as men, but as dangerous animals.

To defeat them Wu-ti had to get horses, horses so fast they could outrun the Huns' steppe ponies, for before the days of aerial bombardment the power of any empire depended on the extent of its horseflesh. But China was not good horse country, and the Chinese were not used to riding. Their past battles had been fought with chariots, but these were unable to compete with the mounted bowmen of the steppe. Although the Chinese had gingerly made some efforts to sit in the saddle, it did not come easily to them. Wu-ti insisted that his armies beat the Huns at their own game and he ordered the training of a light cavalry.

He was rewarded by the discovery of a boy of eighteen called Ho-Ch'u-p'ing, who appointed himself the scourge of the Huns. In 142 BC he split off from the main army with a band of rough-riders, rounded the Gobi Desert, slaughtered the astonished enemy, captured a 'million' animals and made off with a prime minister. The Emperor loved the marvellous boy and kept enlarging his estate by several thousand households, but the boy said he couldn't think of houses as long as a single Hun breathed. He lectured him on principles of strategy and advised him to read Sun Tzu's *Art of War* (one day to become the military gospel of Mao Tse-tung), but the boy said: 'The only thing that matters is how *one's own* strategy is going to work.' He was, one suspects, a little monster. He was nasty to his soldiers; one day in the middle of nowhere they were on the verge of collapse, and he had them level a private football pitch. However, the *enfant terrible* burned himself out and died very young. The Emperor heaped a huge mound over the grave, with a stone horse trampling a Hunnish bowman underfoot.

Elsewhere Chinese diplomacy had been meddling in far-off places. Since nomads always quarrelled among themselves, Wu-ti attempted to persuade other tribes to attack the Huns from the rear. Some years before there had lived on the western frontier of China a people called the Yueh-chih, who had reddish hair and blue eyes and who spoke an Indo-European language similar, at several removes, to Gaelic. The Huns had horribly defeated the Yueh-chih and converted the skull of their king into a drinking cup. The latter had then trekked over the deadly sands of Sinkiang and had installed themselves near the present city of Samarkand. The Emperor sent his ambassador, Chang-ch'ien, to find them in the countries of the Far West and persuade them to return to their old pastures. He was delayed on the way for ten years by the Huns, but managed to escape and continue his journey. But the Yueh-chih had no desire to leave the Trans-Oxiana to become a buffer state in a scrubby waste between two equally rapacious peoples.

That part of the mission was a failure, but Chang-ch'ien had also visited the Kingdom of Ferghana (Ta-yuan). Its inhabitants will have been like the Tajiks who live in the region today, whiskery men with deep-set eyes. They were mad for commerce and lived in mud houses. It was a delicious country, abandoned by Alexander's Greeks not long before. The valleys were strips of emerald between purplish hills. Jade-green streams flowed from the Pamirs through the gardens. White roses twined their way up poplars. There were peaches, apricots, mulberries, the most sumptuous melons in the world, and grapes, several varieties of which Chang-ch'ien took back to China — 'The White Crystal', 'The Vegetable Dragon Pearl', and the long one called 'Mare's Nipple'. The ambassador also reported on the King's stud of horses. They sweated blood, ate alfalfa, and their ancestor had descended directly from Heaven.

From that moment horses and power politics were inseparable for Wu-ti. But it was, apparently, impossible to wheedle the Heavenly Horses out of the King of Ferghana. Then the Emperor heard of another people in the West called the Wu-sun, living in present-day Soviet Kazakhstan. They also had fine thoroughbreds and might be persuaded to attack the Huns from behind. In 111 BC the aging Chang-ch'ien, Wu-ti's Central Asian expert, was dispatched with Imperial gifts, and, with considerable force of character, made the King of the Wu-sun prostrate himself. 'If you do not prostrate yourself, I shall have to take them back.' The ambassador then said the Son of Heaven would gratefully receive the horses as a gift. The King was pleased to send some, but in exchange he required an Imperial Princess.

At this news Wu-ti consulted the Book of Changes. That convenient book replied: 'The Heavenly Horses will come from the North-West,' and so he horse-traded an Imperial

Princess into the wilds of the Far West. The King was called K'un-mo and as a child had been abandoned on the steppe, where wolves were said to have suckled him and birds had dropped gobbets of raw meat from the sky. But to his bride he was a decrepit old man who could only drink a cup of wine with her. The princess wrote a sad little poem which the late Arthur Waley translated:

> A tent is my house,
> Of felt are my walls:
> Raw flesh my food
> With mare's milk to drink.
> Always thinking of my country,
> My heart sad within.
> Would I were a yellow stork
> And could fly to my own home!

Occasionally Wu-ti found time to send her exhortatory messages.

He idolised the Heavenly Horses, until one day his spies told him that Wu-sun horses were not properly Heavenly Horses. True Heavenly Horses belonged only to the King of Ferghana who kept them shut up in his capital. Their whiskers reached their knees. Their tails swept the ground. They had a 'double-spine like a tiger'. Their hooves were 'like a thick wrist'. When the sun was at its height they sweated blood. They could grasp the sun, and travel 1,000 *li* a day (about 300 miles).

Three thousand miles across the Roof of the World, the King of Ferghana had the horses locked in his stables. Wu-ti had to get them from him. All the curiosities of the West, the jugglers or ostrich eggs, were nothing to the Heavenly Breed. First he tried diplomacy by offering the King a golden horse in exchange for real ones. But the people of Ferghana were bored by Chinese presents and evaded the issue. They felt quite safe. Were there not 3,000 miles of saltpans and singing sands between them and the Emperor's anger? Then in a fit of pique the ambassador took a mallet, smashed the gold horse to bits, cursed all present and left. But the King ordered him to be killed on the frontier.

The Celestial Emperor would not be humiliated by any minor monarch, however far away. He commandeered an enormous army, and put General Li-kuang-li, the brother of a court favourite, in charge. In 104 BC, the army disappeared through the Jade Gate, only to reappear hopelessly reduced some months later. Locusts had eaten every blade of grass that year; tens of thousands of men and horses had collapsed and died. But Wu-ti's generals retreated only in the direction of the executioner's axe, and it was stopped just in time to save their necks. Then an even vaster expedition was planned. Wu-ti emptied the jails of criminals; he sent horse-tamers, and water engineers to divert the rivers of Ferghana; he organised relief supply-trains of dried boiled rice for the whole journey. And this time he succeeded. The army besieged the capital of Ferghana. Its inhabitants killed their irritable old king and promised Li-kuang-li a pick of the Heavenly Horses if he would lay off. The latter chose thirty breeding animals (with the promise of two more to be sent annually) and 3,000 of lesser breeds. And the few Chinese who didn't litter the sands with their own bones returned to marquisates and showers of gold. For what could be more glorious for the Emperor than to have the divine steeds browsing on amethyst fields of alfalfa beside the vermilioned eaves of the palace?

What was the Wonder Horse that sweated blood? It is hard, at this distance in time, to say. But one thing is clear. The Kings of Ferghana had got hold of an animal with 'hot blood', and 'hot blood', as any bloodstock expert will tell you, comes from the Near East. Somewhere in North Africa or South-West Asia there had once existed the ancestor of the modern Arab horse: the late Professor Ridgeway said it may have looked like a quagga (an extinct form of zebra), and the Arabs say it all began with Baz, the great-great-grandson of Noah, who captured wild horses and tamed them. Among these early domesticated animals was the horse described by Job: 'The glory of his nostrils is terrible . . . he paweth in the valley . . . swallowing the ground in fierceness and rage . . . '

In modern horse-breeding there are two main streams of blood. One comes from the 'cold-blooded' stocks of the north. The ponies of the Huns had descended from a 'cold-blooded' wild horse that still survives in Outer Mongolia and is named after an obstinate Russian traveller called Colonel Przwalsky. It has an upright bristly mane, a Roman nose, heavy lower jaw and a thick neck that looks as if it is made for battling against headwinds and snowdrifts. The steppe ponies of this northern strain have a lolloping trot and marvellous endurance.

The 'hot-blooded' strain, represented by today's Arabian, is almost another animal. It has a 'dished' gazelle-like skull, flaring nostrils, eyes set well down the head, an arched neck, a flowing mane and tail, a depressed spine with two ridges of muscle along it (the Chinese 'tiger-back'), and a light bounding gallop. On all points it differs from the descendants of Przwalsky's horse. And the blood-sweating? Some say that it is to be explained by a parasitic insect called *Parafiliaria multipapilosa*, but Lady Wentworth, who bred the finest Arabians in England, once had a horse that sweated blood. And she would have been the first to spot a parasite.

How 'hot blood' came to Ferghana is a matter of conjecture. It *had* been in the region for some time. Three centuries earlier, twelve fine thoroughbreds were buried in the ice-bound grave of a tribal chieftain in the Altai Mountains, north of the Wu-sun. 'Hot blood' (mixed with some heavier stock) also coursed in the battle-chargers, bred for Greek cavalry on the Thessalian Plain. One can see it in the flaring nostrils of Selene's horse on the Parthenon (which, allowing for differences of artistic convention, closely resembles Commander Chang's horses). But in some way the Ferghana horses must have been yet more special. Fourteen centuries later, as Marco

Polo passed through the region, he learned of a local breed which claimed a pedigree going back to Bucephalus, the famous Thessalian battle horse of Alexander the Great. Could Wu-ti's Heavenly Horses be descended from the only real love of the other God King?

There are two possible explanations for Wu-ti's horse mania. The more conventional one suggests, of course, that the Chinese army needed the 'hot-blooded' animal, as modern armies need rockets and tanks. The marvellous cavalcade of 'hot-blooded' horses from the Tomb of Commander Chang shows that the new strain was prized for cavalry three centuries later. But there is a suggestion, first made by Arthur Waley, that military operations were not uppermost in Wu-ti's mind when he nearly ruined China to get the Heavenly Breed. Instead his horse-rustling may have been an affair of the spirit.

All religions have propounded a belief in an immortal soul which flies off after death, while some have believed it possible to pre-empt the inconvenience of death by arranging to fly off while the body still breathes. But the soul needs a 'vehicle' — a chariot, a saddle or wings (and we must not forget that for 3,000 years a man came nearest to flight on a galloping horse). Our hobby-horses and merry-go-rounds are the last vestiges of the 'vehicles' in European folklore which helped one 'get out of oneself'.

In Chinese mythology the horse was the magical 'vehicle' which escorted legendary emperors to a happy place in the Far West. It was the 'Friend of the Dragon' and was 'born from the waters of a pool'. Wu-ti had been looking for such an animal all his life. In 121 BC a strange horse had emerged from the Ordos River but that proved a disappointment. When at last the real Heavenly Horses arrived in China he must have felt confident about his imminent take-off. 'They will draw me up,' he wrote in a poem, 'and carry me to the Holy Mountain. I shall reach the Jade Terrace . . . ' And this is why he kept the horses close to the palace, waiting for the event he projected in fantasy.

One morning, when all the omens were favourable, he would descend from his apartments. Sweet music would be playing. He would mount the chariot drawn by the steeds of the wind. Gently they would lift in the air and fly to the Land of Perpetual Peace. The Royal Mother of the West would be standing on her jade ramparts to greet him. She would hand him one of her celebrated peaches that ripened every 6,000 years, and his wizened skin would stretch into the smoothness of youth . . .

1973

ROCK'S WORLD

And over Li Chiang, the snow range is turquoise
Rock's world that he saved us for memory
a thin trace in high air

Ezra Pound, *Canto CXIII*

It is a cold, sunny Sunday in Yunan. On the plain below Jade Dragon Mountain, the villagers of Beisha are letting off fire-crackers to celebrate the building of a house, and the village doctor is holding a feast in his upper room, in honour of his first-born grandson.

The sun filters through the lattices, bounces off rafters hung with corn-cobs and lights up everyone's faces. Apart from us, almost all the guests are members of the Nakhi tribe.

The Nakhi are the descendants of Tibetan nomads who, many centuries ago, exchanged their tents for houses and settled in the Lijiang Valley, to grow rice and buckwheat at an altitude of over 8,000 feet. Their religion was — and surreptitiously still is — a combination of Tibetan Lamaism, Chinese Taoism and a far, far older shamanistic belief: in the spirits of cloud and wind and pine.

The Doctor has seated us, with his four brothers, at the table of honour beside the east window.

Below, along the street, there are lines of weeping willows and a quickwater stream in which some pale brown ducks are playing. Led by the drake, they swim furiously against the current, whizz back down to the bridge and then begin all over again.

The panelled housefronts are painted the colour of ox-blood. Their walls are of mud brick, flecked with chaff, and their tiled roofs stretch away, rising and sagging, in the direction of the old dynastic temple of the ancient kings of Mu.

None of the Doctor's brothers looks the least bit alike. The most vigorous is a leathery, Mongol-eyed peasant, who keeps refilling my bowl of firewater. The second, with bristly grey hair and a face of smiling wrinkles, sits immobile as a meditating monk. The other two are a tiny man with a wandering gaze and a shadowy presence under a fur-lined hat.

Looking across to the ladies' table, we are amazed by the full-fleshed, dimpled beauty of the young girls and the quiet dignity of the older women. They are all in traditional costume, in the celestial colours — blue and white. Some, it is true, are wearing Mao caps, but most are in a curved blue bonnet, rather like a Flemish coif. Our Shanghai friend, Tsong-Zong, says we might well be guests at Brueghel's *The Peasant Wedding*.

Apart from the bonnet, the women's costume consists of a blue bodice, a pleated white apron and a stiff, quilted cape secured with crossbands. Every Nakhi woman carries the cosmos on her back: the upper part of the cape is a band of indigo representing the night sky; the lower, a lobe of creamy silk or sheepskin that stands for the light of day. The two halves are separated by a row of seven disks that symbolise the stars — although the sun and moon, once worn on either shoulder, have now gone out of fashion.

Girls come up from the kitchen with the sweet course: apples preserved in honey, melon in ginger, sour plums in alcohol. More girls then come with the 'Nine Dishes' — the 'Nine Dragons', as they've been called since the Chou dynasty: in this case, cubes of pork fat and winter sausage, water chestnuts, lotus root, carp, taros, bean tops, rice fritters, a fungus known as tree ears, and a heap of tripe and antique eggs that go, like sulphur bombs, straight to the gut.

From time to time, the Doctor himself appears at the head of the stairs, in a white clinician's mobcap and silver-grey cotton greatcoat. He surveys the company with the amused, slightly otherworldly air of a Taoist gentleman-scholar, and flicks his wispy beard from side to side. As soon as the meal is over, he appears again, hypodermic in hand, as if to remind us that healing, even on this 'Big Happy Day', is a work without end.

The grandson's name is Te-Sho: 'Te' for virtue, 'Sho' for longevity. On a sheet of red paper, now pinned to the porch, the old man has written the following:

> The grandfather grants his grandson
>   the name 'Te-Sho'.
> Te is high as the Big Dipper.
> Sho is like the southern mountain.
> Te is valued by the world.
> Sho respected by men.
> Te is an oily rain,
> Sho the fertilised field.
> Long life and health to him, born
>   10.30 am, 9th Moon, 14th Day.

The focus of all this adoration is swaddled in a length of gold-and-purple Tibetan brocade, and has the face of a man born wise. He is on show downstairs, in his mother's lap. The bedroom has white-papered walls to which are pasted scarlet cutouts of characters representing happiness and of butterflies flying in pairs.

Apart from the Doctor's herbal and his English dictionary, the swaddling clothes are the family's only treasure to survive the Cultural Revolution, when Red Guards ransacked the house.

The Doctor takes the baby and cradles him in his arms.

'I have plenty,' he says, gesturing to the revellers in the courtyard. 'Six years ago I had nothing. But now I have plenty.' His wife comes from the kitchen and stands beside him. And with her deep blue bonnet, and smile of tender resignation, she reminds us of Martha or Mary in a Florentine altarpiece.

The Red Guards stripped him of everything, and he was forbidden to practise. 'It was she who saved me,' he says. 'Without her I could not have lived.'

Their son, the father of three weeks' standing, is a young man of twenty-seven in a neat blue Chinese suit. He is a self-taught teacher of English, and now also a student of medicine.

Proudly, he shows us his wedding cup — a porcelain bowl painted with peacocks, on which the village calligrapher has added a couplet by the Tang poet Pai-ju-li:

> One only wishes that people will live
> forever
> And be in couples even at a distance
> of 1,000 li

The calligrapher — a courteous, hook-nosed old gentleman — is the Doctor's cousin and also one of the party. He has spent many years, as an ideological bygone, in jail. But now — in this new, relaxed undoctrinaire China — he has retired to his tiny house by the stream: to practise the arts of seal cutting, brush-work and the culture of orchids. On Tuesday, when we called on him, he showed us a lilac autumn crocus, with a label in Chinese reading 'Italian autumn narcissus'.

The Doctor, too, is a passionate plant collector, though of a rather different stamp. Behind his surgery is a garden with paths of pebble-mosaic where a plum tree casts its shadow, like a sundial, on the whitewashed walls, and there are raised beds for growing medicinal herbs. Most of the herbs he has gathered himself, from the slopes of the Snow Range: heaven's hemp (for the bladder); orchid root (for migraine); *Meconopsis horridula* (for dysentery), and a lichen that will cure shrunken ovaries, or bronchitis if taken with bear's grease.

He owes much of his botanical knowledge to his student days in Nanjing. But some he learned from the strange, solitary European — with red face, spectacles and a terrible temper — who taught him his first smattering of English — at whom, as his retinue passed up the village street, the boys would clamour: 'Le-Ke! Le-Ke!' — 'Rock! Rock!' — and scamper out of reach.

Joseph F. Rock — 'Dr Lock' as the Nakhi remember him — was the Austro-American botanist and explorer who lived in the Lijiang Valley, off and on, from 1922 to 1949. My interest in him goes back many years to a summer evening in the Arnold Arboretum in Boston, when I found that all the trees I liked best bore Rock's name on their labels.

'Tell me,' the Doctor asked on a previous visit, 'why was Le-Ke so angry with us?'

'He wasn't angry with you,' I said. 'He was born angry.'

I should perhaps have added that the targets of his anger included the National Geographic magazine (for rewriting his prose), his Viennese nephew, Harvard University, women, the State Department, the Kuomintang, Reds, red tape, missionaries, Holy Rollers, Chinese bandits and bankrupt Western civilisation.

Rock was the son of an Austrian manservant who ended up as major-domo to a Polish nobleman, Count Potocki. His mother died when he was six. At thirteen, already under the spell of an imaginary Cathay, he taught himself Chinese characters.

Tuberculosis notwithstanding, young Rock ran away to sea: to Hamburg, to New York, to Honolulu — where, without training, he set himself up as *the* botanist of the Hawaiian Islands. He wrote three indispensable books on the flora, then went to Burma in search of a plant to cure leprosy. He 'discovered' Lijiang, thereafter to be the base for his travels along the Tibetan border: to the former kingdoms of Muli, Choni and Yungning, and to the mountain of Minya Konka, which, in a moment of rashness, he claimed to be the highest in the world. (He had miscalculated by about a mile.) Yet, though he introduced hundreds of new or rare plants to Western gardens and sent off thousands and thousands of herbarium specimens, he never wrote a paper on the botany of China.

Instead, he gave his life to recording the customs, ceremonies and the unique pictographic script of his Nakhi friends. Lijiang was the only home he ever knew; and after he was booted out, he could still write, in a letter, 'I want to die among those beautiful mountains rather than in a bleak hospital bed all alone.'

This, then, was the meticulous autodidact, who would pack 'David Copperfield' in his baggage to remind him of his wretched childhood; who travelled '*en prince*' (at the expense of his American backers), ate off gold plate, played records of Caruso to mountain villagers and liked to glance back, across a hillside, at his cavalcade 'half a mile long'.

His book *The Ancient Na-Khi Kingdom of South-West China*, with its eye-aching genealogies and dazzling asides, must be one of the most eccentric publications ever produced by the Harvard University Press.

Here is a stretch of his embattled prose: 'A short distance beyond, at a tiny temple, the trail ascends the red hills covered with oaks, pines, *Pinus Armandi*, *P. yunnanensis*, *Alnus*, *Castanopsis Delavayi*, rhododendrons, roses, Berberis, etc., up over limestone mountains, through oak forest, to a pass with a few houses called Ch'ou-shui-ching (Stinking water well). At this place many hold-ups and murders were committed by the bandit hordes of Chang Chiehpa. He strung up his victims by the thumbs to the branches of high trees, and tied rocks to their feet; lighting a fire beneath he left them to their fate. It was always a dreaded pass for caravans. At the summit there are large groves of oaks (*Quercus Delavayi*) . . . '

No wonder Ezra Pound adored it!

Pound appears to have got hold of Rock's *Na-Khi Kingdom* in 1956, at a time when he was locked up as a lunatic in St

Elizabeth's Hospital in Washington; from it, he extrapolated the upland paradise that was to be, in effect, his lifeline.

Over the last week we have been walking the roads of Lijiang country and finding, to our delight, that the world Rock 'saved us for memory' — to say nothing of Ezra Pound's borrowings — is very far from dead.

At Rock's former lodgings in Lijiang town, we have seen his bookcase, his pigeonhole desk, his wide chair ('because he was so fat!') and the remains of his garden beside the Jade Stream.

At Nuluko (the name means 'the foot of the silver cliffs') his country house is almost as he left it, except that, instead of herbarium specimens, the porch is spread with drying turnip tops. The present occupant, Li Wen Biao, was one of Rock's muleteers; he showed us the master's camp-bed and the washhouse where he would set up a canvas bath from Abercrombie & Fitch.

We have been to Tiger Leaping Gorge and seen the cliff-line plummeting 11,000 feet into the Yangtze. We have watched the Nakhi women coming down from the Snow Range, with their bundles of pine and artemisia; and one old woman with a bamboo winnowing basket on her back, and the sun's rays passing through it:

> Artemisia
> Arundinaria
> Winnowed in fate's tray . . .
> *Canto CXII*

The wild pear trees are scarlet in the foothills, the larches like golden pagodas; the north slopes 'blue-green with juniper'. The last of the gentians are in flower, and the flocks of black sheep brindle the plain.

> When the stag drinks at the salt spring
>   and sheep come down with the gentian sprout . . .
> *Canto CX*

One evening, walking back to town across the fields, I came on a boy and girl reading aloud beside the embers of a fire. Their book was a traditional Chinese romance and, on its open page, there was a picture of Kuan Yin, goddess of mercy.

The Nakhi are a passionate people and, even today, rather than submit to a hated marriage, young lovers may poison or drown themselves, or jump to their death from the mountain.

At the Nakhi Institute in Lijiang, we were shown a pair of pine saplings, adorned like Christmas trees, commemorating two people who killed themselves for love. Rock wrote that such suicides become 'wind-spirits', reminding Pound of Dante's Paolo and Francesca, whose shades were 'so light on the wind', and who, readers of the *Inferno* will remember, fell in love while reading a romance of chivalry.

At Shigu, where the Yangtze takes a hairpin bend, we have seen the Stone Drum:

> by the waters of Stone Drum,
> the two aces . . .
> *Canto CI*

The drum is a cylinder of marble in a pavilion by the willows. The 'aces' refer to two Chinese generals — one lost in legend, the other of the Ming dynasty, whose victory is recorded on the drum itself. Our friend Tsong-Zong raised his hand to the surface and rattled off the characters:

> Snowflakes the size of a hand
> Rain joining sunset to sunset
> The wind quick as arrows . . .
> Commands quick as lightning
> And the bandits loose their gall . . .
> Their black flag falls to the earth . . .
> They run for their lives . . .
> Heads heaped like grave mounds

Blood like rain . . .
The dikes choked with armour and rattan shields
The trail of foxes and the trail of jackals
Have vanished from the battle field . . .

Rock wrote of a tradition that, should the Stone Drum split, a catastrophe will fall on the country. About fifteen years ago, some Red Guards did indeed split it. (It has since been stuck together.) We wondered if, secretly, the iconoclasts had seen the foxes and jackals in themselves.

We have listened to a Nakhi orchestra that in the bad years would practise in secret: on a stringless lute, a muffled drum and a flute turned at a right angle to the mouthpiece.

In the hills above Rock's village is the Jade Dragon Monastery, Yufeng Si, where we have sat with the lama hearing him tell how he would sneak into the monastery at night, on pain of prison or worse, to save the five-hundred-year-old camellia that stretches, trained in a trellis, around the temple court.

Of all the places we have seen, the monastery seems the loveliest. But this is what Rock had to say of it: 'It is the home of rats, whose excrements lie inches deep . . . dangerous to visit . . . books wrapped in dusty silks . . . the most forlorn and forsaken lamasery I know of.'

Also paying his respects to the lama was the Regional Commissioner for Monuments. I asked him about the horribly battered temple, dating from the Tang dynasty, which we could see in the valley below. It is dedicated to the mountain god, Saddo, lord of the Snow Range and protector from calamities.

The Commissioner answered, emphatically: 'The restoration will begin next month,' as if also to say that the world's oldest, subtlest, most intelligent civilisation has now returned to the sources of its ancient wisdom.

In the village of Beisha, around the corner from the Doctor's house, there is another, smaller temple, its garden desolate, its cypresses fallen, its balustrades smeared with graffiti: 'Confess and we will be lenient!'

Here, under Taoist symbols of the Eternal Return, the Red Guards set up their so-called courts. Yet it occurred to us that these ill-tempered scrawls were not, after all, so distant from the spirit of the 'Tao-te-ching' of Lao-tze:

> How did the great rivers and
> seas gain dominion over the
> hundred lesser streams?
> By being lower than they.

The sun goes down behind the mountain, and we must, finally, say goodbye to the Doctor. He is anxious to give me from his pharmacy a plant with the windblown name of *Saussurea gossipiphora*, which only grows on the snow-line. Soon, he hopes to leave his practice in the care of his son and be free to gather herbs in the mountains. He lifts his eyes to Jade Dragon Peak and, suddenly, in his silver greatcoat, becomes the living image of my favourite upland traveller, the poet Li Po:

> You ask me why I live in the
> grey hills.
> I smile but do not answer, for
> my thoughts are elsewhere.
> Like peach petals carried by the
> stream, they have gone
> To other climates, to countries
> other than the world of men.

1986

NOMAD INVASIONS

During the Spring of 376 AD the Roman garrisons on the Danube frontier learned Nomads were on the move. Over the steppe lands that stretched to the east came news that the Gothic kingdom of Ermanarich in the Crimea had fallen to the Huns, an unknown people of mounted archers, bestial in appearance, whose home lay close to the ice-bound ocean. 'No one ever ploughs a field in their country,' wrote the contemporary historian Ammianus Marcellinus, 'or touches a plough handle. They are ignorant of home, law or settled existence, and they keep roaming from places in their wagons. If you ask one of their children where he comes from, he was conceived in one place, born far away and brought up still farther off.' Gothic refugees implored the Roman government for asylum within the imperial frontiers. And, putting themselves under the protection of the Emperor, they were allowed to cross the Danube in their thousands 'like the rain of ashes from an eruption of Etna'. But their hosts failed in the basic obligations of hospitality, and within two years the Goths had revolted and killed the Emperor Valens himself at the Battle of Adrianople. Thereafter the Empire was doomed to further barbarian inroads.

However momentous the fall of the Roman Empire may seem in retrospect, it was merely an episode in a conflict between two incompatible, yet complementary, systems — nomadism and settled agriculture. The arrival of the Huns on their stocky ponies was no new event. The 'unharvested steppe' forms a continuous strip of grazing from Hungary to Manchuria. It was a reservoir of nomad peoples — Cimmerians, Scythians, Sarmatians, and later Avars, Magyars, and Mongols — who migrated up and down it and periodically overflowed on to the sown lands of civilisation. Ancient Mesopotamia and Egypt faced the same problem from the men of the fringe, whose mercurial shiftings in the encircling deserts and mountains were a source of anxiety in times of national ascendancy, of terror in times of collapse. As the Hungarian historian Andreas Alfoldi wrote, there existed along the Rhine and Danube a 'moral barrier' between the barbarian and civilised worlds. The grandiose Roman fortifications, like the Great Wall of China, were simply 'the secondary consequences and the reflection of that moral isolation'. In a modified form the confrontation continues as the barrier of incomprehension between the revolutionary insurgent and established authority.

The quarrel of nomad and settler is, of course, the same as that of Abel the shepherd and Cain the planter and founder of the first city. As befitted a Bedouin people, the Hebrews sided with Abel. Jehovah found his offering of a 'firstling of the flock' more acceptable than Cain's 'fruit of the ground'. Cain's act of fratricide is judged a typical crime of settlement, and as punishment Jehovah sterilises the soil and forces him to wander on a penitential pilgrimage, 'a fugitive and a vagabond'.

True nomads are sons of Ishmael, the wild man, whose 'hand shall be against every man, and every man's hand against him', activated by what Gibbon called 'the spirit of emigration and conquest'. The Book of Joshua, for example, is a paean of praise for the ideal of nomadic insurgency. As the nineteenth-century traveller James Morier wrote of the I'lyats, or wandering tribes of Persia, they 'look down on the *Shehrnishins* (or dwellers in cities) as degenerate, applauding the hardihood and simplicity of manners of those who have no other dwelling place than the tent, and reviling those who recur to the luxuries of a house and the protection of a city.'

In turn the citizen reviled the nomad as a savage wrecker of progress. And, since literature itself is the invention of settlers, the nomadic record looks black in writing. Thus an ancient Egyptian official would write of the Bedouin Hebrews, 'Their name reeks more than the stink of bird droppings', or a Chinese Imperial Secretary of the Eastern Huns,' . . . in their breasts beat the hearts of beasts . . . from the most ancient times they have never been regarded as a part of humanity'. Roman authorities treated the citizens of the Empire as men, outsiders as animals, and their historians could calmly compare the annihilation of a Germanic people to a medical cure (*salubria medicamenta*). Elsewhere, nomad invaders, who migrated onto sown lands, were compared to plagues of locusts and swarms of snakes.

Faced with the acceleration of world population-growth, some modern biologists have diagnosed that the human species is rapidly approaching the 'swarming stage',* thus refining Malthus's 'dismal theorem' that human populations breed up to the level of their food supply, a proliferation that can only lead to global starvation unless checked by mass mortality. Animal species reach the 'swarming stage' when some pressure of natural selection, to which they have been subjected during their evolution, is removed. The result is a population outburst, followed by a neurosis from overcrowding and panic in the face of starvation. Random migrations ensue.

The suicidal march of the Scandinavian lemming to death in the sea is thought by some to shed light on the tragic refugee problems of our day, and a global situation of wandering refugees is predicted. But the apocalyptic idea of total destruction at the hands of migrating hordes is again nothing new. At the time of the Mongol holocaust in the thirteenth century,

* S.R. Eyre, 'Man the Pest: the Dim Chances of Survival', *New York Review*, 18 November 1971, pp. 18ff.

observers confidently announced the end of the world. The Mongol Khan was Antichrist himself, his armies of mounted nomads the Legions of Gog and Magog. The Mongol military machine generated the same sort of anxiety as the nuclear bomb, and for this reason alone the mechanics of a nomadic invasion are of more than passing interest.

The word nomad derives from the Greek *nomos* — a pasture. A nomad proper is a mobile pastoralist, the owner and breeder of domesticated animals. To call a wandering hunter 'nomadic' is to misunderstand the meaning of the word. Hunting is a technique for killing animals, nomadism for keeping them alive. The psychology of the hunter is as different from the nomad's as the nomad's from that of the planter. Nomadism is born of wide expanses, ground too barren for the farmer to cultivate economically — savannah, steppe, desert and tundra, all of which will support an animal population providing that it moves. For the nomad, movement is morality. Without movement, his animals would die. But the planter is chained to his field; if he leaves, his plants wither.

Nomads never roam aimlessly from place to place, as one dictionary would have it. A nomadic migration is a guided tour of animals around a predictable sequence of pastures. It has the same inflexible character as the migrations of wild game, since the same ecological factors determine it. But domestication blunts an animal's innate sense of time and space. The herdsman replaces this loss with his own acquired skill, plotting his annual orbit to suit the needs of his own particular livestock.

A nomad's territory is the path linking his seasonal pastures. The tent-dweller invests this path with the emotional attachment a settler reserves for his houses and fields. Iranian nomads call the path *Il-Rah*, The Way. The 'way' of one tribe intersects with the 'ways' of others, and ill-timed movements lead to conflicts of interest. Herdsmen claim to own their 'ways' as their inalienable property; but in practice all they ask is the right of passage through a given stretch of territory at a fixed time of the year. The land holds no interest for them once they have moved on. Thus for a nomad, political frontiers are a form of insanity, based as they are on the aggregation of farmlands.

Today's nomads, whether they be Quashgais in Iran or Masai in Kenya, are facing their ultimate crisis at the hands of settled administrations. Their way of life is considered an anachronism in a modern state. Nomads are resentful of, and resistant to, change. The 'problem of the tribes' is as much an issue to many a modern government as it was to the rulers of an ancient near-eastern city-state. For life in the black tents has not significantly changed since Abraham, the Bedouin sheikh, moved his flock on his 'journeys from the south even unto Bethel, where his tent had been at the beginning' (Genesis 13:3).

The automatic discipline of pastoralism encourages a high standard of loyalty among close kin. In most nomad cultures the definition of a human being is 'he who goes on migrations'. The word *arab* means a 'dweller in the tents' as opposed to *hazar*, a 'house dweller'. Again, the latter is less than human.

Yet nomads are notoriously irreligious. They show little interest in ceremonial or protestations of faith. For the migration is of itself a ritual performance, a 'religious' catharsis, revolutionary in the strictest sense in that each pitching and breaking of camp represents a new beginning.* This will account for the violence of a nomad's reaction when his migration is blocked. Furthermore, if we assume that religion is a response to anxiety, then nomadism must satisfy some basic human aspiration, which settlement does not. It is paradoxical, but not surprising, that the great religions — Jewish, Christian, Muslim, Zoroastrian and Buddhist — were preached among settled peoples who *had been* nomads. Their

* For the ritual aspects of migrations, see Fredrik Barth, *Nomads of South Persia*, 1964, pp. 146ff.

ceremonial is saturated with pastoral metaphor, their processions and pilgrimages perform the activities of a pastoral migration in mime. The *Hadj*, or holy journey to Mecca, is but an artificial migration for settlers to detach them from their profane homes. What then has given the nomad his bad reputation?

The least helpful view suggests that the 'spirit of emigration and conquest' is a genetically inherited behavioural trait, which, through the pressures of natural selection, is highly developed in the nomad. In his *Evolution of Man and Society* Professor C.D. Darlington maintained that the instincts of a gipsy, like the palaeolithic hunter, were adjusted to a life of wandering, and seriously suggested that the royal families of Europe, as well as the Mongols, had a genetic adaptation to the horse. This had enabled their ancestors to win wars, but on mechanised battlefields had brought them 'headlong to disaster'. But so far the genetic approach to history has been either misleading or malign. The innate superiority of the wandering Nordic *Volk* was a fantasy. And it is not possible to explain Mongol militancy in genetic terms. The Mongols were a people of hunters who broke out onto the steppe, learned the arts of equitation and pastoralism, and left behind their closely related cousins, the Tungus and Samoyed, who were — and are — among the least violent people in the world; 'deformed and diminutive savages', as Gibbon called them, 'who tremble at the sound of arms'.

Others have suggested that the piles of skulls that marked the passage of a Genghiz Khan or the fearsome slave-markets of Bokhara were proof of a primary instinct in man to attack, dominate and kill his own kind, an instinct often suppressed by the institutions of civilised life, but encouraged under the more 'natural' conditions of nomadic barbarism. Again this view is unhelpful. Instead, we should perhaps allow human nature an appetitive drive for movement in the widest sense. The act of journeying contributes towards a sense of physical and mental well-being, while the monotony of prolonged settlement or regular work weaves patterns in the brain that engender fatigue and a sense of personal inadequacy. Much of what the ethologists have designated 'aggression' is simply an angered response to the frustrations of confinement.

A primary need for movement is borne out by recent studies of human evolution. Professor John Napier* has shown that the long-striding walk is an adaptation, unique among the primates, for covering distances over open savannahs. The bipedal walk made possible the development of the manufactory hand, and this led to the enlarged brain of our species. Any human baby also demonstrates its instinctive appetite for movement. Babies often scream for the simple reason they cannot bear to lie still. A crying child is a very rare sight on a nomad caravan, and the tenacity with which nomads cling to their way of life, as well as their quick-witted alertness, reflects the satisfaction to be found in perpetual movement. As settlers, we walk off our frustrations. The medieval Church instituted pilgrimage *on foot* as a cure for homicidal spleen.

The mainsprings of nomadic insurgency must be found within the precarious character of nomadism itself. Arnold Toynbee, following the lead of the fourteenth-century Arab historian, Ibn Khaldūn, could never be accused of underestimating the importance of nomad invasions on the course of history. But in *A Study of History* he favoured the mechanical agency of climatic change to account for the periodic eruptions of nomads from their customary pastures. Travellers in Central Asia, like Sven Hedin or Sir Aurel Stein, had observed that the cities of the Tarim Basin were flourishing in the tenth and eleventh centuries, but two hundred years later lay abandoned after a shift of climate had desiccated the land. This onset of aridity had coincided with the Mongol outburst, and it inspired the American geographer Ellsworth Huntington to plot a sequence of climatic oscillations that would

* John Napier, *The Roots of Mankind*, London, 1971, chapter VIII.

account for every nomad eruption. The idea that the nomads had responded to a climatic challenge admirably commended itself to Toynbee's scheme and was further reinforced by the story of Jacob and his sons coming down to Egypt 'when the famine was sore in the land'. But Jacob came as a suppliant, not a conqueror. Whether or not the insurgents would swamp the civilisation depended on its political state at the time. For Toynbee the nomads were either 'pushed off' the steppe or desert or 'pulled out' of it as if by suction when internal chaos invited them to raid.

But Toynbee's scheme is too simple. Shortage of grazing and population pressures certainly contributed towards the great exoduses. Livy tells of a Celtic king who resorted to predatory expansion, 'anxious to relieve his realm from the burden of overpopulation'. Furthermore, once pastureland is overgrazed, the grass becomes sour and less nourishing. Overgrazing also bares the topsoil which is then carried away in the wind. Dustbowl conditions ensue and the rains do not come any more. But such shifts in climate as there were do not coincide with the invasions. No climatic change took place in Arabia to account for the outpouring of Bedouin warriors in the service of Islam.

Moreover, it does not require a major shift in climate to ruin a stock-breeder. Few climates lack a lean season, a time of mental and physical anguish, which the religions ritualised as Lent or Ramadan. In the desert this coincides with the hot dry phase (Ramadan comes from the Arabic *ramz* 'to burn'), in the north with the last months of winter. At this time the people are weak, the animals weaker. And if the lean season lasts too long, a rich man may face total ruin. (Sheep farmers in New South Wales used to calculate that a thirty per cent drop in rainfall would carry off eighty per cent of the live-stock.) But the lean season is also, in Bedouin terminology, 'the time of the beasts'. The story of David and the Lion reminds us of the danger shepherds faced from carnivorous animals, and wolves will increase their numbers in direct ratio to the availability of edible sheep.

The instability of his profession encourages the nomad to increase and guard his flocks with fanatical obsession. He prefers to eat meat at others' expense and to rustle his neighbour's animals whenever he can. Then he looks about for other alternatives — raids, long-distance trade, and protection rackets as an insurance against disaster. 'The soul of them', Doughty wrote of the Arabian Bedouin, 'is greedy first of the proper subsistence, then of their proper increase. Though Israel is scattered among the most polite nations, who has not noticed this humour in them?' Owen Lattimore, whose knowledge of steppe pastoralism is unrivalled, once said, 'The pure nomad is the poor nomad,' in that he is unburdened by the luxuries of settlement. But in a society where livestock *is* wealth, the pure nomad is the relatively rich nomad. His obsession with increase is dictated by the fact that, once his flocks decline below a certain level, nomadism loses its viability. He and his family are compelled to find employment as agricultural serfs. As Ellsworth Huntington wrote in *The Pulse of Asia*, 'all the nomads I have ever met seemed to be comfortable. When their flocks diminish, they are obliged to seek new homes and to betake themselves to agriculture, leaving only the rich to continue the nomadic life.' Live beasts are the standard medium of exchange, and a man rich in animals has purchasing power to 'buy' wives for himself or his sons, to buy grazing concessions, and to buy his way out of a blood-feud.

Nomads are unstable within their tribal lands as a direct result of their 'growth ideology'. And it can be seen that the maximum amount of activity on the steppe will coincide with a climate favouring the growth of herds. With more animals to defend, there will be more herdsmen needed, and in turn more disputes over grazing rights and more raids. The cattlemen of Abraham quarrelled with the cattlemen of Lot. Knowing neither could control the wayward temper of their cowboys, Abraham suggested a parting of the ways. 'Is not the whole land before thee? Separate thyself I pray thee, before me: if thou wilt take the left hand, then I will go to the right; or if thou depart to the right hand, then I will go to the left' (Genesis 13:9). But once a split-away group trespasses on the pastures of others because of overstocking, old boundaries and agreements are destroyed.

'Sons are the source of wealth' goes a Turkoman proverb. And as we know from the Gospel of St John, a good shepherd owns his own sheep, unlike the hireling who runs away at the first sight of a wolf. The increase of healthy animals demands the increase of healthy sons to look after them. Hence the nomad's exhibitionistic attitude to male potency and his pre-occupation with the genealogy of the male line. All stock-raisers have this obsession for 'fine blood', and human stud-books litter the Old Testament. As economic principle, nomads make no effort to limit births, and a plentiful supply of milk from domesticated animals enables a nomad mother to conceive again immediately after birth. Her first child is weaned early and to some extent this rupture weakens the bond of attachment between her and her infant. The latter deflects its attachment onto animal 'substitutes' and is encouraged to fondle baby animals, remaining 'animal-fixed' for life. Boys are taught to ride as soon as they can walk, if not before. Pere Huc describes this in *Travels in China, Tartary and Thibet*. 'When a mere infant the Mongol is weaned and as soon as he is strong enough he is stuck upon a horse's back behind a man, the animal is put to a gallop, and the juvenile rider, in order not to fall off, has to cling with both hands to his leader's jacket. The Tartars thus become accustomed, from a very early age, to the movements of the horse and by degrees and the force of habit, to identify themselves, as it were, with the animal.'

Warfare — or, at least, violent competition — is endemic to nomadism. The tribe is a military machine, and from the age of four boys are trained in the art of war and defence. They are deputed to tend a few animals on pain of punishment for letting them stray. As a result, they are brainwashed into believing that the care of livestock constitutes one of the main purposes in life. This devotion to animals is invariably accompanied by a weakened regard for the value of human life. The Grand Historian of China, Ssu-Ma Ch'ien, describes the process in his account of the Hsiung-Nu or Eastern Huns. 'The little boys start out by learning to ride sheep and shoot birds and rats with a bow and arrow, and when they get older they shoot foxes and hares which are used for food. Thus all the young men are able to use a bow and act as armed cavalry in times of war.' Furthermore, equitation engenders a sort of Olympian grandeur. As the Russian explorer Colonel Przwalsky quaintly remarked of the Kalmuck nomad, 'His contempt for pedestrianism is so great that he considers it beneath his dignity to walk even as far as the next *yurta*.' The Huns, we are told, bought, sold, slept, ate, drank, gave judgment, even defecated without dismounting.

The territorial instability of the nomad may be contrasted unfavourably with the greater security enjoyed by the 'primitive' hunter and gatherer. The former sees territory in terms of good or bad grazing, the latter exploits his territory gratefully for his basic needs, and refuses on principle to store food for more than a few days. This he can afford to do, since hunters take active steps to keep their numbers constant. Without milk from domesticated animals and without beasts of burden, the mothers must suckle *and* carry their children on long journeys till the age of three or more. Meanwhile, they cannot bear any more children. The hunters have been accused of 'merry squandering' and certainly enjoy a far lower standard of living. But by budgeting for the minimum they lack all incentive to overstretch their frontiers unless forced out by others. 'There has never been the least attempt', wrote Spencer and Gillen of the Central Australia Aborigines, 'made by one tribe to encroach on the territory of another. Now and again they may have inter-tribal quarrels or fights, but there is no such thing as the acquisition of fresh territory.' The hunter's sole motive for travel outside his hunting ground is to 'marry far' in accordance with the incest taboo. For this reason, isolated groups of hunters are interlinked in a network of reciprocal trading agreements and marriage alliances with their neighbours. Fights flare up when — and only when — the parity of these exchanges is broken. Thus 'primitive' war and nomadic insurgency cannot meaningfully be compared to one another.

In their own feuds nomads preserve something of this 'archaic' notion of equivalence. The nomad world is racked with vendettas, but justice is personal, brisk and effective. All parties to a quarrel try to prevent it getting out of hand. The instability in their nomad society lacks the cohesion needed for conquest on a mass scale. The nomad armies were military machines co-ordinated by powerful autocrats. Their cohesion can only be explained in terms of the nomad's interaction with settled civilisation.

It used to suit evolution-minded social scientists to believe that pastoralism preceded agriculture. The hunter learned to tame wild animals. The nomad settled down to grow crops, and the farmer made the inventions on which the first cities depended. Yet nomadism was not a step towards civilisation, but a step away from it. Abraham left the city of Ur to become a nomad. The Central Asian Steppe, like the Great Plains of America, had been under cultivation till the horsemen swept the planters aside.

The great transformation from food-gathering to food-producing, known as the Neolithic Revolution in the Old World, first took place on the flanks of the Fertile Crescent, that great arc of mountains from Palestine to South Persia, where, after the recession of the ice-sheets, the wild ancestors of our sheep and goats browsed over stands of wild wheat and barley. The process by which grains and animals became domesticated was gradual and is not yet fully revealed. The important point to remember is this: at first, stock-breeding and agriculture were practised by the people of the same settlement.

The farmers eventually developed irrigation, and agriculture came down the mountainsides into the rich alluvial valleys with startling increases in yield. Meanwhile, the herdsmen withdrew to the wild places and developed a new order of their own. There they later domesticated the horse to give them greater range. Thus, nomad and farmer are linked to a common past and, to some extent, share common aspirations. If the nomad recovered the mobility of former times, he was also committed to an ideology of growth. The cleavage deprived the farmer of rich sources of animal protein and the nomad of essential grain. Nomad and farmer might hate each other, yet they needed each other. A nomad independent of settled agriculture has probably never existed. Ammianus Marcellinus, it is true, heard that the Hunnish cavalry survived on the blood of their horses and foraged roots alone, just as the Masai suck the blood of their cattle. Such were the iron rations of the campaign; but normally settler and nomad exchange grains and vegetables for hides, meat and dairy produce. An Iranian nomad cannot get through the winter without grain. The Sahara camel man cannot live without dates. In an ideal situation the two cultures live symbiotically side by side.

But the nomadic insurgent has tactical mobility and is expert in guerilla warfare, the art of 'attack and withdrawal' which, according to Ibn Khaldūn, was the practice of the Bedouin nations. 'Raids are our agriculture', goes a Bedouin proverb. The nomad does not take kindly to being ordered about. He looks down on farmers as sub-human rabble and does not feel obliged to treat them as equals. To quote Lattimore, 'when nomad chiefs patronize agriculture it is a subject agriculture that they prefer, exploited under their military protection and practised by imported peasants, between whom and the dominant nomads there is an emphatic social difference.' A character in the *History* of Priscus said this of the Huns: 'being themselves contemptuous of agriculture, they descended on the Gothic food supply and snatched it away like wolves. Eventually the Goths occupied the position of slaves and toiled for the sustenance of the Huns.'

A barbarous taste for 'fire-bright gold' infected the pastoral world. Its incorruptible brilliance relieved the leaden monotony of waste places. 'They had golden earrings because they were Ishmaelites', goes a line from the Book of Judges. The Huns 'burned with an insatiable lust for gold' and their Scythian and Sarmatian predecessors had their goldsmiths perfect ornaments in the celebrated 'Animal Style', an art of seething, snapping monsters where man is a stranger. From the frozen tombs of Pazyryk in the Altai Mountains or that of the Hunnish ruler from Noin-Ula in Mongolia, archaeologists have unearthed precious silks and embroideries, pile carpets and lacquers. Byzantine ambassadors to the camp of Attila noticed that the Hunnish dictator himself ate from a wooden trencher. But his followers wore extravagant silks, garlanded themselves with pearls, and drank from golden bowls encrusted with garnets. Such were the effects of contact with the luxuries of settlement.

The nomad ruler could only attract followers if he rewarded them well. An ungenerous lord was a dead lord. Once the supply of luxuries dwindled, he had a clear choice, blackmail or war. Ssu-Ma Ch'ien records that the Hsiung-Nu appointed a Chinese renegade to handle their diplomatic exchanges with the Imperial authorities; he advised the ambassadors to make sure that their tribute of grain and silks was of fine quality and the right quantity; if not, 'when the autumn harvest comes we will take our horses and trample your crops'. Once the settlers hardened their hearts and the subsidies dried up, the nomad ruler had no alternative but to risk deploying his 'natural' military machine against the glittering metropolises of the plains.

1972

7
PEOPLE

SHAMDEV:
THE WOLF-BOY

Last Easter Saturday, Father Joseph de Souza put on a freshly-laundered soutane and took the bus from Sultanpur to Lucknow, to celebrate Mass in the Cathedral. With him went an eight- or nine-year-old boy whom he was taking to Mother Teresa's Mission of Charity. The boy was unable to speak. Instead, he would clench his fists against his neck, depressing his vocal chords to make a low muted noise halfway between a growl and a howl.

Along the road the bus passed through the forest of Musafirkhana, where, about four years earlier, the boy had been found at play with his foster-brothers — who, it was said, were wolf-cubs.

From Romulus and Remus to Mowgli in Kipling's *Jungle Book*, there have been stories of man-cubs being saved and suckled by wolves: as well as by pigs, sheep, leopards, bears and, recently in the Sahara, by gazelles. No single case has been proved beyond doubt. It is conceivable that Pascal — the name bestowed on the new arrival by the mission Sisters — will turn out to be the exception.

Pascal immediately befriended the orphanage dog — although, one day, he took its ear in his mouth and bit hard. During the first week, he would rip off his clothes, chuck away his food, and when he got hold of a pair of glasses, he clashed them together like cymbals. During the second week, he began to settle down. He learned to greet people with the Hindi salutation 'Namaste!' He liked to travel round the garden sitting upright in the back of a bicycle rickshaw. The Sisters did have to watch him with other children: for sometimes, without warning, he would flick his fingers into their eyes.

One morning, a troupe of Rajasthani entertainers came down the street with monkeys jingling their bells, and a bear on a chain. Someone held up Pascal so he could get a better look — and he, as if suddenly seized with a fit, struggled and tried to throw himself into the bear's arms. A mission-worker, having watched this behaviour, decided to rename Pascal 'Baloo' — like Baloo the Bear in *The Jungle Book* — and wrote a short article about him for one of the Lucknow papers.

The article was syndicated in the foreign press. I was in Benares when I heard of it: I took the train to Sultanpur and looked up Father Joseph, who teaches at a school run by the Sisters of the Little Flowers of Bethlehem. He is a small, wrinkled, optimistic South Indian who has spent forty of his sixty-nine years in the Hindi north. In the hot weather he sleeps alone on the roof of a barrack-like building, at the far end of the compound from the nuns. In the yard below there grew some leggy papayas. A kennel housed a ferocious Alsatian that yanked at its chain, howled, and bared its teeth as I passed. Father Joseph's colleague, Sister Clarice, then gave a tea-party in my honour at which she and two other nuns told their version of Pascal's story:

Early in Easter week a Muslim woman came to the school with news that an 'animal-child' was roaming the western part of the town, scavenging for scraps. The Sisters found him on Good Friday, filthy and abandoned, crouching in a niche in the wall of a mudbrick house. The owners of the house said that a laundrywoman had come to claim him a few days earlier.

'But she didn't want him back,' Father Joseph interrupted,

'seeing he's come from the jungle and all. That's what it is. Once a baby's been touched by an animal, they abandon him and all.'

Father Joseph said that, in the course of his ministry, he had often heard stories of 'wolf-children', but had never set eyes on one. He knew of one case where a mother had lost her child at nightfall, and returned to find a female wolf guarding it.

The Sisters succeeded in tying up the boy and taking him back to the school. When they bathed him, he bit them. He spat out some Cadbury's chocolate. They gave him dal and chapaties, but 'he threw the plate and all'; and when he heard the Alsatian barking, he rushed towards the kennel and tried to get inside. The Alsatian suddenly went quiet. They then put the boy to bed and locked the room.

'I heard him growling in the night and all,' said the old priest − and the morning had found him hunched against the door.

My train got to Sultanpur in the late afternoon. By a lucky coincidence, only a few hours earlier the Sisters had received a visit from the man who originally 'rescued' the boy in the forest. His name was Narsing Bahadur Singh and he was the *thakur*, or headman, of the village of Narangpur, about three miles outside the town.

The thakur owned a food-stall near the railway repair-yards and would often take along his wolf-boy, whom he called Shamdev. He said that Shamdev was always getting lost, or running after pariah-dogs, but usually had the knack of finding his way home. When Sister Clarice taxed him with a rumour she had heard: that he used to exhibit the boy in a booth, for money − he was extremely indignant and went away.

In the evening she and I took a rickshaw to Narangpur. The thakur was still at market, so we sat in his courtyard while a crowd of villagers entertained us with imitations of Sham-dev's antics, growling and baring their teeth. Narsing

Bahadur Singh, when he did appear, was an erect, mild-mannered man in his fifties, dressed in white hand-woven khaki cloth, and with a striped towel draped over his shoulders. He owned six acres of land, planted corn, dal and rice, and was accounted rich. He had, it turned out, a history of adopting stray children. Besides his own two sons, he had brought up four other boys found abandoned in the wild. One of these, a gawky adolescent called Ramdev, was bundling straw into a loft. The thakur was insistent on one point: Ramdev was a mad boy; Shamdev was *not* mad, he was a 'wolf-boy'.

With the help of Sister Clarice's translation, I pieced together an outline of the story: It had happened early one morning about five years ago. It was the dry season but he couldn't be sure what month. He had bicycled to see his cousin, who lived in a village on the far side of Musafirkhana forest, about twenty miles from Sultanpur. On his way back to the main trunk road, the track cut through thickets of bamboo and thornbushes and, behind one of these, he heard the noise of squealing. He crept up and saw the boy at play with four or five wolf-cubs. He was most emphatic that they were not dogs or jackals, but wolves.

The boy had very dark skin, fingernails grown into claws, a tangle of matted hair and callouses on his palms, his elbows and knees. Some of his teeth were broken to sharp points. He ran rapidly on all fours, yet couldn't keep up with the cubs as they bolted for cover. The mother wolf was not in sight. The thakur caught up with the boy, and was bitten on the hand. He did, however, succeed in trussing him up in his towel, lashed him to the pillion of his bicycle, and rode home.

At first Shamdev cowered from people and would only play with dogs. He hated the sun and liked to curl up in shadowy places. After dark, he grew restless and they had to tie him up to stop him following the jackals that howled around the village at night. If anyone cut themselves, he immediately smelled the scent of blood, and would scamper towards it. He caught chickens and ate them alive, including the entrails. Later, when he had evolved a sign language of his own, he would cross his thumbs and flap his hands: this meant 'chicken' or 'food'.

Eventually the thakur decided to wean him off red meat. He force-fed him with rice, dal and chapaties, but these made him sick. He took to eating earth, his chest swelled up and they began to fear for his life. Only gradually did he get used to the new diet. After five months he began to stand: two years later he was doing odd jobs, like taking straw to the cows.

'He's mine,' said Narsing Bahadur Singh, angrily. 'I want him back. I will go to Lucknow to fetch him.'

'I'll take you,' I said.

At six the next morning he was waiting for the taxi, all dressed up in spotless whites. As the taxi passed through the forest at Musafirkhana he pointed to the track, but we couldn't go and see the place because the driver was in a hurry and threatened to dump us and return to Sultanpur.

There were at least a hundred mentally defective children at the Mother Teresa Mission. We were greeted there by an elderly man, Ananda Ralla Ram, who had been a barrister before devoting himself to charity. He turned his legal mind onto the subject of Shamdev and gave the thakur quite a grilling. We tried to explore the story from every angle, in an effort to find a flaw or contradiction. The thakur's answers were always consistent.

When the Sisters brought in the boy, he stood tottering in the doorway, screwing up his eyes to see who it was. Then, recognising his old friend, he jumped into the air, flung himself around his neck, and grinned.

I watched him for about two hours. Nothing much happened. He cuffed a child; he made his growling noises; he made the sign for 'chicken'; sometimes he would point to the sky, circling his index finger as if describing the sun or moon. The callouses had gone, but you could see the scar tissue on his knees. He also had scars on the sides of his head: these, according to the thakur, had been made by the wolf-mother when she picked him up with her teeth.

The thakur left the Mission with me. He had been gearing himself for a scene; but the firm smiles of the Sisters unnerved him. He asked, meekly, if he could come again. He seemed very upset when it was time to say goodbye. So was Shamdev, and they hugged one another.

The discovery of an authentic wolf-child would be of immense importance to students of human and animal behaviour. But though I felt that Narsing Bahadur Singh was speaking the truth, it was a very different matter to prove it.

The best-documented account of Indian wolf-children is that of Kamala and Amala, who, in 1920, were dug out of a wolf lair in Orissa by the Reverend J.A.L. Singh. The younger girl, Amala, died — although her 'sister' lived on for nine years at the orphanage of Midnapore, during which time Singh kept a diary of her adjustment to human life.

Extracts from the diary have recently been republished in a book called *The Wolf Children* by Charles Maclean. On reading through it, I kept being struck by parallels between the girls and Shamdev: their sharpened teeth, their callouses, the craving for blood, the earth-eating, chicken-killing, the love of darkness and their friendship with dogs and jackals. Maclean, however, concluded that the Reverend Singh's story is shot with inconsistencies — and that it does not hang together.

Another investigator, Professor Robert Zingg, collected in his *Wolf Children and Feral Man* all the known texts relating to children reared by animals, as well as stories of The Wild Boy of Aveyron and the legendary Kaspar Hauser. As for Shamdev, by far the most interesting comparisons are to be made with the reports in Major-General Sir W.H. Skinner's *A Journey through the Kingdom of Oudh (1849–50)*: five of his six cases of wolf-children come from the region of Sultanpur. He writes:

Zoolfikur Khan, a respectable landowner from Bankepoor in the estate of Hassanpoor, 10 miles from the Sultanpoor cantonments, mentions that about eight or nine years ago a trooper came to town with a lad of about 9 or 10 years of age whom he had rescued from wolves among the ravines of the road . . . that he walked on his legs like other people when he saw him, though there were evident signs on his knees and elbows of having gone very long on all fours . . . He could not talk or utter any very articulate sound . . . he understood signs and understood exceedingly well and would assist the cultivators in turning trespassing cattle out of their fields . . .

His story could be that of Shamdev.

During the nineteenth century, when such tales were commoner, the most famous 'wolf-man' in India was Dina Sanichar, who lived at the Sicandra Orphanage in Agra from 1867 till his death in 1895. He probably gave Kipling the model for Mowgli. He, too, had a craving for raw meat and, when forced to give it up, would sharpen his teeth on stones.

In zoological terms, there are almost insuperable difficulties in the way of a female Indian wolf actually being able to rear a human baby. First, she would have to lose her own brood: to keep her milk, and to be on the lookout for a substitute cub. She would have to scent the baby but, instead of making a meal of it, allow its cries to stifle her hunger-drives and signal to her maternal instincts. Finally, since a wolf-cub's period of dependence is so much shorter than a human infant's, she might have three litters of her own before her adopted child could fend for itself. She would also have to protect it and post 'Keep off!' signals to other wolves whose hunger might get the better of them.

One alternative explanation is that the wolf-boys or girls are autistic children, abandoned by their parents once they realise their condition; who somehow survive in the forest and, when rescued, seem to *behave* like wolves. Or could it be that the wolves around Sultanpur have a natural affiliation with man? There are no absolute conclusions to be drawn. But I came away convinced that Shamdev's story was as convincing as any other. Someone should get to the bottom of it.

1978

THE VERY SAD STORY
OF SALAH BOUGRINE

It was an early morning last August in Marseilles. A lonely Algerian was walking in the Quartier de la Porte d'Aix, the quarter they call the 'Kasbah'. The streets of the Kasbah are straight but narrow, and residents hang their washing from house to house. Balks of timber shore up the bulging walls of the houses. Black water runs along the gutters, and hungry dogs drive the rats from the rubbish dumps at dawn.

This particular morning, 25 August, at eight o'clock, Algerian traders were beginning their day, stacking heaps of plastic suitcases and tin trunks, laying out leather jackets on old camp-beds, or hanging up the tinsel dresses that are loved by Berber ladies. In the Rue des Chapeliers a street-vendor was arranging his tray of razor-blades, soap and key-chains with medallions of Napoleon III. In the Rue des Présentines a barber opened his plyboard booth, papered inside with pin-ups and prints of the Ka'aba. A butcher in the Rue Puvis de Chavannes hung sheep-carcasses from steel hooks outside his shop, which was painted blood red and protected by a plastic hand of Fatima.

The hotels — Hôtel de l'Armistice, Hôtel des Phocéens and hotels without name — were emptying their sleepy occupants onto the street. In the Quartier des Carmes nearby one set of Algerian sleepers quit their damp mattresses to allow a few hours' sleep to friends who had no bed that night. And in the

Rue de Baignoir the *bain turc* opened the door to its palms, plaster statues of Health and Hygiene, and not-so-healthy goings-on behind.

Mothers of Africa lolloped down the street in multi-coloured cottons, smiling. The ladies of Algeria preferred not to be seen: Kabyles with tattooed faces, veiled Arabs with pale foreheads and wide dark eyes. A few exhausted whores were out among the flower-sellers hoping to catch their share of the morning trade: their mahogany-coloured coiffures were clustered round the Hôtel de Verdun, once a fine town house with a wrought-iron stair-rail sweeping up to its now squalid rooms. Over the door a stucco nymph of the Belle Epoque had been transformed into a Mussulman houri, with jet hair, mascara and moles. Across the street a few elderly French-women crept into the crumbling church of St Théodore to pray. The raking sunlight along the Rue des Dominicaines threw into sharp relief its statue of the Virgin, and played over Arab and anti-racist graffiti.

In the Black's Paradise Bar Senegalese dandies with soulful fingers were dipping their brioches into bowls of café-au-lait, while in the Arab cafés they had tuned into Radio Cairo. In one café two Algerian migrants were sipping mint tea and clacking dominoes onto the table. They were working in France as labourers on an industrial site at Etang-de-Berre. The lonely man who came in and ordered himself a coffee they instantly recognised as their cousin Salah Bougrine. They had all three been born on the same slab of mountain, at Maida, near Sedrata in the east of the country.

Now when an Algerian in France sees a relative, he shouts for joy, pumps his hand, kisses him four times, blesses him in the name of Allah, and asks for family news. But Salah Bougrine greeted his cousins with a blank, uncomprehending stare. He sat beside them. He didn't speak. He drank his coffee, stared into the middle distance, and left without a nod. Poor Salah, they thought, he must be mad!

At two-thirty that same afternoon, the trolley-bus,

Number 72, driven by Monsieur Désiré-Emile Gerlache, was carrying a load of Marseillais to the beach. It halted at a stop north of the Zoological Gardens to take on a new passenger, Salah Bougrine. The driver, who also sold the tickets, asked the Algerian for his money — and received the same negative stare. What M. Gerlache said next is unknown or ill-reported, and the man is dead. He may have said nothing *very* offensive; but he may also have said '*raton*', or '*sale melon*' or '*putain de bougnoul*' or any other French term of abuse for Arabs. For M. Gerlache the matter was simple: 'Here is an Arab who will not pay. Either he pays or he gets off' — and he started shouting abuse.

Bougrine's immediate reaction was to find the money in his pocket, put his ticket in the automatic punching-machine, and sit in the seat behind the driver. As the bus started, however, he pulled a knife from his other pocket and expertly inserted the point under M. Gerlache's left shoulder-blade, where it found the heart. Before the victim had time to fall, the killer withdrew the knife, hooked one arm around the driver's partition, and cut his throat. The bus zigzagged across the Boulevard Françoise Duparc and came to a halt for lack of power, the passengers shrieking '*À l'assassin! À l'assassin!*' Bougrine wounded five of them.

By chance, the motorist who swerved to miss the careering bus was the retired light-heavyweight boxing champion, Gracieux Lamperti. By another chance, he happened to have a short iron crowbar in the car. He prised the bus-door open, thumped the bar onto Bougrine's skull, and laid him out cold. He then left the ladies and gentlemen of the bus to continue the good work — and particularly the ladies, who went at the skull with high heels. They would have carried the work to conclusion had not a company of the Deuxième Corps Cycliste restrained them. The Algerian came out of his coma on 15 September and cannot remember one detail of the events of 25 August, expressing surprise and anguish to the psychiatrists who examined him.

On the surface the Marseillais rose to the occasion. They celebrated the funeral of Désiré-Emile Gerlache in magnificent southern style, with black crêpe, crowds in tears and the chant of *De Profundis*. His fellow-drivers led a blue-uniformed guard alongside the hearse, and announced beforehand they 'would not tolerate any racist demonstration to mark the obsequies of our comrade'. These had, in any case, been forbidden by the police. 'It would be regrettable,' said Monsieur René Heckenroth, the Prefect, 'if following so grave an incident, the public, in an excess of legitimate anger, lapsed into acts unworthy of its history.'

But the killing of Monsieur Gerlache had come at the end of a summer of hate. In fact, both the North African and French communities had been sharpening their teeth for some time. Earlier in the year, politicians in the Midi discovered that anti-Arab policies could capture a valuable slice of the electorate. 'Toulon must remain Toulon,' said the Mayor of Toulon. 'Keep Grasse for the Grassois,' said the Mayor of Grasse, a young man called Hervé de Fontmichel, who found the presence of North African demonstrators offensive to his town's scent-manufacturing image, and illegally turned the fire-hoses on them. About this time, I was told, a Tunisian was given up for dead *after* his arrest and questioning by the Grasse police, but woke up on the municipal garbage tip. At Ollioules, near Toulon, the racists talked of relighting the gas-ovens — but that was only a joke.

It was no joke when they machine-gunned Arab cafés, or threw Molotov cocktails into Arab lodgings. The graffiti campaign was no joke either, if you were an Arab and could read '*Cochonnerie Arabe*', '*Merde aux Arabes*', 'Our city is polluted by Arabs', 'Our mothers, wives and children are menaced by Arabs'. Nor was it a joke to the Algerian who strolled into the Quartier du Panier: the residents strung him up by the feet and pelted him with filth — which was odd in a quarter patrolled by so many policemen.

The revenge killings began the night of Monsieur Ger-lache's death: within a week there were seven dead in Marseilles. There was the case of Ladj Lounès, a thin sixteen-year-old boy with a shock of hair and a cheeky smile. He had been playing football with friends and had gone into a tobacconist's on the Boulevard Madrague-Ville. A dark red Peugeot was waiting for him when he came out. The driver asked him some directions, and he was giving them when the passenger shot him through the head. They put two more bullets in his back as they drove off. The police said Lounès was a car thief and street-trafficker in barbiturates — and that explained everything.

Or there was the case of Mebarki Hamou, workman, forty years old, father of five, who died in the Hospital of the Conception in Marseilles on 29 August. His employer came with gendarmes to his lodging, and took him away for questioning. There was some row over wages. He left the gendarmerie a free man, but was found dying outside on the pavement thirty minutes later.

There have been no arrests. The Government did not even express its regret: although the President of the Republic did say some words about racism ('*Non . . . non . . . et NON!*') and the Ministry of the Interior published a graph to show that the number of North African deaths was nothing unusual for the time of year.

The police report on Salah Bougrine should have calmed things down. His papers showed that he was working in regular employment, in the sewage department in Nice. And the 2,500 francs in his pocket should also have suggested that he was in town to take the boat to Algiers.

This would not do for most Marseillais. To their minds an Algerian with 2,500 francs was up to no good. Was he, perhaps, a hired killer? Or a heroin-pusher? It was always convenient, in Heroin Capital Number One, to pin that business onto Arabs. But Bougrine had no police record. Instead, he had a clinical record. In 1969 he had been attacked in Nice by two Europeans and a French Muslim, who had robbed him of all his savings and split his head open with an axe. The blow had removed an area of his skull 'the size of a galette', and the damage to his brain was 'severe'. He remained in a Nice hospital for over a year. He had been in and out of mental institutions. The facts of his condition speak for themselves.

The events in Marseilles showed that France had run into real trouble with her Algerian minority, and relations with her ex-colony took a further downward turn. Many Frenchmen were upset to be labelled 'racist', and there was considerable heart-searching in the press. The French have a long-cherished belief that they are not, as a people, racist; that racism is an Anglo-Saxon malady they do not happen to share. They will admit to cultural chauvinism, even to the cruelty of, say, the Foreign Legion; but the idea of a colour-bar is alien to them. French colonists always wanted their 'natives' to become brown Frenchmen — and to a degree they were successful. No African leader is going to pay England the compliment of Leopold Senghor: 'Lord, among the white nations, place France on the right hand of God the Father.'

But France had no such luck with Islam — and this time the Government in Algiers was really angry. It was bad enough the coffins coming off the Marseilles boat, and the trite police denials, and the murderers running free. But when we crossed to Algiers, six weeks after the death of Monsieur Gerlache, officials were still howling about an editorial in the right-wing Marseilles newspaper, *Le Méridional*. 'We have had enough,' it said. 'Enough of Algerian thieves. Enough of Algerian vandals. Enough of Algerian loudmouths. Enough of Algerian syphilitics. Enough of Algerian rapists. Enough of Algerian pimps. Enough of Algerian madmen. Enough of Algerian killers.' All of which might make you think the average Marseillais had never heard of a gun, a whore or syphilis.

The days are over when Frenchmen could use this kind of language and get away with it. *Algérie française* is no more and the new Algeria is in capable hands. Its President, Houari Boumedienne, is a self-effacing man, ascetic, difficult and proud; and he has pulled his country out of the fratricidal aftermath of the revolution and the hysteria of Ben Bella's rule. He has the air of a man who is horror-struck by the past, and determined it will not be repeated. The regime has its ghosts of course — but these are apparently sleeping.

The 730,000 Algerian passport-holders in France are the children of the detested colonial marriage, and are shunted to and fro between their divorced parents. When Algerian bureaucrats talk about them, they stiffen with wounded pride and you hear the words 'respect' and 'dignity' repeated and repeated. The events in Marseilles drew from Boumedienne a characteristically sharp reaction. On 19 September he blocked the passage of all future emigrants to France, and added that if the French Government did not protect innocent Algerians from reprisals, he would bring everyone home regardless of cost. He knew he could rightly blame their presence in France on colonial injustice — but not indefinitely. He also knew that the onus was on him to remove the pressures that force a Salah Bougrine to leave his wife and children — and eventually murder a bus driver.

We met Bougrine's father on the chalk-white mountain where he was born. The old man saw our car had broken down, and he left his sheep and came up the hill to help. He had a distinguished manner, with a droopy moustache and scratched-over spectacles. He wore a rather raffish yellow headcloth but his chest was concave; he was coughing badly, and death was perhaps not far away. Yes, yes, his boy was the murderer all right. They had come from town to tell him, and he seemed quite pleased about it.

He did not want us to visit the family farm: but we could see it up the valley, the land bleached and thorny and covered with white dust, the barn that was walls and no roof, and the pile of brushwood for the winter. Trees would not grow on old Bougrine's side of the mountain: only over the pass, on the north flank, there were orchards and poplars for shade. He did have a spring or two, that dribbled moisture all year round, enough to keep the sheep and mules alive. But the cows were in a bad way, quietly complaining, with leathery skin and hollow rib-cages.

'I think they're going to die,' said old Bougrine's neighbour. 'We're in a prison here.'

The *fellah*, or small farmer, is the gut of the Algerian nation.

To the east of Algiers itself are the Kabyles: Berber mountaineers, an ancient people with long faces and hazel eyes; and if you look at their overloaded villages and their cramped, stony terraces of olives and fruit trees, you understand why a third of the men are always away in France. If you look closer at other villages, you will see they are still ruined shells, after the French bombing: another third died in the war.

In the south-east of the country are the Chaouia of the Aurès Mountains. This is wild country, even poorer than Kabylia. It grows cedars and live-oaks, but most of it is bare and rocky, and the snows come early. Then, on the gloomy uplands from Sétif to the Tunisian border, there are the Arabs.

When the *colons* took the best land a century ago, the free farmers retreated to farms of a few stony acres, or to the margins of the *chotts*, or salt-lakes, where the wind drives saline scum ashore and blows off the topsoil. People mistook their poverty for poverty of spirit: but in fact the harsh, dry climate refined the complexity of their emotions. Many, it was true, were sucked into the French towns and entered into the process of becoming good bourgeois. The ones that stayed recalled, in folk memory, a time when the fat lands were theirs, and never lost the hope of their recovery. French Algeria enjoyed periods of uneasy calm, but the colons always lived under the threat of peasant revolt. Unlike Tunisia or Morocco, Algeria had no great cities of her own, and no feudal aristocracy worth the name. The *fellah* was Algeria. He made the revolution. It released in him destructive energies he had neither known nor suspected.

The colons, more than a million of them, have been so pilloried, and their recent history is so unfortunate, that they now deserve an apologist. Nicknamed '*pieds noirs*', or 'black feet', they were frontiersmen by temperament and circumstance: refugees from an ungrateful Europe who had landed in Africa with nothing − and were hardly even French! A government report of 1912 revealed that one in five settlers was of French origin. The exodus of 1962 was not a homecoming but another displacement. Algeria was *la patrie*. The colons were suspicious of metropolitan France and devious in their dealings with her. They did not understand the changes in post-war Europe and were stranded, morally and socially, in the Empire of Napoleon III. They longed to be loved by a France they did not know. Any attempt to give Algerians control of their affairs drew from them hysterical outbursts that ended in their collective suicide. De Gaulle shouted from the balcony '*Vive l'Algérie française!*' − and then betrayed them. Understandably, they are bitter.

The colons loved their country but they loved too much of it. There were, of course, poor honest families, like that of Albert Camus, who had 'never exploited anyone'. But on the eve of the revolution, nine tenths of the country's wealth was in the hands of one tenth of the population. Everything of value belonged to the settlers: or to a residue of 'men devoted to France' − toadying *bachagas* or *caïds* who taxed the peasants to the limit.

You can see their great farms, stranded in wheatfields like half-sunk ships, the grim houses with machine-gun turrets, and the farm-workers' with the roofs caved in. Many look plague-stricken, for the Algerians have left them to the storks and crows, and the orchards are dying for lack of water. It is a usurped, bitter country. On the hills there are many Christian cemeteries, the walls with ragged holes, the tombs upturned, and a shroud of black cypresses. In Algeria you are always aware of cemeteries.

The Night of the Long Knives — literally knives, because the FLN possessed only antique firearms and valued silence — took place at Arris in the Aurès Mountains on 1 November 1955: within two years the revolt had spread all over the country. The FLN chose well in the Aurès. The mountains were the traditional refuge of outlaws, and — for all the French helicopter landings — the rebels never lost control. What followed became the most bloodthirsty of colonial wars. There is a mass of documentation on the behaviour of the French Army; about its inferiority complex over Vichy and Dien Bien Phu; how officers told their men: 'You may rape but discreetly'; how they deflowered Djamila Boupacha with a bottle; how they cleared a million *fellah* from the villages, to cut them off from the FLN and leave the country clear for *la chasse*; and how they massacred whole villages, faked the evidence and blamed the FLN. Then there is the black side of the FLN — very black — and it is still argued in Algiers if those means were needed to achieve that end.

The war still scars the eastern half of the country, from the Kabylia through the provinces of Sétif, Batna and the Constantinois: a sinister undertone of violence that never lets you forget the past. There are wrecked guard-posts, gutted barracks and broken bridges; there is the farm of Le Main Rouge where they brought FLN suspects for torture — and you would have to be blind to forget the war in Arris itself.

It is a big village of rough stone houses, with flat baked mud roofs rising in tiers up the hill. It was Ramadan when we went there and we had to mind our manners. Tempers snap on empty stomachs. In the bazaar there were lots of people with little to do; the boys holding hands and hitting their heads against the wall; the old men hunched in the shade so their turbans seemed to wind around their knees; and the fancy young men back from France, strutting in their wasp-waisted suits and saying yes to policemen. The FLN cemetery is downhill from the village. It is a very big cemetery. In Arris, we were happy not to be French.

The history of the war relates directly to the plight of immigrants in France. The greater part of them comes from Eastern Algeria. They began the revolution; they were the hardest hit by it. Traditional agriculture, difficult enough in peace, was completely dislocated by the war, and centuries of tradition were broken. Then there is the psychological damage to the tortured, and to those who saw their villages burning, their mothers and sisters raped, or their male relatives lined up against a wall and shot. It is said that one million people were killed. Certainly, you can hardly find an immigrant in France without a missing father, brother or son. Salah Bougrine is thirty-six. He was twenty-five when the war ended and seventeen when it began. In those days you learned to use a knife.

The knife is the classic weapon of the high plains' Arab. In his last book, *The Wretched of the Earth*, Franz Fanon, the Martinique-born psychiatrist and hero of the Algerian revolution, explains how the Algiers School of Psychiatry went to endless lengths to prove, with 'scientific' data, that the Algerian peasant was a born killer. He was no suicide: instead, he channelled his homicidal melancholia outwards into murder. The fact that he stabbed several times and often mutilated the body revealed 'primitive impulses uncontrolled by the cerebral cortex'.

This kind of dogma, if believed, was very useful to the coloniser. It gave him tacit permission to treat the native as an animal, even to condone the use of torture with the minimum side-effects to himself. Fanon's refutation of the argument is one of the best things he wrote: he shows how homicidal depressions relate to the degree of brutality applied. No one can hope to remove the scars of the war within eleven years. Nor can one deny that some Algerians are quick on the draw — often with good reason. On two occasions I have heard them say, 'When an Algerian goes to France, he buys a knife!' And in Marseilles what an opportunity! What a selection! Eight-inch switchblades and all the latest cutlery!

The young men of Salah Bougrine's generation fought under the slogan 'Land to the Fellah!' When the colon farmers left, their workmen moved in on the land and farmed it themselves in co-operatives. But there was no land for the dispossessed peasant of the margins. The country was starving: there could be no question of dismembering the old estates and risking further famine. So the young men drifted to the towns, but there were no jobs. Then they heard on the grapevine that France, the old enemy, was the land of jobs: and since the boss had always been the enemy, they set off to earn money from him. Most went for reasons of poverty; some from curiosity; a few because they couldn't sit still. First they went to the white city of Algiers and saw the cars, the shops and the sad-eyed street boys. Then, often without a word of French, they boarded the boat for Marseilles.

The poor young man, crossing the sea to face the Industrial Giant, is a theme for a modern Virgil. If the immigrant is lucky, he will escape with some pay-packets saved up: enough, after a few years, to buy a café or a grocer's shop, or a house and tinsel dresses for his wife. But the risks are high, and the French unfriendly. They have dangerous machines he doesn't understand — and there is always the danger of a nervous breakdown.

The emigrants do bring one big advantage to the Algerian Government. Annually, they remit home one milliard of francs (about a hundred million sterling) and this helps make up the trade deficit with France. It also relieves local unemployment. The nineteenth-century evictions gave Algeria a floating population of landless unemployed: their number, at the time of independence, had risen to two million, with twice as many on the breadline. Boumedienne's administration has staked everything on the generation born after 1962, and hopes to abolish urban unemployment by 1980. The older ones, the ones who are scarred by the war, would slow down the programme if they stayed. 'So,' say the French racists, 'they come and shit on us.'

France, as a young Algerian economist put it to me, is '*la société de la consommation folle*'. A mania for the modern is sweeping the country: modern in the most old-fashioned sense — Frenchmen now want all the things Americans wanted twenty years ago. Supermarkets and shopping-malls are going up in every provincial town, and the new High Paris — west of the Arc de Triomphe — has the appearance of an undistinguished American city. But this soi-disant economic miracle needs labour: and, long ago, French planners realised there would not be enough Frenchmen for the task. Accordingly, they introduced 'la politique nataliste'. They dangled every inducement in front of French motherhood to breed: yet the population graphs obstinately refused to soar. It was then evident that, even if enough babies were born, most would aspire to becoming skilled workmen, and would not want to be stuck in a lower industrial proletariat, doing the underpaid jobs known as 'travaux penibles'.

The solution, in common with other countries in Western Europe, was to rent a lower working-class from abroad — rent rather than buy. This was not, repeat not, the Slave Trade: if the labourer broke down, you could send him back where he came from. Industry was crying out for the able-bodied young men who would arrive from an inexhaustible source, of their own accord, fully grown: you didn't have to feed or educate them till the age of twenty. Some came with entry permits. Some entered illegally over the high passes of the Pyrenees and, when the snow melted, their corpses were found by the dogs of shepherds.

Their effect on the economy was disinflationary. The lower the wages the higher the profits for reinvestment, the more you could keep prices down. Immigrants, too, had another advantage that outweighed their nuisance value. They were desperate for money, bewildered, and therefore, in theory, docile. They would take less pay, they would refuse to strike, and you could use them to bust the strikes of your own workers. You could use the immigrants to divide Communist unions against themselves, and turn the 'Internationale' into a farce. As De Gaulle's Prime Minister, Georges Pompidou, said: 'Immigration is a way of creating a certain détente on the labour market and of resisting social pressures.' Immigration has certainly contributed to the buoyancy of the French economy — but this perhaps set a time-bomb underneath it.

Immigrants are the first to suffer in a crisis, for they serve as an insurance policy against the effects of recession. You can simply lay them off without fear of a revolt. Immigrants, it is true, are a less attractive proposition when they wake up and learn the language; and when they press for higher wages and better housing. On the other hand, if they drift into left-wing politics, you can brand them as subversive and strong-arm them with the police.

On paper, Algerians have an easier time in France than others from the ex-colonial empire, in that the dreaded Circulaire Marcellin-Fontanet does not touch them. This recent piece of legislation aims to end the 'scandalous traffic in men'. But while it forces an employer to house him, it ties the worker's contract to his residence permit. The special status of Algerians stems from the days when France, in theory, stretched from Dunkirk to the Sahara. After the Evian Accords of 1962, there was free entry for all Algerians, but the French have since reduced the number to 25,000 fresh immigrants a year.

For its part, Algeria provides her workers with a card from the Office Nationale de la Main-d'Oeuvre and insists on a clean bill of health. The French police cannot deport a man with an ONAMO card unless he is habitually unemployed or mixes himself in 'undesirable' politics.

The reality is different. The daily life of an immigrant is a sad business. No women. Bad bed. Bad food. If he eats he doesn't save and if he saves he doesn't eat. And always the worst jobs set aside for him: heavy labour in foundries, road repairs, work on construction sites, sewage or garbage disposal.

Many Algerians, of course, rise above this. The Kabyles, who have been longer in the emigration business, are more enterprising than the Arabs, and will not be pushed around. I heard of £6 an hour being paid to Kabyle specialists in dry-dock construction. But the usual wage is the legal minimum (SMIG) of 5.50 francs an hour (about 50 pence). Admittedly, this is three times the wage in Algeria, but in France money drifts away three times faster.

Then there are the clandestine workers — the so-called '*touristes*', who have slipped into France without a permit. To small businesses they are the most valuable of the lot, since they can be put to work on a daily basis, paid in cash, no names given and no questions asked. Without them there would be fewer swimming-pools and fewer *maisons provençales* in Provence.

There is always a climate of fear. Many of the immigrants' troubles come from the *harkis*: Algerians 'loyal to France', or those who got on the wrong side in the war. If *harki* means 'auxiliary soldier' to the French, it means 'traitor' to an Algerian patriot. 10,000 of them were shot after Independence, and the ones that got away to France are often out for revenge. Some try, without great success, to be Frenchmen and will ally themselves to any right-wing cause. Others hope for an amnesty in Algeria, and curry favour with the immigrants. They are a pathetic lot. It was a *harki* who axed Salah Bougrine in 1969.

French workers have no great love for the Algerians, at best they are a convenient evil which saves them from *les travaux pénibles*. But cheap Algerian labour removed a peg from the unions' bargaining position: and an old French expression for strike-breaker is 'bedouin'. In times of trouble the unions mumble the formulae of International Socialism, but that does not stop their members from complaining: 'They eat our bread.' 'They pay no tax.' 'They fill our hospitals.' 'They take our money abroad.' I heard French workers protesting they would gladly do the dirty jobs if only the employers would pay properly — but somehow it didn't ring true.

Another source of trouble comes from the Maoist or Trotskyite Left: students and staff from the universities, who use Algerian immigrants as shock-troops in their confrontations with the Right. From time to time they pour into the Algerian quarters and smear them with revolutionary graffiti. The sex-starved boys get all worked up over the girls, and follow them to political meetings they know nothing about. But the Leftists are a broken reed when things go wrong — and it is the Algerians who get hurt.

The vehemence of one Algerian social worker amazed me: '*Cette cochonnerie de la Gauche!*' he sneered. 'Chile! Chile! . . . Always Chile! And when our people get killed they run like mice for their holes.'

Last summer, on a day when the mistral was blowing, a lecturer in political science was arrested with fire-canisters in the act of setting fire to the forest between Marseilles and Aix.

'You can't arrest me,' he said to the police, and explained that this was political propaganda by the deed.

Algerians *are* victims of their own country's anti-Zionist propaganda. We went one evening to a reunion called by the Amicale des Algériens en France at Fos-sur-Mer, the vast new industrial complex at the mouth of the Rhône. The building contractors were laying off 3,000 men, so there were great difficulties. One of the men who saw us there was a middle-aged Algerian from Barika on the high plains. He introduced himself two days later on the Algiers boat. He was a cheerful man and something of a clown. He had had enough of France, and was going home for good. His brother was a shepherd.

'All the big companies in France are controlled by Jews,' he announced. 'And these Jews pay the *pieds noirs* to kill us because we are fighting with our Palestinian brothers. I am happy to say there are no Jews left in Algeria. I'd kill a Jew if I saw him in Algeria.'

The real danger, however, comes from the *pieds noirs*. If the Midi is a centre for racist outbursts, there is one good reason for it. The least enterprising Algerians settle here, because the climate reminds them of home and they dread cold, austere cities like Metz or Lille. But the *pieds noirs* themselves have settled here for precisely the same reasons. They are not popular, and have a complex about not being entirely French. Most, it is true, are hard workers and are happy to mind their own business. But a minority acquired a taste for *ratonades* (Arab hunts) during the last days of the OAS, and have drifted into organisations of the Far Right, or into the underworld. Others have gone into the police. They say the Marseilles police is 50 per cent *pied noir*. There are bound to be problems.

It was a shock for us to find ordinary citizens in Marseilles screwing up their faces and saying they'd like to kill Arabs. The Marseillais are an open-hearted people who enjoy coarse pleasures and are mercifully immune to art. Theirs is the one great city in France that does not advertise the grandeur of the past, or oppress you with the weight of its monuments. It is also an ethnic layer-cake which has opened its doors to all kinds of travellers and immigrants, from Spanish Anarchists to Smyrna Greeks, Armenians and African sailors — '*la marine au charbon*'. Portraits of Napoleon, after Ingres, still hang as political propaganda in the Corsican cafés of the Panier. The whole world knows Marseilles is crooked, and it used to announce the fact cheerfully. But the city of individualists is turning its back on the sea, and, caught in the new prosperity, begins to hate strangers and be secretive and suspicious.

The heroin business is in bad shape. In the Sixties, when business was wonderful, the Corsican milieu bosses had a tacit agreement with the Gaullist administration that heroin could be processed in or around Marseilles as long as it was exported to America and such places, and not sold on the streets of

France. The bosses called in many new recruits, and these collectively seem to have lost their heads and broken all the rules. The U.S. Federal Narcotics Bureau has enjoyed several good seasons, and, for reasons of face, the present French Government has been forced to clamp down. The 'untouchables' remain untouched. But lower down the heroin hierarchy, casualties have been heavy: Tony the Eel, Petit Francis, Big Arm, Johnny Cigar and Benedetto Croce the Financier. Mémé Guerini is still in prison for taking his brother's killer 'for a ride in the country'. So is the wizened Marcel Boucan, skipper of *Le Caprice des Temps*, who panicked and threw himself overboard when the police made a search — they went on to find half a ton of heroin. Joseph Cesari, the biggest heroin chemist of them all, is dead: hanged by himself in prison, his body covered with acrid burns. Dead, too, are Jo Lomini, 'the Toreador', and Albert Bistoni, the one they called 'The Aga Khan'. It was an April evening on the Vieux Port. Three leather boys stepped out of their car and gunned the Tanagra Bar. The Toreador was a little too slow and the Aga Khan was too old and heavy to move. They also shot dead the patronne, Carmen Ambrosio, 'as she joked with a candidate barmaid'. It was a dangerous business, breaking the rules.

The police are, by all accounts, corrupt. There was the case this summer of the 'incorruptible' Commissaire Bezart, corrupted into taking bribes by a pair of prostitution racketeers. His clients, and later accusers, were a spectacular blonde called Mireille Mesas and her ex-footballer husband. They behaved with marvellous composure and a suitable sense of outrage in court, and the policeman is now behind bars.

Certainly, Algerians in Marseilles do not believe one word of what the police say — and the police reports on the sudden deaths of North Africans do not fill one with confidence: 'Probable act of vengeance on the part of a co-religionary.' 'Skull broken from waste material falling from lorry.' 'Settlement of accounts within the narcotics trade.' This is not to say

258

Algerians are saints. They, too, lie and exaggerate, but their versions of police brutality ring true, and on balance I believed them.

I went to see a very imposing police commissioner, imposing in every sense. He was relaxed and smiling, his silver-capped teeth winking at his secretaries, and when he dismissed my suggestions as fantasy ('A policeman's self-respect is at stake' etc.), I almost believed him as well. But he was too convincing. He did his act once too often, and I ended up not believing a word.

The Algerian Vice-Consul took us one day to a strike-meeting at the shipyard at La Ciotat. Algerians are employed here to clean up after the solderers, and for the past year their lives had been made a hell by their 'chief', a *pied noir* ex-corporal. Algerians do not have much experience of striking, and at La Ciotat it was considered a brave move. They did not want money, only the removal of the corporal. The contractor did his best to be agreeable, and the man was transferred to other work. The older Algerians could speak a little French and the young ones none, but they were all under terrible strain, the boys had deep-cut stress lines of a kind I didn't see in Algeria. They never walked alone in La Ciotat.

The consul took us to the *bidonville* where they lived. It was not pretty: the kind of sight you expect in Calcutta but not the South of France. The huts were situated in the middle of the municipal garbage tip: rickety plyboard shacks or wrecked delivery vans, patched with sheet plastic to keep out the wind. We looked out over the acres of filth, the fires that blew acrid smoke in our faces, and the whole place seething with rats in the middle of the day. 'The French landscape is beautiful,' said the consul. '*La douce France* if you don't look too hard.' There was nowhere else in La Ciotat for the men to go. Besides, they felt safer here than in the town: even though two French boys, in September, stuck the barrel of a sub-machine-gun through the fence and fired.

The men were brooding and listless. They put on a cheerful

show for the consul, but couldn't keep it up. One newcomer, Mebarak ben Manaa Aich, a fair-haired boy from Sétif, had injured his shoulder terracing for gas-tanks. He was plainly terrified and had taken to his bed, but we noticed he had the spirit and the Muslim love of flowers to tear a page from a bulb-merchant's catalogue, showing two gladioli, and had pinned it to the wall. The consul pointed to a shack even more tumbledown than the others. It was the Shanghai Bar. 'There's always hope,' he said melodramatically, 'if they can call that the Shanghai Bar.'

Nor is Camp Colgate a pretty sight. It began life as an Allied prisoner of war camp, then it was a centre for Jewish refugees, and then it became the biggest *bidonville* in Marseilles, for Algerians and their families. The city authorities are pulling it down, and the inmates will get better housing: no small task when the size of the average family is 9.7 persons. But that afternoon there were the usual tired and hostile stares, and the screaming children playing over broken glass, and a party of French press-photographers clicking their shutters like visitors to a zoo. We went inside the Mosque: an old Nissen hut. There were red carpets on the floor. The walls were painted pale green and on them hung strings of rosary beads and the Name of Allah. The Imam Bashir was softly reading the suras of the Koran to a circle of worshippers, and somehow there was a notion, not lost, of all men equal in the sight of God.

Another evening we went to an immigrant lodging near the Porte d'Aix. There were sixteen men in three small squalid rooms. One was an airless cellar. None was cheap. The men gave us coffee and Coke, and told a long drawn-out story about a North African corpse and how the police said it had fallen from a window, which it hadn't. Then the landlord's rent-man came in, very hysterical: a slug-fingered fellow in a shiny brown raincoat. He shrieked at us: these lodgings were for workers. Workers only! No one who wasn't a worker had any business there. We weren't workers and we weren't wanted. He wasn't a worker either and he showed us his white hands. And that was our only contact with one of the famous 'sleep-merchants'.

The Quartier de la Porte d'Aix is squalid. Its poverty is particularly offensive when compared to the wealth that encircles it. But it is at least alive. Algerians do not feel strange or threatened there, and it is one of the few places in France they have made their own. The Marseillais, on the other hand, cannot wait to pull it down; for in their eyes it is a future breeding ground for cholera — or, worse, insurrection. The Algerians may be an unpleasant necessity, but that is no reason why one should allow them to choke the centre of the city. One day, North African demonstrators so clogged the Rue d'Aix that weekend motorists could not get onto the Autoroute. The Gaullist Deputy and Minister, M. Joseph Comiti, said the Algerian quarter was a gangrene — and the way to combat gangrene is to cut it out.

Responsibility for cutting out the gangrene rests with the Socialist Mayor of Marseilles, M. Gaston Defferre, who surveys from an office of Louis Quinze splendour the masts and blue awnings of the Vieux Port. He is a paradoxical man in his sixties, a Protestant, a resistance hero, a yachtsman, a fighter of duels, a ruthless administrator, an adroit politician of the Left who enjoys the active support of the Right, a rich newspaper proprietor and a lover. He has just taken a third wife, Edmonde Charles-Roux, the novelist and former editor of French *Vogue*. He is still ambitious for power (and would become Minister of the Interior in Mitterand's first cabinet). In 1965 he stood as Socialist candidate in the presidential elections. His party is at present allied to the Communists, but he will not sing the 'Internationale' and winces at being called 'Comrade Defferre'. In interview he gives out virtually nothing: there is little point in repeating what he said. Behind the tough façade I had the impression of a naïve man, somewhat trapped by intrigues not necessarily of his own making.

Gaston Defferre has no great love for the Arabs. His newspaper, *Le Provençal*, loudly champions the State of Israel. But he is reputed to control the right-wing *Le Méridional* and, if so, he should have had retracted the anti-Algerian rant I quoted from that newspaper. Anyway, he has taken the first steps to pull down the Kasbah: 'We make it known that the whole quarter of the Porte d'Aix will be demolished and rebuilt. It will not be easy, but we have promised it.'

It will not be easy, because when the demolition begins tempers will snap. But the City will win, and there will be offices and shops, apartment blocks and underground car parks. And the Algerians will have gone home or been housed in the sterile banlieue. And there will be no more Soirées de Ramadan. No Big Leila dancing naked round a goldfish-bowl. And nowhere to go for one Nigerian sailor who already senses the end: 'I go for get wooman, but is soo expensive! One emission cost three poun! O Sir, London is a heaven place. Marseilles is finish.'

Cutting out the gangrene will please a group of three gentlemen I visited before leaving, the self-appointed Committee for the Defence of Marseilles, which was founded on the evening of Monsieur Gerlache's death. They had a small room off the Canebière, bare but for posters with a red fist and the title '*Halte à l'Immigration sauvage!*' All three had fleshy noses and disagreeable mouths. They looked quite impressive sitting down, but when they stood up they had very short legs. They did at least speak their minds. But I thought of the bright new offices in Algiers, and the smart young executives, and the eyes of the Third World narrowing on Europe if the racists continue. Wasn't it time, I asked, to bury the hatchet?

'Monsieur, you are suggesting we take our pants down?'

'Not that,' I said.

1974

DONALD EVANS

The World of Donald Evans by Willy Eisenhart
(Harlin Quist Books, 1981)

On the night of 29 April 1977, a fire, sweeping through a house on the Stadhouderskade in Amsterdam, caught the American artist Donald Evans on the staircase and burned him to death. He left behind him, scattered among collections on both sides of the Atlantic, several thousand miniature watercolours in the form of postage stamps. These stamps were 'issued' in sets by forty-two countries, each corresponding to a phase, a friendship, a mood, or a preoccupation in the artist's life. In style, they more or less resemble 'colonial' stamps of the late nineteenth century. The sets were then mounted on the black album pages of professional philatelists, a background that showed up the singularity of each stamp as a work of art in its own right while, at the same time, allowing the artist to play games of pattern and colour on a grid.

In Muslim theology, God first created the reed pen and used it to write the world. Less ambitious, Donald Evans used the same sable brush, a Grumbacher No 2, to paint a limpid, luminous world — a kind of Baudelairean *pays de Cocagne* — that would, nevertheless, mirror his own life and the life of his times. The result is a painted autobiographical novel of forty-two chapters, whose original pages, like the pages of some illuminated manuscript, have wandered abroad: indeed, the chances of reassembling them are as remote as the chances of realising the peaceable world they portray.

Fortunately, Donald Evans kept a meticulous record of all his work and entered each set of stamps in a catalogue, which grew as his work grew and which he called *Catalogue of the World*. The master copy — and several Xerox copies — survived him.*

Whether by accident or design, his life was short, circular, and symmetrical; his one obsession — the painting of postage stamps. He painted them during two five-year periods: as an introverted schoolboy from the ages of ten to fifteen; then as an adult, from twenty-six to thirty-one. The fact that he believed he had 'peaked' at sixteen or seventeen; that he had, by thirty, relived his childhood; that there are reasons for supposing that, in his eyes, the Catalogue was complete; that, having worked on the tropical zones of his world, he should have been painting the stamps of an icebound, polar country when he himself was consumed by fire — all go to reinforce the impression of symmetry.

When his friends recovered from the horror of his death, they began to celebrate his exemplary life, and to puzzle over the pieces. Because Donald Evans was so secretive, and because of his habit of slotting friendships into compartments, the autobiographical complexity of his work might well have escaped notice, or at least lain dormant, were it not for the detective work of Willy Eisenhart, who has prepared a key towards the elucidation of his subject in a cool, tranquil text that reminds one of the best American reporter style of the 1920s. It is also a very beautiful book.

Donald Evans was born on 28 August 1945, the only son of a real estate appraiser in Morristown, New Jersey. His mother kept a neat green lawn and was a member of the local gardening club. As a boy, he built sandcastles, and cardboard villages

* *Catalogue of the World* was published in facsimile by Uitgeverij Bert Bakker, Amsterdam, in 1980.

and palaces. He pored over maps and encyclopaedias and dreamed the geography of a world that would be better than the one in which he lived. He also collected stamps — and, at the time of the coronation of Elizabeth II, drew his own commemorative issue for the coronation of his own imaginary queen.

By ten, this precocious autodidact was hard at work on his own private philately. At first, to quote Eisenhart, the stamps 'were crudely drawn and crudely perforated with his mother's pinking shears, but he quickly became more accomplished. He began to outline the stamps in pencil and then fill them in with his pen and brush, and he solved the technical problem of the perforations by pounding out rows of periods on an old typewriter.'

By fifteen he had filled three volumes of a 'World Wide Stamp Album' with postal issues from mythical countries such as Frandia or Doland, Slobovia or Kunstland East and West. Each country had its own complicated history — 'of invasions, federations, liberations'. Each, in some way, expressed his 'romantic' yearning for the remote and exotic, or the private concerns of his family and friends. Then he started going to football games; he set his sights on college, and he stopped making stamps.

There followed ten conventional years — not so conventional by the standards of his home town — but conventional enough for a middle-class American boy coming of age in the Sixties with a contribution to make in the arts. He wanted to be a painter and painted enormous abstract expressionist canvases in the manner of de Kooning. He graduated in architecture at Cornell. He travelled to Europe; looked in on the Warhol Factory; learned to dye and weave textiles; smoked marijuana; did yoga; took an interest in Gurdjieff; and was always falling in and out of love.

After leaving Cornell, he came to New York where he lived in a sparsely furnished apartment in Brooklyn Heights and got a job as an architectural designer in the office of the architect

Richard Meier. But the scale of the city dwarfed and depressed him. He felt apart from the pushy exhibitionism of its artists. His love affairs were unhappy and he retreated back into his shell, back to the introverted world of his childhood — and its stamps. One day he happened to show his stamp album to friends who encouraged him to continue it. He did so — and left the United States.

In February 1972, he packed his watercolours and a stack of perforated papers and flew to Holland where a friend had rented a cottage 'behind the Dike' (*Achterdijk*) near a village not far from Utrecht. Immediately he set to work on the stamps of a 'Dutch' country called Achterdijk.

During the Vietnam years, young Americans flocked to Holland as they had flocked to Paris in the Twenties. But for Donald Evans Holland was not a hippy heaven of easy sex and easy drugs. He felt reborn there; and, one day, after stamping an antique envelope with the postmark 'Achterdijk', he addressed it to an imaginary correspondent, '*De Heer Naakt-geboren*' (Mr Naked-Born) — which was a surrogate name for himself. He loved the flat wind-blown landscapes of Holland and the high varied skies. He liked the open-mindedness of the Dutch, and paid them the compliment of learning their language. He liked the abstract beauty of Dutch brickwork; the compact scale of the architecture; and, from the seventeenth-century masters, he appropriated certain techniques, of drawing and watercolour, that were perfect for his stamps.

Donald Evans lived, off and on, in Holland for his five remaining years — in lofts, rented rooms, and tiny apartments. He was, by temperament, hypochondriac: when it was found that his chest troubles were caused by a vestigial third lung, he had it removed and recorded the event, from his hospital bed, with the stamps of twin kingdoms called Lichaam and Geest, which means 'Body and Soul'. He was also liable to bouts of wandering fever; and he even invented a capital city called Vanupieds (Barefoot Vagabond) to describe his habit of roaming around the world. Many artists moan about being chained to their studios, but Donald Evans could set up in a railway waiting room. Perhaps the very portability of his work states his contempt for the arts and pretensions of settled civilisation — the nomad's contempt for the pyramid.

His colour sense was as faultless as his draughtsmanship. A set of his stamps sits on a page like butterflies in a case. And, needless to say, he loved butterflies and came up with a country for them — Rups, which is the Dutch for 'caterpillar'. He himself said he had no originality, and that he preferred to work from photographs or given images: yet one flat panorama of Achterdijk has the 'breathed-on' quality of a sepia-wash landscape by Rembrandt. His art was so disciplined that it was patient of receiving anything that happened to attract him — zeppelins, barnyard fowls, penguins, pasta, a passion for mushroom hunting, Sung ceramics, shells, dominoes; drinks at the Bar Centrum; windmills that were 'abstract' portraits of friends; the vegetable market at Cadaques, or a recipe for pesto from Elizabeth David's *Mediterranean Cooking*: his way of recording the pleasures of food and drink reminds me, somehow, of Hemingway.

He never set foot in Asia, but as a boy he had been fascinated by camel-trains and caravansaries and had invented desert countries for his stamp album. Later, he liked reading British travel books about the Middle East and, to create a country called Adjudani — the Persian for 'Jewish' — he borrowed images from Wilfred Thesiger's *The Marsh Arabs*. To my delight, he also borrowed an image from me — the photo of a Timurid tomb-tower taken in an Afghan village on the Russian frontier.

As a boy, too, he had dreamed of the South Seas. Now he dreamed up a coral archipelago — Amis et Amants — a 'French' colony populated by happy, friendly, amorous blacks: the stamps of one issue, titled *Coups de Foudre*, show a row of storm-blasted coconut palms, each painted in a different colour combination to suggest the different thunderbolts of love. Or there were the Tropides — tiny islands in Vermeer-like dots and dashes. Or the arctic country of Yteke, named after a Dutch dancer friend who could only perform in a cold climate.

He had no literary gifts himself. Sometimes he thought of writing — or of getting someone else to write — an accompanying text; but in the end he preferred to leave each stamp as a window into his world, and the rest to the imagination. His favourite modern writer was Gertrude Stein — perhaps because he learned from her the value of the variant within the repetition. In a 'commemorative' issue painted in her honour, he inscribed a set of stamps with texts from her *Tender Buttons*, the prose poem of 1914, which was first published by another Donald Evans, an American poet.

By common consent, the art of the drop-out generation is a mess — and the art of Donald Evans is the antithesis of mess. Nor is it niggling. Nor is it precious. Yet I can't think of another artist who expressed more succinctly and beautifully the best aspirations of those years: the flight from war and the machine; the asceticism; the nomadic restlessness; the yearning for sensual cloud-cuckoo-lands; the retreat from public into private obsessions, from the big and noisy to the small and still. On one of his Gertrude Stein stamps he inscribed these haunting lines from her *Valentine to Sherwood Anderson* which could also serve as his epitaph:

> Let us describe how they went. It was a very windy night and the road although in excellent condition and extremely well-graded has many turnings and although the curves are not sharp the rise is considerable. It was a very windy night and some of the larger vehicles found it more prudent not to venture . . .

1981

8

TRAVEL

ON YETI TRACKS

This April, having spent the hottest part of the year in the Central Australian desert, I felt the urge to get out of that tired red country and clear my head among some mountains. I had always wanted to walk in the valleys around Mount Everest and remember, as a boy, going to a slide-lecture of the Hillary-Tensing climb and forming a very vivid impression of rivers rushing with snowmelt, bamboo bridges, forests of rhododendrons, Sherpa villages and yaks. I wanted to see the Tibetan Buddhist monasteries that lie on the Nepalese side of the frontier. As for the Yeti, I wanted to explore, at first hand, that nebulous area of zoology where the Beast of Linnaean classification meets the Beast of the Imagination.

From Sydney, I called my wife and told her, firmly, to meet me in Nepal.

'I can't,' Elizabeth said in a dispirited voice. Her favourite aunt was having her ninetieth birthday party in Boston.

'The offer's open,' I said. 'Call me if you change your mind.'

'I've changed it.'

The Everest region is known as Khumbu Himal and to reach it you must either trek for a week over three high passes, or fly to Lukla where the airstrip tilts off the mountainside at an angle of 25°. The weather was foul: a series of cyclones in the Bay of Bengal had made nonsense of the forecast. Twice we took off, ran into turbulence, and returned to Kathmandu. On our third try, the pilot nosed the plane under a purplish cloudbank, threaded along a forested valley, and finally approached the runway from below rather than above.

The passengers cheered as we bounced onto the gravel; the bags were chucked clear and, as the plane reloaded, we took our first gulps of thin air. Sir Edmund Hillary could be seen striding about shaking hands with a film crew. High above, I heard a cuckoo, not a kookaburra, calling. Then Elizabeth, who is also an amateur botanist, pointed to a tree with huge white flowers that seemed to hang out of the clouds.

'Look!' she called. '*Magnolia campbelli.*'

A dashing young Sherpa pressed forward and introduced himself as our sirdar. His name was Sangye Dorje — which means 'Thunder-Lion'. He moved with a certain military precision; and in his peaked cap, his waisted green tunic, boots and breeches, he could have played the role of a Kalmuck lieutenant in a pre-war Soviet movie. He was always cheerful, always resourceful, and had the habit of prefacing his statements with 'I have something to say', and of closing with 'That is all I have to say'.

The cook was his old school friend Nima Tashi, who was a wizard at sticky cakes and whose left cheek was scarred with a yak-horn cornada. The third Sherpa, Pasang Nuru, was forever whirling prayer-wheels. Lastly, the cook's boy, Tham, a Magar from Central Nepal, was a shy doe-eyed boy of infinite sweetness and theatrical temperament, who wore a scruffy red knitted cap as if it were Pulcinello's.

Mountain Travel, the organisation which had made our paltry arrangements as well as those of the Everest Expedition, had promised us ten porters. But most Sherpas were off planting potatoes and, anyway, we were better off with three yaks — or rather, three dzoms, which are a cross between a yak and a cow.

We strolled around Lukla while they loaded up. Woodsmoke drifted placidly from the houses; the windows were painted in bright Tibetan colours; the fields were knee-high in green barley, and there were apple trees in flower. Behind the village we saw the remains of a crashed Twin Otter, whose fuselage served as a latrine, its wings as a goat-fence, and its engines as an ornament to the Buddha Lodge Hotel. At Lukla, the windsock is also a prayer-flag.

On coming back I pointed to a hermitage high on the mountainside among red rhododendrons.

'Who lives there?' I asked Sangye.

'One nun.' He screwed up his face, and grinned. 'But now not a nun because she make a baby.'

'Who was the father?'

'One monk.'

The cloud cleared as we started up the road to Namche Bazaar. The road was about three feet wide. The wind soughed in the pines; the river echoed in its gorge; the mountains glittered and the dzom-bells clanged. Sangye and Pasang whistled between their teeth, thwacked the animals on the rump, shouted, 'DZOM! DZOM!' and we all felt the exhilaration that comes at the start of a journey.

'Sherpa' means 'Easterner' in Tibetan; and the Sherpas who settled in Khumbu about 450 years ago are a peace-loving Buddhist people from the eastern part of the plateau. They are also compulsive travellers; and in Sherpa-country every track is marked with cairns and prayer-flags, reminding you that Man's real home is not a house, but the Road, and that life itself is a journey to be walked on foot.

Sangye said that each thread blown from a prayer-flag was a prayer blown straight to Heaven.

Every half mile or so, we would pass a wall of stone slabs, each one carved with the mantra *Om mani padmē Hum* – 'Om! Jewel in the Lotus! Hum!' (The jewel in question is Avalokiteśvara, the Buddha of Infinite Compassion, while the Om and Hum represent the Height and Depth of the Universe.) Sangye was very anxious we should walk round these prayer-walls in a clockwise direction, that is, to follow the Way of the Heavens — 'Or else,' he said, 'everything will go wrong.' When Elizabeth forgot, he smiled and said, 'Never mind! Not so many OMs on that one!'

We stopped for the night at Phakhding in a grove of pines beside the river. In the next-door camp was an expedition of British Army officers, one of whom wore a T-shirt reading 'The Falkland Islands are beautiful and British'. Another officer said the War had been a 'necessary bit of blood-letting, what?'

'Idiots,' I said to myself, as I rolled over to sleep.

Around ten next morning we stopped at the tea-house of an old Japanese solitary — a character from the travel diaries of Bashō, with a long wispy beard and baggy red trousers that shone with dirt. He was hoeing his vegetables and, while his boy made the tea, he came over to talk. He was an expert in the grafting of fruit trees. In Japan he had worked for the Government forestry service and had come here, on retiring, eight years ago.

'I had no children,' he said. 'I had no house. Why should I not come and live among these mountains?'

After crossing the torrent of Bhote Khosi, the track then zigzagged up a cliff and we had our first view of Everest to the east. Streams of snow were blowing off the summit. On ahead was Khumbu Ylha, the Sacred Mountain of the Sherpas, rearing its triangular peak above a throne of puffy white clouds. We kept passing short, brown, bandy-legged men bent double under loads of rice and millet which they were carrying to the Saturday market at Namche.

'Lowlanders,' said Sangye contemptuously. 'From five days down.'

Namche is a small town built in terraces around the bowl of a valley, like the seats of an Ancient Greek theatre. Its merchants traffic in every kind of leftover from mountaineering expeditions: Spanish quince paste, French packet soup, Swiss crampons, German oxygen cylinders, freeze-dried cheesecake from the U.S.A., and British bully-beef. The market began at sunrise and, from our campsite, sounded like a swarm of bees. I saw a party of monks arriving to buy provisions. Most of them were wearing European cast-offs — the yellows, reds and oranges of high-altitude gear corresponding to the orthodox colours of Tibetan Lamaism.

Before leaving for Thame Monastery, we visited the town *gompa*, which is the equivalent of the parish church. In the courtyard an aged lama was chatting to a scrawny Tibetan already loaded up with buffalo-skins. The man was a smuggler. To reach Tibet he would have to avoid the Chinese Army, cross two glaciers, and climb a pass of 19,000 feet. The lama was about to bless him. He needed it.

Inside the *gompa* we were shown into a dusky room lit with flickering butter lamps and frescoed with the bestial or benevolent Tibetan divinities, whose identity we tried to puzzle out. We saw a rather down-at-heel statue of Guru Rimpoche, the legendary proselytiser of Tibet. I then paused in front of a bull-headed, thousand-armed Demon and said, facetiously enough, that anyone who believed in such a creature was in a fit state to 'see' the Yeti.

All along the track to Thame there were clumps of blue iris and gentians the size of sapphire studs. Soon we came to a lovely wood of birch trees, leafless as yet, with peeling orange bark and beards of jade green lichen festooned from their branches. We passed through stands of pale pink rhododendrons and, as we ambled along, I asked Sangye Dorje whether he believed in the Yeti.

'I do,' he said, and went on to explain how there were two

kinds of Yeti: the *mih-teh* which killed people, and the *dzu-teh* which killed only animals.

'But Yeti', he added sombrely, 'is also some kind of God.'

He promised that when we got to his own village, Khumjung, he would introduce me to a woman who was actually attacked by the beast. Usually, he said, a person who looked into Yeti's eyes was doomed to die: but she had been the exception.

Nima Tashi and Tham had gone on ahead to cook lunch. We found them boiling rice and lentils in the ruins of a water-mill and, while we waited, we lay on the turf and watched the cumulo-nimbus playing games to outwit the sun. Later, in the village of Thome (which means 'Way Up') we ran in with some novice monks coming back from market. They were all singing at the tops of their voices. The smallest was walloping out the rhythm on an oil-can, and a wizened old monk followed wearing purple rags and a sou'wester.

'Ask him', I said to Sangye, 'whether *he* has ever seen the Yeti.'

'Not I,' the old man smiled. 'But my aunts did.' His two aunts had been pasturing their sheep when the whole flock suddenly poured off the mountain with the Yeti in pursuit.

'How did it look?' I asked.

'Bigger than a man,' the monk said, 'with terrible yellow eyes, arms almost touching the ground, red hair growing upwards from the waist, and a white crest on top.'

'Likely story,' murmured Elizabeth.

I thanked the monk and walked on ahead with one of the novices. His name was Pama Jhablan. He was sixteen, and had a head of bootbrush hair and an extremely determined expression. He spoke excellent English, having lived for seven years in Darjeeling, which he seemed to think was some kind of Gomorrah. He said he would never kill a living thing, NEVER, NEVER, not even if a monster attacked him. The idea of taking a woman was NOT POSSIBLE, and he looked forward to living his whole life in the mountain monastery.

'All my life,' he repeated with some insistence. 'IN PRAYER.'

It was snowing when we got to Thame Og. There were a few rough stone houses reminding you of houses in the west of Ireland, and mounds of yak dung in the potato fields. We spent a freezing night at 12,500 feet and, at sunrise, climbed to the monastery, which lay perched on the side of a cliff. My friend Pama was there to show us the preparations for the Mani Rimdu Festival. He thumped the great drum. Then he allowed me to handle the skin of a 'fish-monster' which I had seen strung up among the dance masks: it was, I believe, a pangolin.

He also tried to sell me an engraved amber bead which, so he said, had been given him by his mother.

'Keep the bead,' I said, and slipped him the money as we went away.

We walked until mid-afternoon and had reached the outskirts of Khumjung when Sangye called out, 'Bruce! You remember about the Yeti lady? There she is!'

We shinned over the wall and greeted Lakpa Doma, a handsome woman in her thirties with polished red cheeks and a dazzling smile. She wore heavy gold earrings, a striped Sherpa woman's apron, and was mattocking her field while her old mother cut potato slips for planting.

This was Sangye's version of her story:

One day in 1974 she was tending her family's yaks in a summer pasture near Macchermo when the Yeti sprung on her from behind a rock, dragged her to the stream, but then dumped her and went on to slaughter three of the yaks simply by twisting their horns. The beast had the same yellow eyes, big brow-ridges and hollow temples. Some policemen came up from Namche to examine the yak carcasses and stated, categorically, that the killer had never been a man.

'I suppose it was a *dzu-teh*?' I said.

'It was,' said Sangye Dorje.

We waved goodbye to the ladies and came to the door of Sangye's house, where we were to spend the night. We picked our way through a pitch–dark woodstore and climbed upstairs into a long warm room with brightly polished tables, bright rugs and a rack of copper cauldrons decorated with swastikas. His mother served countless cups of Tibetan tea and we peered at his baby boy, asleep in a pile of sheepskins.

Then, at sunset, we went to call on the Ger Lama.

He was a holy wanderer, who came here from Tibet about twenty-eight years ago, living in caves and herdsmen's huts until he persuaded the villagers to help him build a hermitage. He had been once to Kathmandu, but never again. Mountains and solitude, he said, were essential to a life of prayer. He received us, sitting cross–legged in a small scarlet room painted with lotus flowers. His alarm clock, his books and sacred images were all well within his reach. One day, he said, he would return to Tibet, but whether in this life or the next, he was unsure. He blessed us each with a scarf of white gauze, and we went away, marvelling.

Next morning we went to see the famous 'Yeti scalp' which is preserved at the Khumjung *gompa*. The guardian had goitre. From a locked box he pulled out a hairy leather cap shaped a bit like a Mongol helmet, moulded in one piece and dyed with henna. There were several neat holes pierced around the lower edge, probably for the attachment of a brim.

'Must be some kind of dance hat,' I said.

'But what's the skin?' whispered Elizabeth.

'Old goat,' I whispered back; for this 'scalp' and the one at Pangboche are supposed, according to expert opinion, to be made from a wild goat called the serow.

'But whatever it is,' I went on, 'it's certainly not a fake.'

I put a banknote in the guardian's hand, and we left the village.

'Well?' asked Sangye sometime later. He sounded quite anxious. 'What did you think about Yeti?'

We were walking to Gokyo along the vertiginous track that follows the flank of Khumbu Ylha. Yaks were grazing up to the skyline, and in among them was a herd of wild goats, their reddish hair blowing about in the breeze. The day was bright and cloudless and the snowy peaks across the valley seemed to be cut from cardboard.

'I don't know,' I said to Sangye, not sure what to say. For what, indeed, could one say? What did I, or any other Westerner, really know about the Yeti?

I knew, for example, that Yetis or similar species had been knocking about European literature since the Elder Pliny (Natural History VII, 9) described a race of 'wild men' who lived in the Mountains of Imaeus (the Eastern Himalaya), moved with astonishing speed, and had huge feet turned back-to-front. I knew that the Sherpas, too, believed that Yeti had his feet turned back. I knew that several tough-minded mountaineers, such as Eric Shipton or Sir John Hunt, had not only photographed Yeti footprints in the snow, but had heard the Yeti shrieking. I also knew that Hillary's 'scientific' expedition had failed to find the least trace of the creature, had sent the Pangboche 'scalp' to America for analysis, and had suggested that the 'tracks' were those of the snow-leopard or Tibetan blue bear, enlarged by the melting sun.

Of course, I reflected, it was *just* conceivable that some giant orang-outang-like ape had survived in the High Himalaya: but I, for one, was sceptical. I believed, rather, that Yeti was (for want of a better term) a creature of the Collective Unconscious. Man, after all, is the inventor of his own monsters. Babies 'see' monsters long before they are shown them in picture books. Milarepa, the Himalayan sage, 'saw' a Yeti at the entrance to his cave. St Anthony 'saw' his fantastical menagerie in the Desert. Hairy 'devils' did actually 'possess' the Salem witches; and only a few weeks earlier I had watched, in a school near Alice Springs, some Aboriginal children drawing an ape-like ogre from their mythology — in a continent that never saw an ape until the coming of the whites.

I believed, too, that the people most likely to 'see' Yetis were either simpletons or schizophrenics; religious ascetics or the very poor (both liable to protein deficiency); or those at high altitude with a diminished supply of oxygen to the brain. Perhaps Yeti was a mountain hallucination. But how could I explain this to Sangye?

'You're right,' I said, funking the issue. 'Yeti must be some kind of God.'

Around midday we reached a ridge where a well-heeled party of American bird-watchers had stopped to rest beside a Buddhist shrine. We talked to the wife of a San Francisco broker, who owned her own computer software business and seemed a bit puffed. We also had an intense conversation with a lone trekker, a Jewish Bruce from Boston, who wangled two eggs from our picnic and pitied our ignorance of computer technology.

Near Everest Base Camp, this Bruce had run into a professional Yeti hunter, a Scotsman, and had asked him for news of the Loch Ness Monster.

'Bah!' the Scot had snapped. 'Only loonies look for the Monster.'

We slept under a pale moon at the yak-herding settlement of Labharma where Sangye had the key to a hut. Stalactites of soot hung from its rafters. Over the hearth there was a rack for drying cheese and, on the door, a set of claw marks.

'Probably a Yeti,' Sangye sniggered: the Yeti was by now our standing joke.

The Yeti was even more of a joke in the morning when we

got to Macchermo and inspected the scene of Lakpa Doma's rape. Sangye growled; Pasang pulled a Yeti-face, and I imitated the walk of Groucho Marx. We then climbed up alongside the Ngozumpa Glacier and came out into a blinding bright landscape of snow and naked rock and green lakes half-frozen over. On a patch of open water a ruddy shelldrake was nibbling at some weed. Elizabeth was watching him through binoculars when I happened to turn round — and blinked.

'Look!' I blurted out. 'Yeti tracks!'

'Oh yeah?' drawled Elizabeth, and went on watching the shelldrake.

'Look at them!'

On the north-facing slope behind us there was a line of very strange footprints. They were each about fifteen inches long, wider at the toe than the heel, and on some you saw — or thought you saw — the imprint of a giant big toe. They approached the base of an almost vertical bank, stopped, continued on the slope higher up, and finally petered out along a rocky ridge. I reckoned that the creature had jumped at least eight feet into the air and twelve along. The tracks were perhaps a day old and had melted a little: even so, I could see that they hadn't been made by any of the usual contenders — yak, blue bear, snow-leopard, langur monkey, human or human hoaxer. No hoaxer could have jumped that high, yet the Sherpas say that Yeti habitually jumps his own height and more. The strange thing was that its foot had scuffed the snow on the way up — unless it really was a Yeti-with-the-feet turned-back, in which case the jumper had been jumping down.

I was sure there must be some logical explanation and called Sangye over.

'Did you ever,' I asked, 'on any of your treks, see anything like them?'

'Never,' he said, darkly. 'They were not made by men.'

'Then who made them?'

'Same as Yeti.'

I still have no idea what these 'Yeti tracks' were. My whole life has been a search for the miraculous: yet at the first faint flavour of the uncanny, I tend to turn rational and scientific. After this excitement, the whole party was infected with Yeti-fever and kept 'seeing things' on every mountain. On Cho Oyu we thought we saw Reinhold Messner manoeuvring across an ice-fall. He was on the mountain that day, but not where we could see him, and the 'thing' we did see turned out to be a pinnacle of rock, doubling and tripling as our eyes watered in the wind.

We camped at Gokyo and in the afternoon I climbed the summit of Gokyo Ri where, gasping for oxygen at 18,000 feet, I propped myself against a stone cairn and, while the wind ripped at the prayer-flags, gazed dully at the ring of blue-and-white peaks — Cho Oyu, Everest, Lhotse, Nuptse and, far to the east, the cone of Makalu.

The sky was all but cloudless; a stream of grey vapour crept up the valley from India, and above it, in the opposite direction, a few shreds of cumulus came blowing out of Tibet. I could see the Gyubanare Glacier snaking down from the Pass of Shangri La. And it occurred to me how easy it would be, in this incandescent atmosphere, to 'see' the real Shangri La as described by the mystics — the Valley of Eternal Youth, always lying somewhere to the North, where the houses are roofed with gold and the streambeds shimmer with precious stones.

Back at the camp, Sangye had shut himself in his tent with an old shaman and the two were chanting hymns to propitiate the Mountain Gods. The shaman said that sometimes people saw a monastery floating in the middle of Gokyo Lake. At sundown it started to freeze. I had a headache and could only sleep fitfully. All night I heard, or imagined, strange rumbles and half-expected a hairy hand to rip through the roof of the

tent. It was good to see the dawn and Elizabeth stirring in her
sleeping-bag.

'Did you sleep?' I asked.

'No,' she yawned. 'I heard funny noises.'

'What kind of noises?'

'Thumps.'

After Gokyo the weather turned sour. Clouds hung below the
snowline and snowflakes whizzed in our faces. We stopped at
a tea-house called 'Cho Oyu View' where the boy called out
'Milik tea or balak tea?' and gave us boiled potatoes and hot
chile peppers. We got stuck behind a caravan of fourteen yaks
nose to tail which Elizabeth said looked like a 'hairy black
centipede'. Across the main valley we saw the monastery of
Thyangboche and heard the weird music of horns and
cymbals carried on the morning wind. When, after two days,
we got to Pangboche, we realised from the continuous stream
of porters and white men with rucksacks that we'd rejoined
the Everest trunk-route.

Pangboche *gompa* is a square red-washed building with the
presence of a Palladian villa and an alley of windblown junipers leading up to it. Among its treasures is the second
'Yeti-scalp'. It is the oldest shrine in the Khumbu and was
founded by Sangye Dorje's namesake, an aerobatic lama who
lived about four hundred years ago and could fly back and
forth across the Himalayas at will.

The guardian, a poetic soul reeking of rancid yak butter,
removed the altar frontal and showed us a dent in the rock
where the lama had landed. Like other Tibetan levitators, this
Sangye Dorje seems to have had little control of his airbrakes
and was always leaving dents in the landscape where he
crashed. Cases of concussion, however, are unknown.

On the upper floor, we saw the lama's portrait, which
showed a young man with luminous white skin and masses of
flowing chestnut hair. Apparently, he'd been very proud of

this hair but, on settling at Pangboche, had obeyed an ascetic impulse, chopped it off, chucked it out, and the junipers had sprouted where it fell.

We then inspected the 'scalp', which was identical to the Khumjung specimen, except that there were rather more holes. I also saw, stored in a rack with the ceremonial masks, a pair of cartwheel hats made of the same reddish goat skin, thus confirming my impression that they all belonged to some kind of ritual costume. The guardian, however, had a different tale. This particular Yeti, he said, had fallen for the young lama; had grown tame in his company; had learned to fetch his wood and water; and when it died, the lama had cut off the scalp and kept it in memory of their friendship.

'Hm!' said Elizabeth. 'Beauty and the Beast!'

We pressed on eastward, but the weather disintegrated terribly. We had intended to climb Kalar Datar, an easy peak from which, on a clear day, you get the best view of Everest. There seemed little point in fog and snow, so we holed up in the rest-house at Pheriche and read. Some of the trekkers looked rather emaciated and were far too obsessed by their next meal to listen to cock-and-bull stories about the Yeti. Eventually, after three dismal days, we decided to beat it back to a warmer altitude.

On the way we stopped at Thyangboche where the novices put on a horn concert for our benefit. At Kyangzuma we saw a musk deer flitting past; and we watched the mating dance of the Impeyan pheasant, a dazzling bird whose plumage seemed to be composed of electricity. Once we got below Namche, every leaf had burst open and Elizabeth's botanical enthusiasms took over, she yanked at branches, sniffed flowers, and called out Latin names with the conviction of a woman who knows her own mind. We also met a young English climber who had found, on the edge of a glacier, a scuba diver's flipper.

'So,' I said to myself. 'The Yeti hoaxer!' — until I remembered that no flippered hoaxer could possibly have jumped eight feet into the air — or, for that matter, jumped down backwards.

Then we went down to Lukla to catch the plane.

We arrived in a rainstorm and, for three days, we waited for the cloud to clear. Lukla was full of stranded trekkers, some of whom had missed their cheap charter flights, and mooned about with an air of quiet desperation. Elizabeth called them the 'down-at-the-mouthers'.

Other passengers were more vocal and kept haranguing the poor Nepali airline official with lists of their business appointments in London, Washington or Abu Dhabi. The most vociferous of all was a journalist who had flown in, against advice, for one night, and had intended to fly out the next day. He had been stuck for a week. In a voluminous blue down-jacket, he would waddle to the airline office to complain. He said that 'for professional and personal reasons' he HAD to be in Geneva on Tuesday. He implied the Nepali pilots were cowards. He demanded an Air Force helicopter. Had anyone radioed for the helicopter?

'Yes,' the Nepali nodded, smiling dreamily into the fog.

Obviously, every time there was a fog, the tourists started yelling for helicopters.

'He should take up Tantric Buddhism,' I said, when the journalist was out of earshot. 'Then he could learn to levitate.'

1983

285

A LAMENT FOR
AFGHANISTAN

Anyone who reads around the travel books of the Thirties must, in the end, conclude that Robert Byron's *The Road to Oxiana* is the masterpiece. Byron was a gentleman, a scholar and an aesthete, who drowned in 1941 when his ship to West Africa was torpedoed. In his short life he travelled as far as China and Tibet, and to most of the countries nearer home. In 1928 he published *The Station*, an account of a visit to the monasteries of Mount Athos, and followed it up with two pioneering volumes on Byzantine civilisation, which, at that time, received scant consideration from academic circles. He had some lively prejudices. Among the targets of his abuse were the Catholic (as opposed to the Orthodox) Church; the art of Classical Greece; the paintings of Rembrandt; Shakespeare — and when his Intourist guide protested that the plays could never have been written by a grocer from Stratford-upon-Avon, he murmured, 'They are exactly the sort of plays I would expect a grocer to write.' In 1932, attracted by the photo of a Seljuk tomb-tower on the Turkoman steppe, he set out on a quest for the origins of Islamic architecture. And, if it is fair to place his earlier books as the work of a dazzlingly gifted young amateur, it is equally fair to rank *The Road to Oxiana* as a work of genius.

I write as a partisan, not as a critic. Long ago, I raised it to the status of 'sacred text', and thus beyond criticism. My own copy — now spineless and floodstained after four journeys to Central Asia — has been with me since the age of fifteen. Consequently, I am apt to resent suggestions that it is a 'lost book' or in need of being 'rescued from the library shelves'. By a stroke of luck, it was never lost on me.

Because I felt the death of Robert Byron so keenly, I sought out his friends and pestered them for their reminiscences. 'Very cross,' they said. 'An awful tease.' 'Surprisingly tough.' 'Abrasive.' 'Incredibly funny.' 'Fat.' 'Rather hideous . . . eyes like a fish.' 'Wonderful imitation of Queen Victoria.' By the time I was twenty-two, I had read everything I could — by and about him — and that summer set out on my own journey to Oxiana.

In 1962 — six years before the Hippies wrecked it (by driving educated Afghans into the arms of the Marxists) — you could set off to Afghanistan with the anticipations of, say, Delacroix off to Algiers. On the streets of Herat you saw men in mountainous turbans, strolling hand in hand, with roses in their mouths and rifles wrapped in flowered chintz. In Badakhshan you could picnic on Chinese carpets and listen to the bulbul. In Balkh, the Mother of Cities, I asked a fakir the way to the shrine of Hadji Piardeh. 'I don't know it,' he said. 'It must have been destroyed by Genghiz.'

Even the Afghan Embassy in London introduced you to a world that was hilarious and strange. Control of the visa section rested with a tousle-haired Russian émigré giant, who had cut the lining of his jacket so that it hung, as a curtain, to hide the holes in the seat of his trousers. At opening time, he'd be stirring up clouds of dust with a broom, only to let it settle afresh on the collapsing furniture. Once, when I tipped him ten shillings, he hugged me, lifted me off the floor and bellowed: 'I hope you have a very ACCIDENT-FREE trip to Afghanistan!'

No. Our journeys were never quite accident-free: the time a soldier lobbed a pick-axe at the car; the time our lorry slid, with gentle resignation, over the cliff (we were just able to jump off); the time we were whipped for straying into a military area; the dysentery; the septicaemia; the hornet sting; the fleas — but, mercifully, no hepatitis.

Sometimes, we met travellers more high-minded than ourselves who were following the tracks of Alexander or Marco Polo: for us, it was far more fun to follow Robert Byron. I still have notebooks to prove how slavishly I aped both his itinerary and — as if that were possible — his style. Take this entry of mine for 5 July 1962 and compare it with his for 21 September 1933:

In the afternoon we called on Mr Alouf the art dealer. He took us to an apartment filled with French-polished 'French' furniture, most of it riddled with worm and upside down.

He had recently converted to Catholicism and, on showing us a signed photograph of Pope Pius XII, crossed himself fervently and rattled his dentures.

From a cupboard he produced the following:

A Roman gold pectoral set with blue glass pastes. A forgery.

A neolithic marble idol with an erect phallus, on an accompanying perch. The perch was genuine, the idol not.

Thirty Syro-Phoenician funerary bone dolls.

A 'Hittite' figure, bristling with gold attributes, perhaps the one Byron saw in 1933. A fake.

Various worrying gold objects.

A collection of Early Christian glasses (genuine). 'I have many glasses', said Mr Alouf, crossing himself, 'covered with crosses. But they are in the bank.'

Finally, a marble head of Alexander the Great. 'I have refused twenty thousand dollars for this piece. TWENTY THOUSAND DOLLARS! All archaeologists agree mine is the only genuine head of Alexander: Look! The neck! The ears!' Perhaps — but the face was entirely missing.

From the Levant we would go on to Teheran. There was more money about than in Byron's day and many more Europeans after it. But the Shah was a pale copy of his father and already he, too, looked pretty silly, and the men around him queasy. One day we went to see Amir Abbas Hoveyda in his office at the Iranian Oil Company (he was not yet Prime Minister): 'A man with big eyes and despairing gestures. He seemed trapped behind the enormity of his desk. He offered us the use of his helicopter in case we should need it.'

Once Byron gets to Iran, his search for the origins of Islamic architecture really gets under way. But to construct, out of stone and brick and tile, a prose that will not only be readable but carry the reader to a pitch of excitement requires talents of the highest calibre. This is Byron's achievement. His paean of praise for the Sheikh Lutf'ullah Mosque in Isfahan must put him at least in the rank of Ruskin. One afternoon, to see how it was done, I took *The Road to Oxiana* into the mosque and sat, cross-legged, marvelling both at the tilework and Byron's description of it.

The 'experts' will carp that, while Byron may have had lyrical powers of description, he was not a scholar — and, of course, in their sense he wasn't. Yet, time and again, he scores over sound scholarship with his uncanny ability to gauge the morale of a civilisation from its architecture, and to treat ancient buildings and modern people as two facets of a continuing story.

Already in *The Byzantine Achievement*, written at twenty-five, there is a haunting passage that tells in four sentences as much about the schism of the Western and Eastern Churches as any number of portentous volumes:

The existence of St. Sophia is atmospheric; St. Peter's, over-poweringly, imminently substantial. One is a church to God; the other a salon for his agents. One is consecrated to reality, the other to illusion. St. Sophia, in fact, is large, and St. Peter's is vilely, tragically small.

On the subject of Iran, he is even more clairvoyant. On reading *The Road to Oxiana* you end up with the impression that the Iranian plateau is a 'soft centre' that panders to megalomaniac ambitions in its rulers without providing the genius to sustain them.

As is well known, the late Shah-in-Shah saw in the ruins of Persepolis a mirror image of his own glory and, for that reason, held his coronation binge about a mile from the site, in tents designed by Jansen of Paris, where a riff-raff of royalty could dine with the ghosts of his soi-disant predecessors.

Read, therefore, Byron's comments on Persepolis in the light of the pretensions and downfall of the Pahlevi Dynasty:

The stone, owing to its extreme hardness, has proved impervious to age; it remains a bright smooth grey, as slick as an aluminium saucepan. This cleanness reacts on the carving like sunlight on a fake old master; it reveals, instead of the genius one expected, a disconcerting void . . . My involuntary thought as Herzfeld showed us the new (newly excavated) staircase was: 'How much did this cost? Was it made in a factory? No, it wasn't. Then how many workmen for how many years chiselled and polished these endless figures?' Certainly, they are not mechanical figures; nor are they guilty of elaboration for their own sake; nor are they cheap in the sense of lacking technical skill. But they are what the French call *faux bons*. They have art, but not spontaneous art . . . Instead of mind or feeling, they exhale a soulless refinement, a veneer adopted by the Asiatic whose own artistic instinct has been fettered and devitalized by . . . the Mediterranean.

If you pursue this vein, you will find that, under the bravura passages, Byron is expounding a very serious thesis — and one of crucial importance for understanding our own time. All he finds most admirable in Persian art — the tower at Gumbad-i-Kabus, the Seljuk Mosque in Isfahan, the incomparable mausoleum of the Mongol Khan Uljaitu, or the buildings of Gohar Shad — results from a fusion (one could say, a chemical explosion) between the old Iranian civilisation and the peoples of nomad stock from the Oxus Basin and beyond. You even feel that Byron's favourite character, Shir Ahmad Khan, the Afghan Ambassador to Teheran, belongs among these first-rate monuments: in other words, genius visits Iran from the north-east.

Certainly — in Byron's day and mine — to cross the Afghan frontier, after the lowering fanaticism of Meshed, was like coming up for air. 'Here at last', he wrote of Herat, 'is Asia without an inferiority complex.' And it is this moral superiority of the Afghans, together with a fear of the centrifugal forces spinning in Central Asia, that has scared the Russians and the bunch of seedy traitors who have sold their country. (May they boil in Gehenna!) So when I read that the Heratis have been sending women's dresses and cosmetics to the cowards of Kandahar, I think back to a dress I once saw flapping in the old clothes bazaar in Herat — a gown of flamingo crêpe with sequined butterflies on the hips and the label of a boutique in Beverly Hills.

Even in Kabul, the unlikely was always predictable: the sight of the King's cousin Prince Daud at a party, the old 'Mussolini' blackshirt, with his muddy smile and polished head and boots, talking to — who? — Duke Ellington, who else? The Duke in a white-and-blue spotted tie and blue-and-white spotted shirt: he was on his last big tour. And we know what happened to Daud — shot, with his family, in the palace he usurped.

I can guess what's happened to the crippled Nuristani boy, who brought us our dinner from his village up the mountain. We had camped by the river, and he came down the rock face, swinging his crutch and his withered leg and, somehow, hanging on to the dish and a lighted firebrand. He sang while we ate — but they have bombed the village and used gas on the inhabitants.

I can guess, too, what happened to Wali Jahn. He took me to safety when I got blood-poisoning. He carried me on his back through the river, and bathed my head, and made me rest under the ilexes. But when we came back, five years later, he was coughing, deep retching coughs, and had the look of someone going down to the cold.

But what have they done to Gul Amir the Tadjik? He was ugly as sin with an unending nose and silver earrings. You never saw anyone so devout. Every time he wanted a rest, 'There was no God but God . . . ' but as he bowed his face to Mecca, he would squint out sideways and, when I fell in the river trying to cast a trout fly, God was forgotten in a peal of girlish giggles.

Where now is the Hakim of Kande? We stayed in his summerhouse under a scree of shining schist and watched the creamy clouds coming over the mountain. In the evening we saw a girl in red creeping out of a maize field: 'The corn is high,' he said. 'In nine months there will be many babies.'

What's become of the trucker who admired my ear-lobes? We left him in the middle of the road. His carburettor had clogged and his hashish pipe had clogged, and the pieces were all mixed up, on the road, and we were in a hurry.

Or the houseboy at the Park Hotel in Herat? He wore a rose-pink turban and, when we asked for lunch, said:

'Yessir! Whatyoulike? Everthing!'

'What you got?'

'No drink. No ice. No bread. No fruit. No meat. No rice. No fish. Eggs. One. Maybe. Tomorrow. YES!'

Or the man in Tashkurgan who took me to his garden? It was a very hot and dusty afternoon and Peter was looking for traces of the Bactrian Greeks. 'Go and find your Greeks,' I said. 'Give me your Marvell and I'll find a garden' – where I really did stumble on melons as I passed and had green thoughts in a green shade.

Or the mad woman in Ghazni at the Tomb of Mahmud? She was tall and lovely and she stared gloomily at the ground and rattled her bracelets. When they opened the doors, she flung herself on the wooden balustrade, and flapped her crimson dress and cawed like a wounded bird. Only when they let her kiss the tomb did she fall silent. And she kissed the inscription, as if each white marble letter contained the cure for her sickness.

This is the year — of all years — to mourn the loss of Robert Byron, the arch-enemy of Appeasement, who said, 'I shall have warmonger put on my passport,' when he saw what the Nazis were up to. Were he alive today, I think he would agree that, in time (everything in Afghanistan takes time), the Afghans will do something quite dreadful to their invaders — perhaps awaken the sleeping giants of Central Asia.

But that day will not bring back the things we loved: the high, clear days and the blue icecaps on the mountains; the lines of white poplars fluttering in the wind, and the long white prayer-flags; the fields of asphodels that followed the tulips; or the fat-tailed sheep brindling the hills above Chakcharan, and the ram with a tail so big they had to strap it to a cart. We shall not lie on our backs at the Red Castle and watch the vultures wheeling over the valley where they killed the grandson of Genghiz. We will not read Babur's memoirs in his garden at Istalif and see the blind man smelling his way around the rose bushes. Or sit in the Peace of Islam with the beggars of Gazar Gagh. We will not stand on the Buddha's head at Bamiyan, upright in his niche like a whale in a dry-dock. We will not sleep in the nomad tent, or scale the Minaret of Jam. And we shall lose the tastes — the hot, coarse, bitter bread; the green tea flavoured with cardamoms; the grapes we cooled in the snow-melt; and the nuts and dried mulberries we munched for altitude sickness. Nor shall we get back the smell of the beanfields, the sweet, resinous smell of deodar wood burning, or the whiff of a snow leopard at 14,000 feet.

1980

9

TWO MORE
PEOPLE

ERNST JÜNGER:
AN AESTHETE AT WAR

Diaries, Volumes I–III by Ernst Jünger
(Christian Bourgois, 1981)

On 18 June 1940, Mr Churchill ended his speech to the Commons with the words 'This was their finest hour!' and, that evening, a very different character, in the grey officer's uniform of the *Wehrmacht*, sat in the Duchesse de la Rochefoucauld's study at the Château de Montmirail. Her uninvited guest was a short, athletic man of forty-five, with a mouth set in an expression of self-esteem and eyes a particularly arctic shade of blue. He leafed through her books with the assured touch of the bibliomane and noted that many bore the dedications of famous writers. A letter slipped from one and fell to the floor — a delightful letter written by a boy called François who wanted to be a pilot. He wondered if the boy was now a pilot. Finally, after dark, he settled down to write his diary. It was a long entry — almost two thousand words — for his day, too, had been eventful.

In the morning, he had discussed the risks of getting burned alive with a tank driver in oil-soaked denims: 'I had the impression that Vulcan and his "ethic of work" was incarnate in such martial figures.' After luncheon, he had stood in the school playground and watched a column of ten thousand French and Belgian prisoners file past: ' . . . an image of the dark wave of Destiny herself . . . an interesting and instructive spectacle' in which one sensed the 'mechanical, irresistible allure peculiar to catastrophes'. He had chucked them cans of beef and biscuits and watched their struggles from behind an iron grille; the sight of their hands was especially disturbing.

Next, he had spotted a group of officers with decorations from the Great War, and invited them to dine. They were on the verge of collapse, but a good dinner seemed like a reversal of their fortunes. Could he explain, they asked, the reasons for their defeat? 'I said I considered it the Triumph of the Worker, but I do not think they understood the sense of my reply. What could they know of the years we have passed through since 1918? Of the lessons we have learned as if in a blast furnace?'

The absent duchess had reason to thank the man who nosed in her private affairs. Captain Ernst Jünger was, at that moment, the most celebrated German writer in uniform. No catastrophe could surprise him since for twenty years his work had harped on the philosophical need to accept death and total warfare as the everyday experience of the twentieth century. Yet he tempered his assent to destruction with an antiquarian's reverence for bricks and mortar, and had saved the château.

Indeed, he had saved a lot of things in the blitzkrieg. A week earlier, he had saved the Cathedral of Laon from looters. He had saved the city's library with its manuscripts of the Carolingian kings. And he had employed an out-of-work wine waiter to inspect some private cellars and save some good bottles for himself. Bombs, it was true, had fallen in the La Rochefoucaulds' park. A pavilion had burned out, leaving in one window a fragment of glass that 'reproduced exactly the head of Queen Victoria'. Otherwise, after a bit of tidying up, the place was just as its owners had left it. Moreover, Captain Jünger had other reasons for feeling pleased with himself.

'*The Maxims* [of La Rochefoucauld] have long been my favourite bedside reading. It was an act of spiritual gratitude to save what could be saved. For properties of such value, the essential is to protect them during the critical days.'

Easier said than done! 'The route of the invasion is strewn with bottles, champagne, claret, burgundy. I counted at least one for every step, to say nothing of the camps where one could say it had rained bottles. Such orgies are in the true tradition of our campaigns in France. Every invasion by a German army is accompanied by drinking bouts like those of the gods in the *Edda*.'

A junior officer remarked how strange it was that the looting soldiers destroyed musical instruments first: 'It showed me in a symbolic fashion how Mars is contrary to the Muses . . . and then I recalled the large painting by Rubens illustrating the same theme . . . ' How strange, too, that they left the mirrors intact! The officer thought this was because the men wanted to shave — but Jünger thought there might be other reasons.

These diaries — three volumes of them — have recently reappeared in France, where the translation of Jünger's work is a minor literary industry. To English-speaking readers, however, he is known by two books — *Storm of Steel* (1920), a relentless glorification of modern warfare, and *On The Marble Cliffs*, his allegorical, anti-Nazi capriccio of 1939 that describes an assassination attempt on a tyrant and appears, in retrospect, to be a prophecy of the von Stauffenberg bomb plot of 1944.

Yet Jünger's partisans — more French perhaps than German — claim for him the status of 'great writer', a thinker of Goethean wisdom, whose political leanings toward the extreme right have robbed him of the recognition he deserves. Certainly, the scale of his erudition is titanic: his singularity of purpose is unswerving, and even at eighty-five he continues to elaborate on the themes that have held his attention for over sixty years. He is — or has been — soldier, aesthete, novelist, essayist, the ideologue of an authoritarian political party, and a trained taxonomic botanist. His lifelong hobby has been the study of entomology: indeed, what the butterfly was to Nabokov, the beetle is to Jünger — especially the armour-plated beetle. He is also the connoisseur of hallucinogens who took a number of 'trips' with his friend Albert Hofmann, the discoverer of lysergic acid.*

He writes a hard, lucid prose. Much of it leaves the reader with an impression of the author's imperturbable self-regard, of dandyism, of cold-bloodedness, and, finally, of banality. Yet the least promising passages will suddenly light up with flashes of aphoristic brilliance, and the most harrowing descriptions are alleviated by a yearning for human values in a dehumanised world. The diary is the perfect form for a man who combines such acute powers of observation with an anaesthetised sensibility.

He was born in 1895, the son of a pharmacist from Hanover. By 1911, bored by the conventional world of his parents, he joined the Wandervogel Movement and so became acquainted with the values of Open Air, Nature, Blood, Soil, and Fatherland: already he was the expert beetle-hunter who spent many happy hours with his killing bottle. Two years later, he ran away to the Sahara and joined the Foreign Legion, only to be brought back by his father. In 1914, on the first day of war, he enlisted in the 73rd Hanoverian Fusiliers and emerged in 1918, 'punctured in twenty places', with the highest military decoration, the *Croix pour le Mérite*, an enlarged sense of personal grandeur, and in possession of a meticulous diary that recorded the horrific beauty of trench warfare and the reckless gaiety of men under fire. The Fall of Germany was thus the making of Jünger.

* For a description of Jünger's 'tripping', see Albert Hofmann, *LSD - My Problem Child*, McGraw-Hill, 1980, chapter 7, 'Radiance from Ernst Jünger'.

Storm of Steel made him the hero of a generation of young officers who had given all and ended up, if lucky, with the Iron Cross, Gide praised it as the finest piece of writing to come out of the war. Certainly, it is quite unlike anything of its time — none of the pastoral musings of Siegfried Sassoon or Edmund Blunden, no whiffs of cowardice as in Hemingway, none of the masochism of T.E. Lawrence, or the compassion of Remarque. Instead, Jünger parades his belief in Man's 'elementary' instinct to kill other men — a game which, if played correctly, must conform to a chivalric set of rules. (In a later essay, 'Battle as Inner Experience', he sets forth his views on the innate gratifications of hand-to-hand fighting.) Finally, you end up with a picture of the war as a grim, but gentlemanly, shooting party. 'What a bag!' he exclaims when they capture 150 prisoners. Or: 'Caught between two fires, the English tried to escape across the open and were gunned down like game at a *battue*.' And how strange it was to gaze into the eyes of the young Englishman you'd shot down five minutes before!

Even in his early twenties, Jünger presents himself as an aesthete at the centre of a tornado, quoting Stendhal, that the art of civilisation consists in 'combining the most delicate pleasures . . . with the frequent presence of danger'. At Combles, for example, he finds an untenanted house 'where a lover of beautiful things must have lived'; and though half the house gets blown to bits, he goes on reading in an armchair until interrupted by a violent blow on his calf: 'There was a ragged hole in my puttees from which blood streamed to the floor. On the other side was the circular swelling of a piece of shrapnel under the skin.' No one but a man of Jünger's composure could describe the appearance of a bullet hole through his chest as if he were describing his nipple.

After the war, he took up botany, entomology, and marine biology, first at Leipzig, then in Naples. Like so many others of his generation, he was saturated by the garbled form of

Darwinism as doctored for nationalist purposes. Yet he was too intelligent to fall for the cruder versions of the theory that led members of the German scientific establishment to condone the slaughter of Gypsies and Jews — recognising, as he did, that any theory is also the autobiography of the theorist and can but reflect an 'infinitesimal part of the whole'. His pleasures in biology tended toward the Linnaean classification of species — aesthetic pleasures that offered him a glimpse of the Primordial Paradise as yet untainted by Man. Moreover, the insect world, where instincts govern behaviour as a key fits a lock, had an irresistible attraction to a man of his utopian vision.

By 1927, he was back in Berlin where his friends were a mixed bag that included Kubin, Dr Goebbels, Bertolt Brecht, and Ernst Toller. He became a founding member of the National Bolshevist Caucus — a zealous, extremist political party that flourished for a while in late Weimar, negligible in its effect on history, though not without interesting theoretical implications. These so-called 'Prussian Communists' hated capitalism, hated the bourgeois West, and hoped to graft the methods of Bolshevism onto the chivalric ideals of the Junkers. Their leader, Ernst Niekisch, visualised an alliance of workers and soldier-aristocrats who would abolish the middle classes. Jünger himself was the ideologue of the movement and, in 1932, published a book that was to have been its manifesto.

The Worker (Der Arbeiter) is a vaguely formulated machine-age utopia whose citizens are required to commit themselves to a 'total mobilization' (the origin of the term is Jünger's) in the undefined interests of the State. The Worker, as Jünger understands him, is a technocrat. His business, ultimately, is war. His freedom — or rather, his sense of inner freedom — is supposed to correspond to the scale of his productivity. The aim is world government — by force.

Not surprisingly, the movement petered out. Niekisch was later arrested by the Gestapo and was murdered, in 1945, in jail. As for Jünger, his war record gave him a certain immunity from the Nazis and he retreated into a private, almost eremitic, life of scientific contemplation and *belles lettres*. Though he deplored Hitler as a vulgar technician who had misunderstood the metaphysics of power, he did nothing to try to stop him, believing anyway that democracy was dead and the destiny of machine-age man was essentially tragic: 'The history of civilization is the gradual replacement of men by things.' Yet, again and again, he insists that the wars of the twentieth century are popular wars — wars, that is, of the People, of the *canaille*, and not of the professional soldier. From his viewpoint, albeit an oblique one, National Socialism was a phenomenon of the left.

Throughout the middle Thirties, Jünger wrote essays, travelled to the tropics, and kept a cold eye on the Fatherland. By 1938, at the time of the Generals' Plot, he seems to have flirted with resistance to Hitler, and one night at his house at Ueberlingen, near Lake Constance, he met a young, patriotic aristocrat, Heinrich von Trott zu Solz (whose elder brother, Adam, was the ex-Rhodes scholar and friend of England who would be hanged for his part in the von Stauffenberg plot of July 1944*). What passed between them, Jünger does not relate. What is certain is that the visit gave him the idea for a story.

On the Marble Cliffs is an allegorical tale, written in a frozen, humourless, yet brilliantly coloured style that owes something to the nineteenth-century Decadents and something to the Scandinavian sagas. The result is a prose equivalent of an art nouveau object in glass, and the plot is much less silly than it sounds in précis:

Two men — the narrator and Brother Otho (not to be distinguished from Jünger himself and his own brother, the poet Friedrich Georg) are aesthetes, scientists, and soldiers

* For a biography of Adam von Trott zu Solz, see Christopher Sykes, *Troubled Loyalty*, Collins, London, 1968.

who have retired from war to a remote cliffside hermitage, where they work on a Linnaean classification of the region's flora, and harbour a lot of pet snakes. Far below lies the Grand Marina, a limpid lake surrounded by the farms, the vineyards, and cities of a venerable civilisation. To the north there stretches an expanse of steppe-land where pastoral nomads drive their herds. Beyond that are the black forests of Mauretania, the sinister realm of the Chief Ranger (*Oberförster*) with his pack of bloodhounds and gang of disciplined freebooters in whose ranks the brothers once served.

The *Oberförster* is planning to destroy the Grand Marina:

He was one of those figures whom the Mauretanians respect as great lords and yet find somewhat ridiculous — rather as an old colonel is received in the regiment on occasional visits from his estates. He left an imprint on one's mind if only because his green coat with its gold-embroidered ilexes drew all eyes to him . . . (His own eyes), like those of hardened drinkers, were touched with a red flame, but expressed both cunning and unshakeable power — yes, at times, even majesty. Then we took pleasure in his company and lived in arrogance at the table of the great . . .

As evil spreads over the land 'like mushroom-spawn over rotten wood', the two brothers plunge deeper and deeper into the mystery of flowers. But on a botanical expedition to the Mauretanian forest in search of a rare red orchid, they stumble on the *Oberförster*'s charnel house, Köppels-Bleck, where a dwarf sings gaily as he scrapes at a flaying bench:

Over the dark door on the gable end a skull was nailed fast, showing its teeth and seeming to invite entry with its grin. Like a jewel in its chain, it was the central link of a narrow gable frieze which appeared to be formed of brown spiders. Suddenly we guessed that it was fashioned of human hands. . .

The brothers' discovery of the orchid gives them a 'strange feeling of invulnerability' and the strength to continue their studies. But one day, just before the *Oberförster* launches his attack on the Marina, they are visited by one of his henchmen, Bracquemart, and the young Prince of Sunmyra.

Braquemart is a 'small, dark, haggard fellow, whom we found somewhat coarse-grained but, like all Mauretanians, not without wit.' The Prince, on the other hand, is 'remote and absent-minded' with an 'air of deep suffering' and the 'stamp of decadence'. This pair, of course, is planning a *coup d'état*, which fails when the *Oberförster* unleashes his blood-hounds. The leader of the pack is called Chiffon Rouge, i.e. Red Flag, and, in a scene of appalling ferocity, everyone gets mangled and killed except for the two brothers, who are saved by the miraculous intervention of their own pet lance-head vipers. Later, at Köppels-Bleck, they find the heads of the two conspirators on poles, Bracquemart having killed himself first 'with the capsule of poison that all Mauretanians carry'. But on the 'pale mask of the Prince from which the scalped flesh hung in ribbons . . . there played the shadow of a smile intensely sweet and joyful, and I knew then that the weak-nesses had fallen from this noble man with each step of his martyrdom . . . ' — which description can be compared to the photo of Adam von Trott, as he heard the death sentence, in the People's Court, five years after Jünger wrote his book.*

On the Marble Cliffs sold 35,000 copies before it was sup-pressed early in 1940. How it slipped through the censor machine of Dr Goebbels is less of a mystery when one realises that Braquemart was modelled on Dr Goebbels himself who was flattered and amused by it, and later alarmed by its popularity among the officer caste. Jünger himself claimed then — as now — that the fable is not specifically anti-Nazi, but

---

* Sykes, *op. cit.*, p. 447: 'Yet the expression on his face showed an extraordinary serenity, and there is almost the suspicion of a smile. His loyalty was no longer troubled.'

'above all that'. And I don't doubt that he conceived it as a contemptuous, sweeping, Spenglerian statement on the destruction of the old Mediterranean-based civilisation of Europe: the *Oberförster* could, at a pinch, stand for Stalin as well as Hitler.

At a meeting of the Nazi Party, Reichsleiter Boulher is supposed to have said: 'Mein Führer, this time Jünger has gone too far!' but Hitler calmed him down and said: 'Let Jünger be!' All the same, the writer's friends advised him to get into uniform; and so by the fall of 1939 he found himself with the rank of Captain, posted to the Siegfried Line, convinced, by now, that the private journal was the only practical medium for literary expression in a totalitarian state.

In his introduction to his diaries, Jünger invokes the story of seven sailors who agreed to study astronomy on the Arctic island of St Maurice during the winter of 1633, and whose journal was found beside their bodies when the whaling ships returned the following summer. The fate of Jünger's journal is to be that of Poe's 'Ms. found in a Bottle' — a record thrown into an uncertain future by a man who may die tomorrow, yet who cherishes his writing as a man 'cherishes those of his children who have no chance of surviving'.

Their German title, *Strahlungen*, means 'Reflections' — in the sense that the writer collects particles of light and reflects them onto the reader. They are surely the strangest literary production to come out of the Second World War, stranger by far than anything by Céline or Malaparte. Jünger reduces his war to a sequence of hallucinatory prose poems in which things appear to breathe and people perform like automata or, at best, like insects. So when he focuses on occupied Paris, the result is like a diorama in the Entomological Department of a natural history museum.

The opening pages find Jünger in April 1939 at a new house in

Kirchhorst near Hanover, putting the final touches to *On the Marble Cliffs* and having bad dreams about Hitler, whom he calls by the pseudonym of Kniébolo. By winter time, he is exchanging desultory fire with the French batteries across the Rhine. He saves the life of a gunner, and gets another Iron Cross. Among his reading: the Bible, Melville's *Bartleby the Scrivener*, and Boethius's *Consolation of Philosophy*. He sleeps in a reed hut, in a sleeping-bag lined with rose-coloured silk, and on his forty-fifth birthday a young officer brings him a bottle of wine with a bunch of violets tied round the neck.

After the invasion of France, there is a gap until April 1941 when he surfaces in Paris as 'Officer with Special Mission attached to the Military Command' — his job: to censor mail and sound out the intellectual and social life of the city. And he remains in Paris, with interruptions, until the Americans are at the gates.

He presents himself as the zealous Francophile. They and Germany have everything to offer each other. Indeed, every-thing does point to collaboration. Pétain's armistice is still popular; anti-Semitism flourishing; and Anglophobia given an enormous boost by the sinking of the French fleet at Mers-el-Kebir. There is even talk of avenging Waterloo and, when Stalin enters the war, '*Les Anglo-Saxons travaillent pour Oncle Jo.*' Besides, Jünger's French friends are determined the war shall cramp their style as little as possible. And how well-mannered the newcomers are! What a relief after all those years of Americans in Paris!

In the first weeks, Captain Jünger is a tourist in the city of every German soldier's dream. He lives at the Hotel Raphäel, and goes on long walks alone. He inspects the gargoyles of Nôtre-Dame, the 'Hellenistic' architecture of La Madeleine ('A church if you please!'), and notes that the obelisk in the Place de la Concorde is the colour of a champagne sorbet. With his friend General Speidel, he goes to the Marché aux Puces; idles the hours away in antiquarian bookshops, and, sometimes, goes to watch a revue of naked girls: many are the daughters of White Russian émigrés, and with one small, melancholic girl he discusses Pushkin and Aksakov's *Memoirs of Childhood*.

Paris is full of strange encounters. On Bastille Day, a street-player sets aside his violin to shake his hand. He rounds up drunken soldiers from a *hôtel de passe* and talks to a gay, eighteen-year-old whore. On 1 May he offers lilies-of-the-valley to a young vendeuse: 'Paris offers all manner of such meetings. You hardly have to look for them. No wonder: for she is built on an Altar of Venus.' He takes another girl to a milliner's, buys her a green-feathered hat 'the size of a hummingbird's nest', and watches her 'expand and glow like a soldier who has just been decorated'. Meanwhile, his wife reports from Kirchhorst the contents of her very intellectual dreams.

Then the restaurants. He gets taken to Maxim's but takes himself to Prunier — 'the little dining room on the first floor, fresh and smart, the colour of pale aquamarine.' 'We lived off lobster and oysters in those days,' he told me — though by 1942 the average Parisian was next to starving. One night he dines at the Tour d'Argent: 'One had the impression that the people sitting up there on high, consuming their soles and the famous duck, were looking with diabolical satisfaction, like gargoyles, over the sea of grey roofs which sheltered the hungry. In such times, to eat, and to eat well, gives one a sensation of power.'

Jünger's entry into the higher circles of collaboration begins with a lunch on the Avenue Foch, given for Speidel by Ferdinand de Brinon, Vichy's unofficial ambassador to the Occupant. There is a vase of startling white orchids 'enamelled, no doubt, in the virgin forest to attract the eyes of insects'. There is Madame de Brinon, Jewish herself but sneering at the *youpins* (Jews). There is Arletty, whose latest film is showing in the cinemas. (After the Liberation, accused of a German lover, she will turn those eyes on the judge and murmur '*Que je suis une femme . . .* ' and get off.) But the star of the party is the playwright Sacha Guitry, who entertains them with anecdotes: of Octave Mirbeau, dying in his arms and saying: '*Ne collaborez, jamais!*' — meaning: 'Never write a play with someone else!'

At a lunch in Guitry's apartment, Jünger admires the original manuscript of *L'Education sentimentale* and Sarah Bernhardt's golden salad bowl. Later he meets Cocteau and Jean Marais, 'a plebeian Antinous', and Cocteau tells how Proust would receive visitors in bed, wearing yellow kid gloves to stop him from biting his nails, and how the dust lay, 'like chinchillas', on the commodes. He meets Paul Morand, whose book on London describes the city as a colossal house: 'If the English were to build the Pyramid, they should put this book in the chamber with the mummy.' Madame Morand is a Rumanian aristocrat and keeps a grey stone Aztec goddess in her drawing room: they wonder how many victims have fallen at its feet. When Jünger sends her a copy of *The Worker*, she sends a note to his hotel: 'For me the art of living is the art of making other people work and keeping pleasure for myself.'

Thursday is the *salon* of Marie-Louise Bousquet, the Paris correspondent of *Harper's Bazaar*, who introduces her German guest to his French 'collaborationist' colleagues — Montherlant, Jouhandeau, Léautaud, and Drieu la Rochelle, the editor of the *Nouvelle Revue Française*, whose own war book, *La Comédie de Charleroi*, is a tamer counterpart to *Storm of Steel* — Drieu who will kill himself after several attempts, in 1945, leaving a note for his maid: 'Celeste, let me sleep this time.' On one of these Thursdays, Jünger brings an officer friend and his hostess says: 'With a regiment of young men like that, the Germans could have walked over France without firing a shot.'

Then there is Abel Bonnard, a travel writer and Vichy Minister of Education, who loved German soldiers and of whom Pétain said: 'It's scandalous to entrust the young to that *tapette*.' They talk of sea voyages and paintings of shipwrecks — and Jünger, who sees in the shipwreck an image of the end of the world in miniature, is delighted when Bonnard tells of a marine artist called Gudin, who would smash ship models in his studio to get the right effect.

He visits Picasso in his studio in the rue des Grands August-ins. The master shows a series of asymmetrical heads which Jünger finds rather monstrous. He tries to lure him into a general discussion of aesthetics but Picasso refuses to be drawn: 'There are chemists who spend their whole lives trying to find out what's in a lump of sugar. I want to know one thing. What is colour?'

But Paris is not all holiday. Shortly after his arrival, Captain Jünger is ordered to the Bois de Boulogne to supervise the execution of a German deserter, who has been sheltered by a Frenchwoman for nine months. He has trafficked on the black market. He has made his mistress jealous, even beaten her, and she has reported him to the police. At first, Jünger thinks he will feign illness, but then thinks better of it: 'I have to confess it was the spirit of higher curiosity that induced me to accept.' He has seen many people die, but never one who knew it in advance. How does it affect one?

There follows one of the nastiest passages in the literature of war — a firing squad painted in the manner of early Monet: the clearing in the wood, the spring foliage glistening after rain, the trunk of the ash tree riddled with the bullet holes of earlier executions. There are two groups of holes, one for the head and one for the heart, and inside the holes a few black meat flies are sleeping. Then the arrival — two military vehicles, the victim, guards, grave diggers, medical officer and pastor, also a cheap white wood coffin. The face is agreeable, attractive to women; the eyes wide, fixed, avid 'as if his whole body were suspended from them'; and in his expression something flourishing and childlike. He wears expensive grey trousers and a grey silk shirt. A fly crawls over his left cheek, then sits on his ear. Does he want an eye band? Yes. A crucifix? Yes. The medical officer pins a red card over his heart, the size of a playing card. The soldiers stand in line; the salvo; five small black holes appear on the card like drops of rain; the twitching; the pallor; the guard who wipes the handcuffs with a chiffon handkerchief. And what about the fly that danced in a shaft of sunlight?

The effectiveness of Jünger's technique intensifies as the war proceeds. The atmosphere in which he clothes the Military Command reminds one of a Racine tragedy, in which the central characters are either threatened or doomed, and all numbed into elegant paralysis by the howling tyrant offstage. Yet, though the clock ticks on toward catastrophe, they are still allowed to hope for the reprieve of a negotiated peace with the Allies.

Earlier in 1942, German officers can still raise a toast: 'Us — after the Deluge!' By the end of the year, it is apparent that the Deluge is also for them. After lunching with Paul Morand at Maxim's, Jünger sees three Jewish girls arm in arm on the rue Royale with yellow stars pinned to their dresses, and, in a wave of revulsion, feels ashamed to be seen in public. Later, on a mission to the Caucasus in December, he hears a General Müller spell out the details of the gas ovens. All the old codes of honour and decency have broken down, leaving only the foul techniques of German militarism. All the things he has loved — the weapons, the decorations, the uniforms — now, suddenly, fill him with disgust. He feels remorse but not much pity, and dreads the nemesis to come. By the time he gets back to Paris, the Final Solution is in full swing, the trains are running to Auschwitz, and a Commander Ravenstein says, 'One day my daughter will pay for all this in a brothel for niggers.'

Letters from home tell of nights of phosphorus and cities in flames. Cologne Cathedral is hit by bombs, and a man from

Hamburg reports seeing 'a woman carrying in each of her arms the corpse of a carbonized infant'. After a terrible raid on Hanover, Jünger asks the art dealer Etienne Bignou to bring up from his safe Douanier Rousseau's canvas, *La Guerre, ou la Chevauchée de la Discorde*. 'This picture is one of the greatest visions of our times . . . [It has] an infantine candour . . . a kind of purity in its terror that reminds me of Emily Brontë.'

He checks his address book and crosses out the names of the dead and missing. He reads the Book of Job. He visits Braque. He has his copy of *Catalogus Coleopterorum* rebound, and works on an 'Appeal to the Youth of Europe', to be called The Peace. A hermaphrodite butterfly gives him the idea for a treatise on symmetry and, in one brilliant aside, he writes that the genius of Hitler was to realise that the twentieth century is the century of cults — which was why men of rational intelligence were unable to understand or to stop him.

Meanwhile, with hopes of an Allied invasion, Paris recovers her perennial toughness. The Salon d'Automne of 1943 is particularly brilliant. 'Artists', he observes, 'continue to create in catastrophe like ants in a half-destroyed anthill.' Women's hats have taken on the shape of the Tower of Babel. Frank Jay Gould, an American trapped in France, reads *On the Marble Cliffs* and says: 'This guy goes from dreams to reality.'

Suddenly, in February 1944, Jünger has to dash to Berlin to rescue his son Ernstel who, in a moment of enthusiasm, has blurted out: 'The Führer should be shot!' He succeeds in getting Dönitz to reduce the sentence, but from now on he is under suspicion from the Gestapo. Back in Paris, he gets a whiff of the plot to assassinate Hitler and, one evening in May, he dines with Karl-Heinrich von Stölpnagel, the commander-in-chief. The general is tremendously erudite and plunges into a discussion of Byzantine history, of Plato, Plotinus, and the Gnostics. He is 'Hitler's biggest enemy' but he is also tired and tends to repeat himself. 'In certain circumstances,' he says, 'a superior man must be prepared to renounce life.' They talk into the night. Both men are botanists and they talk of the nightshade family — nicandra, belladonna — the plants of perpetual sleep.

After the Normandy landings, his friend Speidel — the man who will 'forget' the order to V-bomb Paris — tells of his visit to Hitler, now sunk in demented vegetarianism, yelling of 'new weapons of destruction'. When the July Plot fails, Von Stölpnagel tries to blow his brains out, but blinds himself only, and is strangled in a Berlin prison. Jünger, who had a date to dine with him that evening, comments thus on the futility of the enterprise: 'It will change little and settle nothing. I have already alluded to this in describing the Prince of Sunmyra in *On the Marble Cliffs*.'

Panic at the Hotel Raphäel. The Americans are near, and the salon hostesses gearing for a change. At a last luncheon for her German friends, Florence Jay Gould comes back from the telephone, smiling: '*La Bourse reprend.*' It's time for goodbyes. A last Thursday with Marie-Louise Bousquet, who says: 'Now the Tea-Time boys are coming.' A last conversation with the Princesse de Sixte-Bourbon. A last bottle of Chambertin 1904 with its art nouveau label. And here is his last entry for Paris:

14 August, en route

Sudden departure at dusk. In the afternoon, last farewells. I left the room in order and put a bouquet on the table. I left *pourboires*. Unfortunately I left in a drawer some irreplaceable letters.

The rest of Captain Jünger's war is not a happy story. Relieved of his functions, he goes home to Kirchhorst where he sorts out his papers, reads tales of shipwrecks, reads Huysmans's *A Rebours*, and waits for the rumble of American tanks. When a telegram comes with news of Ernstel's death on the Italian front, he loses the will to be clever and reveals the stricken horror of a parent who has lost what he loves the

313

most. A photo of Ernstel hangs next to that of his protector, General Speidel, in his library.

Jünger refused to appear before a 'de-Nazification' tribunal on the grounds that he had never been a Nazi. But the whole course of his career put him outside the pale for the post-war German literary establishment. If his ideal was 'the desert' then he was condemned, until recently, to stay in it. Since 1950 he has lived in the beautiful, rolling country of Upper Swabia, at Wilflingen, in a house that lies opposite a castle of the Barons von Stauffenberg, where, by coincidence, Pierre Laval was interned after his escape from France in 1944. (Siegmaringen, Marshall Pétain's residence and the scene of Céline's *D'un Château à l'autre*, is only a few miles down the road.)

My own visit to Jünger five years ago was an odd experience. At eighty, he had snow-white hair but the bounce of a very active schoolboy. He had a light cackling laugh and tended to drift off if he was not the centre of attention. He had recently published a book describing his experiments with drugs, from his first sniff of ether to lysergic acid, and was about to publish an enormous novel called *Eumeswil*. The ground floor of the house was furnished in the Biedermeier style, with net curtains and white faience stoves, and was inhabited by his second wife, a professional archivist and textual critic of Goethe. Jünger's own quarters upstairs had the leathery look of a soldier's bunker, with cabinets for beetles on the landing and a sea of memorabilia — fossils, shells, helmets from both wars, skeletons of animals, and a collection of sandglasses. (In 1954 he wrote *A Treatise on the Sandglass* — a philosophical meditation on the passage of time.)

If I had hoped for more memories of Paris under the Occupation, I was disappointed. In answer to questions, he simply recited an excerpt from the diary, though occasionally he would rush to the filing cabinet and come back with some *pièce justificative*. One of these was a letter from his friend

Henri de Montherlant, quoting a remark of Tolstoy: 'There is no point in visiting a great writer because he is incarnate in his works.' Since I had an interest in Montherland, I was able to draw Jünger out a little further, and he returned again from the filing cabinet, this time flourishing a rather blotchy sheet of Xerox paper on which was written:

> Le suicide fait partie du capitale
> de l'humanité,
>
> Ernst Jünger
> 8 juin 1972.

This aphorism of Jünger's dates from the Thirties, and the story goes that Alfred Rosenberg once said: 'It's a pity Herr Jünger doesn't make use of his capital.' But the scene you have to imagine is this:

Montherlant, dying of cancer, is sitting in his apartment on the Quai Voltaire, surrounded by his collection of Greek and Roman marbles. On his desk are a bottle of champagne, a revolver, a pen, and a sheet of paper. He writes: '*Le suicide fait partie . . .*'

Bang!

The blotches were photocopies of blood.

1981

ON THE ROAD WITH
MRS G.

Mrs Gandhi's secretary — her Assistant Private Secretary — called to say that she would be driving at four-thirty in the morning to Pantnagar Agricultural University where the riot police had shot some peasants. Estimates of the numbers dead varied from thirteen to four hundred.

'If you want to see Madame in action,' he said, 'don't throw up the chance.'

We left Delhi in the half-light: Mrs Gandhi's air-conditioned Chevrolet leading a procession of five cars. Our driver had been to the Doon School with Sanjay Gandhi, and his nickname was Dumpy. His companion was a tall, dark, graceful girl who had been a model in New York and wore a painted Rajasthani sari.

'Isn't Mrs G. rather marvellous?' she said.

Later, when the hired claque whizzed by in a minibus, she said: 'Do look! There go the rowdies!'

At Rundrapur, Congress-Indira workers had put together a fair-sized, if rather taciturn crowd. But once the Rowdies started bawling 'Indira Gandhi Zindabad!' people came running from all directions and jammed the yard outside the Guest House. The police had to bash a way for her to pass upstairs. A man shouted in my ear: 'Everyone is waiting for

Indiraji. The people have love for her.'

Mrs Gandhi wore a green-and-white striped sari, and sat down to a breakfast that never came. I introduced myself.

'Oh! *that's* who you are!' she said. 'I can only give you my little finger to shake because there's something the matter with the others.'

She offered round a piece of soap in case anyone wanted to wash. From time to time, she stepped out onto the balcony and glowered at the outstretched palms and betel-stained mouths of the crowd.

Notwithstanding the imperial nose and the great brooding eyes, she seemed small, frail and nervous. She had a tic in her left cheek, and kept rolling her tongue round the right side of her mouth. My immediate impulse was to protect her.

She went into the bedroom, and a hysterical young man in glasses tried to barge past her Sikh bodyguards.

'Let me see her!' he shrieked. 'You're the ones who ruined her reputation during the Emergency.'

The town of Pantnagar lies on a fertile plain of sugar plantations and maize-fields. Along the horizon, the foothills of the Himalayas flickered in the heat haze.

The local farmers are Jats. They are a caste of peasant proprietors who have resisted every attempt to make them share their land with the landless. They employ a shifting workforce of Purbias: a poor, landless caste from the eastern half of the state. About 6,000 Purbias are employed on the Agricultural University's farms: only Purbias died in the shooting.

News of the atrocity had filled the Delhi newspapers for five days: the date fell on the fifty-ninth anniversary of the Amritsar Massacre. Worse, the men involved in the shooting were Jats. Jats had control of the University and were running it as a private fief. The Vice-Chancellor, a Mr D.P. Singh, was a Jat, and he was the nominee of Mrs Gandhi's arch-enemy, the Home Minister of the ruling Janata Government, Charan Singh.

Charan Singh left Mrs Gandhi's cabinet in 1977 with the comment, 'She never speaks the truth, even by mistake!' He is an obdurate seventy-six-year-old, an agricultural economist and a Gandhian. He abhors the city and heavy industry: India is to be saved by its independent peasant farmers. At his prompting, the Janata is channelling investment away from the industrial to the rural sector. The reaction of big business has been to pump money into Mrs Gandhi's campaign.

Charan Singh also heads the movement for her arrest and trial — although he bungled it last October. The police officer turned up with the wrong kind of warrant. (She had fixed this through spies inside the Ministry.) So, by the time he returned with the right warrant, she had phoned the entire press corps and was staging a monumental scene in the front garden.

'Handcuff me!' she screamed. 'If I'm a common criminal, I demand to be handcuffed.'

In the kitchen, the cook — whom I managed to interview — was shredding documents with an Italian noodle-cutter belonging to Rajiv Gandhi's wife, Sonia.

Owing to a heart-condition, Charan Singh did not show up at Pantnagar in the summer heat. Nor did any member of the Janata Government. But Mrs G. was not going to let the opportunity slip.

At noon, the cars halted by a grain-mill where, half an hour after the main shooting, a police platoon had gunned down five workers as they were having lunch. Dr Pant, a serene, bearded academic, showed us round.

'Pure barbarity!' he muttered. 'How could any civilised government permit such a thing?'

Mrs G. took little notice but strode round the exhibits with a grim face. She peered at a pool of caked blood on the grass. She peered at a lamp post buckled by bullets, and at a bullet-hole through a boy's shoulder. Then she met the widows. She gave them no consolation. Instead, she offered her jagged three-quarter profile to them and the photographers. The widows seemed quite pleased.

At the University campus an excitable crowd was waiting. Mrs G. mounted a canopied podium, and the speeches began. Members of the Provincial Armed Constabulary — the PACs — strutted about in perfectly pressed khaki. In one of the buildings some students had begun a 'fast till death' — which they called off the moment she left.

My friend of the afternoon was Sanjay's wife, Menaka — a pretty, freckle-faced girl dressed in scarlet kurta-pyjamas. She had not had an easy time. Her father, Lt Col Anand, was thought to have siphoned funds away from Sanjay's Maruti car factory and diverted them to Congress-I. Last June he was found shot dead in a field, lying on newspapers full of the scandal. A note at his side read 'Sanjay worry unbearable'. Neither dogs nor vultures had touched the corpse for two days. The gun was missing. The arms were rigid. It was an odd kind of suicide.

'Come on, Brucie.' Menaka took my hand. 'Come and watch me do my fishwife act!'

She led me to the Children's Park where the PACs had pitched camp.

'Show me your rifles,' she screeched at a kind-faced sergeant.

'I can't, Menakaji.'

'You showed them when you murdered people. Why can't you show them to me?'

She raised her camera.

'Please, Menakaji, don't photograph me. I have a wife and a mother. We had nothing to do with the killing. It was the 10th Battalion from Meerut.

The 10th Battalion had been transferred.

319

The speeches ended and Mrs Gandhi went to inspect the scene of the crime: at a crossroads between the student hostel and some staff bungalows.

The trouble began when some non-Jats among the students and staff encouraged the Purbias to strike for higher pay. A local Congress-I politician got in on the act. The Vice-Chancellor panicked and asked for a detachment of police. About a thousand Purbias first prayed in their temple and then set off in a protest march towards the administrative building. The PACs blocked their path — and they sat down.

The students, confined to their hostel, had a grandstand view from the roof. They saw the police officer fire a single shot into the air, and saw his men fire straight into the crowd. Some of the strikers ran for an open drain where we saw their sandals still floating on the surface. Others rushed for the bungalows but were dragged out and bayoneted. There was a list of 81 dead: 160 were missing.

Yet the cheerful crowds milling around Mrs G. gave the event the air of a race-meeting. A senior student boasted it was he who had persuaded her to come. He knew all along that the Jats had planned the massacre for that morning.

'In which case,' I said, 'why didn't you stop the Purbias from marching to their deaths?'

He shrugged and walked away.

A Janata supporter said the whole thing had been set up by agents-provocateurs.

'And now let me show you something absolutely gruesome,' said a bright-eyed boy from Kerala. He pointed to a bed of zinnias and petunias, in which there was a reddish smear, buzzing with flies.

'The brains of a murdered man,' he added, melodramatically. 'Pantnagar produces the best seeds in India. Now human seeds have been sown in the canefields.'

The police, he said, loaded the bodies onto a truck, burned

them with gasoline in the canefield, and ploughed in the remains.

'And even now, Sir, in that place you will smell putrefaction and burnt flesh!'

The students dug up the bones and took them to the laboratory, but the verdict passed on to Charan Singh pronounced them the bones of jackals.

'This is a question mark,' Mrs G. said to me in Delhi two days later. 'Whether the bones were jackals or whether people were burned in the fields, that has not been proved. What the students say is: "Why did they set fire to the fields? They must be hiding *something*." But when we talked to Dr Pant he wasn't sure whether the bones were human or not.'

'So you think the shooting was planned in advance?'

'It's very difficult to say,' she said. 'I mean, it seems so senseless. I always find it very difficult to believe in anything for which you can't find a cause. It all seems so cruel . . .'

Delhi

Mrs G. lives in a low white bungalow, No. 12 Willingdon Crescent, a few doors away from her father's house, Teen Murti. It is an excellent spot for staging a political comeback, because Teen Murti is a museum and place of pilgrimage. She shares these cramped quarters with her two sons, Rajiv and Sanjay, their wives, and Rajiv's two children. The cook has to prepare meals at the oddest hours, for the family and a couple of exhausted Irish wolfhounds. From time to time Mrs G. goes on fast — and will then order quantities of deep-frozen trout.

Access to Mrs G. is controlled by the Assistant Private Secretary, R.K. Dharan: people say she is a puppet in his hands. He was once a tourist guide at the Red Fort. It was he who persuaded Sanjay there was a loophole in the constitution which would enable them to call a State of Emergency — although it is doubtful, in retrospect, if either was sufficiently literate to interpret a document of this kind. But Sanjay persuaded his mother. R.K. took their orders to the President, and most of the Opposition went to jail.

R.K.'s office was in a garden shed. His hair was heavily pomaded, and he wore a white bush jacket. He seemed very anxious to make a good impression, and said we could call him 'R.K.'. There was a stack of books and magazines on his desk.

We talked for a while until the phone rang.

'Excuse me, Sir,' he said, 'Madame is calling.'

He waddled off towards the bungalow, but hastened back and, removing the top-most book, inserted it into the middle of the pile.

'Psst!' I called to my photographer friend Eve Arnold. 'Watch the door. I'm damned if I'm not going to see what that book is.'

The author was Chatpathi Rao, and the title *Mimicry and Mono-acting*. It was a handbook for ventriloquists.

In another shed visitors had congregated for the *darshan*, or morning audience. At 9.15 Mrs G. emerged from behind the bamboo blind of the verandah. Someone handed her a black umbrella. She swept past a bed of red roses, and swept on to greet the crowd.

There was a minor hullaballoo when Sanjay and Menaka came out with armfuls of papers and drove off to Tis Hazari Court, where he was in the dock.

Sanjay makes a very odd impression: plump, balding, with thick, bright, downcurving lips. He is, of course, his mother's blind spot. As a boy, he was a near-delinquent and she had to rescue him from various scrapes. In England he worked as an apprentice in the Rolls-Royce factory. In India, his Maruti people's car was a fiasco. During the Emergency, he drew up the list of people to be locked away. Finally Mrs G. could bear the loneliness of dictatorial rule no longer. She overrode him – and called the election she lost.

The Janata has a variety of criminal charges against him: the murder of a dacoit, the illegal bulldozing of slums in the Muslim quarter, frauds at Maruti factory. But the charge they are pressing is that he burned a satirical film called *Kissa Kursee Kaa*, *The Story of a Chair*.

Mrs G. received us in a white room bare but for a vase of gladioli, one or two paintings, some lumps of quartz crystal and a spiky modernistic sculpture. Her chair was stationed beneath a photo of Pandit Nehru in profile. She presented herself as a modern, practical housewife: indeed the only one capable of ordering the affairs of India. She kept turning her hands over as if rinsing them – and knew exactly how to time the intervals between her smiles.

But the interview was a bitter disappointment. Most of it consisted of petulant and rambling attacks against unidentified enemies. She attributed her election defeat to the 'vicious propaganda of outside forces', and when I asked her to name them, she said, 'I couldn't do that.'

Her reasons for calling the Emergency made even less sense. She implied that Jayaprakash Narayan's non-violent resistance movement had been leading India towards a civil war, like Bangladesh:

'My chief ministers said, "Well, if you want to be a martyr that's all right for you, but there's no reason why you should force us into the same situation."'

I asked about her plans:

'I have no plans.'

I asked about her political beliefs:

'I really think I am a socialist because I believe in the basic things.'

I asked about the secret of her attraction for the Indian masses:

'Basically, I am a sympathetic person and that's what creates a bond.'

When I slightly overstepped the mark, she countered with a crack at the English:

'There were these refugees . . . pouring over the border from East Pakistan. So I said to my cabinet, "We'll have to send them back. We can't feed all those people." "Well," they said, "we can't send them back." So I said, "Then let them go to England or some rich place."'

The only real point of interest was her description of looking after her mother as she died of T.B. in a Swiss sanatorium. It was in Switzerland that she first read the story of Joan of Arc.

'Rather morbid it sounds now,' she said, 'but I didn't think of it in those terms. It was the sacrifice of Joan of Arc that attracted me, the girl who gave up her life for her country . . . '

Over the next couple of weeks she repeatedly harped on the theme of Joan of Arc. Often, when there was a lull in the conversation, she would start up the familiar refrain: 'Joan of Arc . . . the girl who gave up her life for her country . . . '

Only when I switched off the tape-recorder did the conversation take an interesting turn: 'Why did you put Rajmatas Jaipur and Gwalior into jail?'

'*I* didn't put them in jail. It was nothing political. They were in for some kind of currency fiddle.'

'You have said the Janata Government is a *kitchri*. In England we have the same word, "kedgeree".'

'Yes, we used to have it for breakfast at Teen Murti. Lady Mountbatten taught my father's cook how to make it: smoked haddock, rice and hard–boiled eggs. But in India *kitchri* means a "mess". I'll say it again and again, "The Janata is a mess."'

'Do you think Mr Bhutto will hang?'

'People who come to me from Pakistan say, "Yes, he will."
After all there's been no little movement to save him inside the
country and that's what gave them the encouragement. I'm
sure he did order the murder. He comes from a part of the
country where life is incredibly cheap.'

Mrs G. met Bhutto in Simla after the Indian victory in East
Bengal.

'What was he like?' I asked.

'Well, when he came to see me he was extremely
frightened. We were standing together outside the Governor's
House and the crowd was looking on. It wasn't a hostile
crowd or anything. But he said to me, "I don't like the look of
that crowd. Couldn't you wave at them or something?" So I
said, "No. Wave at them yourself. After all, it's your show."
So he waved and they waved back. But even after we got
Bhutto and his daughter inside, it took us quite a lot to get
them calmed down.'

'But he was rather charming, wasn't he?'

'He was extremely nasty to me.'

Cochin, Kerala

After a whistle-stop round of speeches at Bombay airport, we
have followed Mrs G. to Kerala where she hopes to mend a
split within the Congress Party. Her faction here is quite
strong: a Kerala MP, Mr C.M. Stephen, is her Leader of the
Opposition in Lok Sabha, or Lower House. But she has been a
controversial — not to say hated — figure since 1960, when she
persuaded her father to boot out the elected Communist State
Government.

They put on a good show at the airport. Chanting crowds
cheered her and Mr Stephen to a white Mercedes that
belonged to a local drink concessionaire. We followed in a
taxi.

On the outskirts of town, a lathi-charge was coming down
the street. The anti-Indira demonstrators dropped their black

flags and scampered away from the 'hard hats'. We swerved. A man fell close to the taxi and was clubbed in the gutter. At the fourth blow blood spurted over his face. Sixty-one casualties were taken to the General Hospital. No one was killed.

Mrs G. installed herself in the Old Divan's residence: a wooden building wherein, in the ground-floor saloon, there were ferns in a brass jardinière, watercolours of Venice and a print of the *Madonna of the Rocks*.

At sunset black clouds banked up and burst: but the downpour did not prevent about a quarter of a million drenched figures from filing past to pay their respects.

Mrs G. reviewed them from a balcony on the top storey, seated on a chair which had been placed on a table. She jammed a torch between her knees, directing the beam upwards to light her face and arms. She rotated the arms as if performing the mudras of Lakshmi, Goddess of Wealth. One group of marchers carried mock corpses, wrapped in orange cloth and with names in devanagari script. They were the three old men of the Janata: Morariji Desai, Jagjivan Ram and Charan Singh.

'They'll stop at nothing,' Mrs G. laughed, 'but I suppose it's all right.'

I was sitting on the table.

'Do get me some more of those cashew nuts.' She turned to me. 'You've no idea how tiring it is to be a goddess.'

The rain cleared and I went into the street to join the marchers. Their pupils dilated as they gazed in adoration at the tiny illuminated figure.

An hour later, I was sitting again behind Mrs G. on the podium of the Cochin Stadium: but the rally was a dismal performance. She spoke in English, in a thin, whining voice, and listed a catalogue of accusations against the Janata.

'No control . . . strife . . . no law and order . . . atrocities are commonplace . . . no homes for the homeless . . . Harijans

(Untouchables) burned alive . . . lathi charges . . .
strengthening the voice of the voiceless they are mo
ested in haranguing me . . . But we have something
important, the love of the people. We can feel the pulse of
masses . . . '

She had not felt the pulse of this mass. Thousands and
thousands turned their backs, and, in the arc lights, we
watched the upper tiers draining, and snaking for the exits.

At the breakfast press-conference Mrs G., dressed in a crisp
flower-printed sari, demonstrated her flawless technique for
dealing with a roomful of men. She poured from the teapot in
her best memsahib manner. If anyone presumed to ask an
awkward question, she said, '*Do* have another cup of tea!'

One journalist, bolder than the rest, was not to be put off.

'Why,' he asked, 'when you were in power, did you throw
out the foreign press? Why are you now courting the foreign
press?'

She looked hard in my direction: 'I don't see the foreign
press.'

At eight sharp the motorcade set off north for Calicut. Mrs G.
sat on the back seat of the drink concessionaire's Mercedes.
We followed in far greater comfort and style, in the doctor's
car: an immaculate white Humber Super Snipe with the Red
Cross flag fluttering from the bonnet.

'What could go wrong with Mrs Gandhi?' I asked the
doctor.

'She might get stoned,' he said wearily. 'But the worst we
expect is an allergy to flowers.'

The doctor had already surprised us with the bust of Stalin in
his living room. This was his story:

Sometime in the Fifties, he was a house-man at the General
Hospital in Newcastle-on-Tyne. Among his patients was a
Conservative MP who was expected to die of a bloodclot

approaching his heart. The MP wanted to die, but wanted to live until Saturday when his racehorse was running at Longchamps. On Friday evening came news that the horse had been kicked and couldn't run.

'Damn it,' said the MP. 'I'd have known what to do. Feed him a couple of pounds of onions.'

The doctor, remembering an ayurvedic cure, asked, 'Do you ever eat onions?'

'Hate onions,' said the MP. 'Always have.'

'Well, I'm going to feed you two pounds of onions.'

They forced the onions down the MP's throat. The clot dissolved — and the man lived.

The doctor took out his album of press-cuttings. *Time* showed a smiling young man in horn-rimmed glasses: the discoverer of carraganen, a chemical contained in onions that was a powerful anti-coagulant and might conceivably transform heart-surgery.

But you couldn't patent an onion: the rest was a sad tale. He came back to India. No one took any notice. He now worked for a private clinic in Cochin owned by a man I felt was completely deranged.

On the way we passed pink-eared elephants, brick-kilns and churches that looked like Chinese pagodas. Most of the slogans were welcoming. But from time to time a string of old shoes was suspended across the road: the worst of all Hindu insults.

One graffito read, 'Indira Gandhi is a notorious fascist witch'.

At every village Mrs G. got out of the car, mounted a platform decked with Congress-I flags, and thanked the crowds for their 'warm and dutiful welcome'. As the morning wore on, more and more garlands of jasmine and marigolds were festooned around her neck: each one had a banknote pinned to it. The heat had the effect of moving her to shriller and shriller rhetoric: 'The full force of the Government is on one small woman.'

Eve Arnold and I go through alternative phases of 'Love Indira' or 'Loathe Indira'. Today was 'Love Indira' day.

At the approach to Calicut, the Black Flag boys were out in force. Mrs G., slumped under her mound of flowers, got through unscathed, but the Humber Super Snipe, like some stately relic of the Raj, was obviously mistaken for her car. A small rock smashed the driver's window and hit him on the head. Another rock smashed my window and landed in my lap. The flying glass lightly grazed my scalp and the side of my neck.

Suitably patched up, I went to the afternoon press-conference where Mrs G. was again handing round cups of tea.

'Good Heavens, Mr Chatwin,' she said, 'whatever happened to you?'

'I was stoned, Mrs Gandhi.'

'That's what comes of following me around.'

But when the conference broke up, she rushed towards me: 'Are you sure you're all right? Have they really got all the glass out? Well, thank Heaven for that! Do you want to lie down?'

No. I did not want to lie down. But Eve did. She was wilting in the heat.

Mrs G. sized up the situation and led Eve into her own bedroom where her briefcase was open and papers were strewn about. She laid her down on the bed and let her sleep for two hours. She then returned with the eternal cup of tea, and said she needed the room to change.

It was, of course, excellent public relations. It was also very pleasant behaviour.

I talked to Mrs G.'s secretary, Nirmala Deshpande, a small,

determined spinster who is very vociferous on the subject of her employer. Miss Deshpande was sitting on the floor unthreading the banknotes from the garlands.

'Look what we got on the way,' she said, stuffing them into a bag. 'The people give her what they have.'

One of Mrs G.'s secrets, she said, was her stamina. Physically, she could outpace every other Indian politician. In the elections of Andhra and Karnataka she went to bed once in sixteen days.

For dinner at the Circuit House we had real mulligatawny soup made of fresh pepper and asafoetida. Then we went to another evening rally. The Black Flag boys had rioted in the afternoon and the Security Guards were taking no chances. Rifles and sub-machine-guns glinted in the moonlight. Mrs G., as usual, was completely fearless: but I did wish she'd make a better speech and not rant on about 'witch-hunts against me and my family'.

After all, it was *she* who locked up the Opposition.

Mrs G. left Calicut at 3.30 am on her way to Manipur, a tribal area on the Burmese border which was out of bounds for foreigners.

Eve and I went to Madras and to the temples at Mahabalipuram, and then returned to Delhi. The mood had changed, drastically. When we first arrived, most people thought Mrs G. was finished. Now, they were tempering their words.

A by-election had been called in the constituency of Azamgarh in Uttar Pradesh. The Congress-I candidate, a Mrs Kidwai, stood a good chance of winning. If she did win, it would mean the Hindu heartland had forgiven Mrs G. for the Emergency — and that nothing would stop her coming back.

One Delhi journalist had it all worked out: Janata was Weimar: 12 Willingdon Crescent was Hitler's cell in Landsberg Castle.

Delhi talk:

'All this nonsense about the 700 million. As far as we're concerned, there are 700 Indians and we know them all.'

'Moraji's quite right. There should be an auto-urine therapy clinic in every Indian village.'

'We've got to stop behaving like Hamlets.'

'She can't come back with all those flunkeys and syco-phants. She's got nobody to come back with.'

'Hindus have always worshipped power for power's sake. In the Hindu pantheon, the male god is passive, whereas the mother-goddess, his *Shakti*, is the active partner.'

'The atmosphere around Mrs Gandhi has always reminded me of *Arsenic and Old Lace*' (Piloo Mody, one of her ex-cabinet ministers).

No aspect of the Emergency was more surreal or more damaging to Mrs G. than Sanjay's programme for sterilising the Muslim men and bulldozing the slums of Old Delhi. The two went hand in hand. If you refused sterilisation, you were bulldozed and packed off to a shanty-town.

Rukhsana Sultana — a gorgeous girl and friend of Sanjay — had been, semi-officially, in charge of the programme.

When I called on her, she was wearing a mass of flowered grey chiffon, and sunglasses in a darkened room. Before she took up 'social work', she had run a jewellery boutique. Her servant brought in some red plush boxes, from which she pulled strings of emeralds, alexandrines, rubies and pearls.

'All our vasectomies', she said, 'were done in a lovely air-conditioned cellar. I and my workers had to sweat it out on the street.

'At my first vasectomy,' she went on, 'I simply passed out . . . The blood and all. But after a while I got used to it. Three minutes on the table . . . snip . . . snip . . . and they were away . . .

'In India one's got to have family planning. We were brilliant. We were idealistic. But we were young and inexperienced and we were victims of vicious propaganda. I must tell you, none of us was working for money. We all came from prosperous families. Our idealism was selfless.'

The programme ended in the famous riot at the Turkman Gate in which at least fifty people were killed.

'But I'm sure she's coming back,' said Rukhsana. 'The people of India have to have one leader. They worship Mrs G. like a god. Indians are only capable of worshipping one God.'

'I thought they worshipped a lot of gods.'

'Hundreds of gods! Thousands of gods! But all manifestations of the same OM. You know what is OM? Well, for them Mrs G. is a manifestation of the OM.'

Azamgarh, Uttar Pradesh

We got here by taxi from Benares in the sweltering May heat. The fields were grey: the cultivators had nothing much to do but wait for the monsoon. Azamgarh itself was a dusty, almost shadeless town on the banks of a sluggish river. There was one hotel. It was full.

In the restaurant — if it could actually be called a restaurant — we overheard three Congress-I workers weighing the pros and cons of getting a Muslim stooge to burn a copy of the Ramayana — and so cause an incident. A very young Delhi journalist was eating his dahl and chapatis. He raised an eyebrow as we came in, as if to say, 'The Brits!'

After a meagre lunch Eve and I set off in search of a bed and, after threading through a mass of rickshaws, were shown a squalid communal doss-house.

'There's nothing for it,' she said. 'We'll have to go back to Benares.'

'We mustn't give up.' I said. 'I think if we're very nice to that young journalist, he'll give up his room for you.'

He was still in the restaurant.

'Can I introduce you to Mrs Arnold?' I said.

'Not Eve Arnold!' He jumped up. 'Your pictures of Joan Crawford are absolutely fabulous!'

Eve almost fainted with pleasure — and it all worked out as I hoped. She got the room and Rajiv (as I shall call him) and I joined a long line of sleepers on the roof.

Rajiv was an exhilarating companion. He had been everywhere in India roughing it. He could take in Hindi and spit it out in English from the sides of his mouth. The Janata candidate was not much in evidence, but we called on Mrs Kidwai: a nice, stout, motherly woman who had set up her headquarters in a ruined rajah's palace on the riverbank. She had carefully modelled her style on Mrs G.

A man asked me, 'Excuse me, Sir. Is she Indiraji's niece?'

Mrs G. was expected to arrive at the border of the constituency around three. While Eve took a nap, Rajiv and I followed Mrs Kidwai's car. But as we passed a clump of ancient mangoes, we saw the green-and-orange flags of the Janata. Rajiv shouted, 'Vajpayee!' — and we tumbled out of the car.

Atal Behri Vajpayee, the Foreign Minister — perhaps the best Foreign Minister India has had — was addressing a crowd assembled in the shade. He had silver hair, a square intelligent face, a dramatic use of gesture, and mastery of metaphor. His audience clung to every word. The level of discourse made Western electioneering seem like some barbaric rout. This was true democracy.

'The squabbles of the Janata', he said, 'are not so unhealthy. All Indians like to squabble.

'Take a bowl of milk,' he continued. 'It hangs over the fire on a rope of five strings. Think of those strings as the Janata. The cats playing round the fire think they are going to snap. But they don't snap. The cats get tired of waiting and fight among themselves . . .

'But this is no ordinary election, my friends. Had it been so, why would Indira Gandhi have bothered to visit you for the last five days?'

Mrs G. and her bandwagon turned up on time. She wore the look of victory. On the window of her used Ford Falcon was an advertisement: 'Go naked in the SUN. Action-packed weekly.' A Jeep-load of Sikh bodyguards followed. One was a vast and sinister man with ice-blue eyes and a turban to match. Proudly, he showed me the revolvers nestling in his rolls of fat.

'She's coming back,' he said, 'like de Gaulle.'

At dusk, they propped her above the roof of the Jeep and, with the torch shining upwards, she really did look like an image on a juggernaut.

Bilaria Ganj, Azamgarh

Mrs Kidwai began the speeches while Mrs G., in vengeful vermilion, glared at the crowd. She then rose to speak and told such outrageous lies that Rajiv and I, crouching under the platform, made a commotion of protest.

'There are no compulsory sterilisations in this part of the country,' she continued blandly.

'Liar!' shrieked a voice from the crowd. 'I have been sterilised!'

He was a shy, frail boy shaking with nerves. He wore steel-framed glasses and a black cap. He was a Muslim divinity student.

'Murderess!' he shouted, as the Sikh bodyguards bore down on him. 'She killed my friend. She put my teacher in prison. And my father! And my grandfather! Why shouldn't I call her a murderess?'

The Sikh in the ice-blue turban clamped his hand over the boy's mouth, and dragged him away.

Around five in the morning, Mrs G. dipped herself in the Ganges. She did not want to be photographed, so her secretary gave us the wrong time and the wrong place.

We returned to the Circuit House where a splendid breakfast was being prepared. The place was so nineteenth-century in atmosphere that one half-expected the sound of braying English voices.

Mrs G. sat at the head of the table flanked by her faithful ex-Minister of Railways, Mr Kamlapathi Tripathi, and a local Congress-I politician. I sat next to the politician, and on my right sat the Congress-I Youth Leader for Delhi. He had bad gums.

Mrs G.'s face was working wrathfully. What she knew — and we did not yet know — was that Sanjay had been arrested in the night and put in Tikhar fort.

'Permit me to ask you, Sir,' asked Youth-for-Delhi, 'which varsity in England did you attend?'

'It was in Scotland,' I said, 'I went to Edinburgh.'

'It is not possible!'

'It is possible.'

'Edinburgh was my father's varsity.'

'He was probably a medical student.'

'How could you know that?'

'Indians who come to Edinburgh are nearly always medical students.'

'And which was the subject of your study?'

'Archaeology,' I said. 'But I also learned some Sanskrit.'

'Sanskrit, yes. Language of the Ancient Aryans!'

'Correct.'

'Tell me, Sir, have you ever heard of the Greek Philosopher Plato?'

'I have.'

'He came to India to learn about the Ideal State from the ancient Brahmins.'

335

'Plato in India?' Mrs G. piped up. 'I knew he was in Greece, but I never knew he came to India.'

'Oh! but he did!' Youth-for-Delhi warmed to his theme. 'And shortly after his visit, some Brahmins travelled all the way to Germany taking with them their sacred vision symbol, the swastika . . .'

A look of utter disgust passed across Mrs G.'s face. She gave me a filthy look as if it were my fault for having lured her into this ridiculous exchange. In a far corner of the room Rajiv was having a tumultuous row with the ice-blue turban, who accused us of 'abusing Mrs Gandhi'.

I was pro-Indira that morning: she seemed so bizarre and eccentric. I felt that anyone who aspired to rule India was bound to end up a bit barmy.

But Eve was down on her and, as a real pro, intuitively spotted her chance. I overheard snatches of her honeyed words. She had photographed so many facets of Indira's life: in a crowd, talking to villagers, to politicians or to her grandchildren. The one thing missing was the spiritual dimension.

Mrs G. obviously needed time to think, yet I was un-surprised when the two of them made for the old Club Room, and locked the door. They stayed there fifteen minutes. Then Mrs G. re-emerged, entirely cool and collected, and set about receiving a stream of well-wishers.

'I really got her this time,' said Eve. 'Here, come and have a look!'

She had prevailed on Mrs G. to sit meditating in the lotus position on a splay-legged coffee-table, at one side of which stood a jardinière with an aspidistra. Behind these hung an English hunting print: *The Quorn take a fence*.

'What a picture!' said Eve.

We parted in Benares. I took the train to Sultanpur to investi-gate the story of a wolf-boy. Eve had things to do in Delhi.

I returned around lunchtime the day she was due to take the night flight to London. She had been forced out of her hotel room at twelve, and was waiting in the lobby. We went upstairs to my bedroom. I had hardly set foot through the door when the phone rang.

'Hello, is that you, Bruce?' came a crisp voice. 'It's Indira here!' She had not called me Bruce before.

'You know I'm a little bit worried about one of those photos Eve took of me in Benares. She wanted to show the spiritual side of my character — and of course I am a Kashmiri Brahmin. But we have so many different religions in India. We have Buddhists, we have Jews, Muslims, Hindus, Parsees, Christians. I don't want to favour one religion over another. I wonder if you'd mind not publishing it with the article?'

I clamped my palm over the mouthpiece:

'She doesn't want the photo published with the article.'

'Great!' said Eve. 'I could make the cover of *Time* with that picture!'

'Of course,' I said to Indira, 'we won't publish it with the article.'

'Well, that's very kind,' she said. 'When are you coming to see me again?'

'We've seen a lot of each other lately.'

'No. No. I'd love to see you again. Why don't you drop in for coffee tomorrow? I'll expect you at 10.30.'

Delhi

That evening I called on Mrs G.'s deadly foe, the Rajmata of Gwalior who is a very orthodox Hindu.

'I've just come back from Benares,' I said, 'where Mrs Gandhi dipped herself in the Ganges.'

'Sacrilege!' said the Rajmata.

She described her time in Tikhar fort during the Emergency. H.H. Jaipur was in the next cell, and spent most of her time reading the *Memoirs of Saint-Simon*.

337

'But I'm no great reader,' she said. 'I was an ordinary girl who happened to marry a maharajah. So I decided to take this opportunity to meet the kind of women one would never normally meet — prostitutes, murderesses and so on. They would come to my cell at five o'clock. We called it The Gwalior Club . . .'

Around the same hour H.H. Jaipur was in the habit of taking her bath, into which she always put a lot of bath-essence. An open drain ran along the balcony.

'The women loved it,' she said. 'They would get down on their knees and smell the scented water.'

Delhi
12 Willingdon Crescent

The news from Azamgarh had come in. Mrs G.'s candidate had a majority of 35,385 votes.

'Yes,' she said, as she poured the coffee, 'we are quite pleased with the result. Of course, we expected some rigging and that's why we made as much noise as possible.'

Sanjay's arrest had also helped: 'People came up and said, "Our son is taken away."'

All she wanted was reassurance about the photo, yet she felt obliged to launch into a monologue: 'What the women in the villages need is cheaper potatoes. I say to my people, "If the women in the villages don't get cheaper potatoes, how are they going to live?"'

I cut her short.

'Well,' I said, 'it's been a very interesting time since I last saw you. A wolf-boy's been found. They've taken him to Mother Teresa's orphanage at Lucknow.'

'Like Mowgli?' said Mrs G.

'Yes.'

'I've always heard about those wolf-children but I've never actually seen one. Will the child ever talk? It would be very interesting to know what it was like to be brought up by a

338

wolf-mother.'

'No,' I said, 'I'm afraid he won't. If any child is deprived of human speech during his early years, the frontal lobes — which deal with speech and symbolic thought — will fail to develop.'

'How old was the child when it was found?'

'About five or six.'

'Well, Sanjay didn't speak until he was six . . .

'But we knew a family in Bombay whose children didn't speak until they were eight! AND THEY WERE PERFECTLY NORMAL!'

Silence.

She looked utterly stricken and all too human. I was sitting quite close to her and brushed her hand.

'Don't worry,' I murmured.

Gradually, she resumed the conversation. I was amazed to hear her say the word 'Thatcher'.

'Quite a different personality!' she said. 'How that woman wants to be PM! When she came here to Delhi she was so nervous. I felt like telling her, "If you want to be PM that badly, you'll never make it."'

London

I called Eve the evening of my arrival — to hear how the photos had turned out.

'Come over right away,' she said.

She was very agitated.

'What did you *do* with that roll of film I gave you in Benares? . . . It's incredible,' she said.

'Out of your hundred-odd rolls, there was one dud . . . She hexed you,' I said.

Everyone knows the rest of the story: the electoral triumph, the death of Sanjay, the storming of the Golden Temple, the assassin's bullet. As I watched the press and TV pictures of the funeral, I felt immeasurably sad. One saw Mrs Thatcher, with her pearls and prurient lips, peering at the flower-filled bier, as if saying to herself, 'Can she really be dead?' Yes. Indira had found her martyrdom. Politically, she was a catastrophe: yet she was still the little girl who wanted to be Joan of Arc. I loved her for that — and still do.

1978

10
CODA

THE ALBATROSS

In *In Patagonia* I suggested that the Albatross which hung from the neck of the Ancient Mariner was not the Great Wandering Albatross but a smaller black species: either the Sooty Albatross or the Black-browed. The Sooty is the likelier of the two. It is a streamlined bird that keeps to the open sea. I think I saw one off the south-east coast of Tierra del Fuego. The Black-browed is everywhere, in the Magellan Strait and the Beagle Channel, and resembles a large Greater Black-backed Gull.

On the south side of the Beagle Channel is the Chilean island of Navarino, with its naval base at Puerto Williams. I hoped to walk around the coast and get a glimpse of Hermit Island, which is the breeding colony of the Black-browed Albatross. The wind and the rain drove me back.

East of the naval base there is a row of shacks in which live the last of the Fuegian Indians — the Indians Darwin mistook for the 'missing link'. He compared their language to the 'grunts of animals', being unaware that a young Fuegian spoke as many words as Shakespeare ever wrote.

Most of the Fuegians on Navarino are half-bloods. But I met one old man, Grandpa Felipe, who was said to be almost pure. He was a frail old man, mending his crab-gear. He had never been strong. He had watched his wife die. And all his children die.

'It was the epidemics,' he said — and whenever he said the word *epidemias*, it sounded as a mournful refrain.

The Fuegians were as skilful canoers as the Eskimoes.

A year and a half later, when *In Patagonia* was in press, I went to the island of Steepholm in the Bristol Channel. My companion was a naturalist in his eighties. The purpose of our visit was to see in flower the peony that is supposed to have been brought here as a medicinal herb by monks from the Mediterranean.

I told my friend the story of how, in the nineteenth century, a Black-browed albatross had followed a ship north of the Equator. Its direction-finding mechanisms had been thrown out of line. It had ended up on a rock in the Faroe Islands where it lived for thirty-odd years and was known as 'The King of the Gannets'. The Hon. Walter Rothschild made a pilgrimage to see it. Finally, it was shot, stuffed and put in the Copenhagen Museum.

'But there's a new Albatross,' the old man said. 'A female bird. She was on Bass Rock last year, and I think she's gone to Hermaness.'

Hermaness, at the tip of Unst in Shetland, is the ultimate headland of the British Isles.

From my flat in London, I called Bobby Tullock, the Shetland ornithologist.

'Sure, she's on Hermaness. She's made a nest among the Gannets and she's sitting proud. Why don't you come and see her? You'll find her on the West Cliff. You can't miss her.'

I looked at my watch. It was nine o'clock. I had time to get to King's Cross Station before the night train left for Aberdeen. I put on my boots and packed a bag.

There was a hold-up on the tube. I almost missed the train. I ran down the platform at the last minute. The sleeping-car attendant was a craggy white-haired Scot in a maroon uniform with a gold braid. Beside him stood a small dark young man, waiting.

I was out of breath.

'Have you got a berth?' I asked.

'Aye,' said the sleeping-car attendant. 'If you don't mind sharing with that!'

He jerked his thumb at the little man.

'Of course not,' I said.

The man jumped into the upper bunk. I tried to talk. I tried English, French, Italian, Greek. Useless. I tried Spanish and it worked. I should have guessed. He was a South American Indian.

'Where are you from?' I asked.

'Chile.'

'I have been in Chile. Whereabouts?'

'Punta Arenas.'

Punta Arenas on the Straits of Magellan is the southernmost city in the world.

'I was there,' I said.

'I come from Punta Arenas. But that is not my home. My home is Navarino Island.'

'You must know Grandpa Felipe.'

'*Es mi tio*.' 'He is my uncle.'

Having exceptional powers of balance, the young man and his brother found work in Punta Arenas as refuellers of the light-buoys at the entrance to the Magellan Strait. In any sea they would jump onto the buoy and insert the fuel nozzle. After the fall of Allende, the brother got a job with an American oil company, using his talent on off-shore rigs. The company had sent him to the North Sea oil field. He had asked for his brother to join him. They would each earn £600 a week.

I told him I was travelling north to see a bird that had flown from his country. The story mystified him.

Two days later I lay on the West Cliff off Hermaness and watched the Albatross through binoculars: a black exception in a snow field of Gannets. She sat, head high and tail high, on her nest of mud, on her clutch of infertile eggs.

I too am mystified by this story.

1988

345

CHILOE

The island of Chiloe is celebrated for its black storms and black soil, its thickets of fuchsia and bamboo, its Jesuit churches and the golden hands of its woodcarvers. Among its shellfish there is an enormous barnacle — the *pico de mar* — which sits on one's plate like a miniature Mount Fuji. The people are a mixture of Chonos Indian, Spanish and sailors of every colour, and their imagination churns with tormented mythologies.

The Cathedral of Castro was built of corrugated sheet and painted an aggressive orange in honour of the Holy Year. Luggers with ochre sails were becalmed in the bay. At a café in the port sat an immensely distinguished, silver-haired man with long straight legs.

He was a Sikh. Long ago, longer than he cared to remember, he was batman to an English colonel at Amritsar. One of his duties was to take the colonel's daughter out riding. Their eyes met. She was excommunicated by her family, he by his. Their life in England was a succession of hostile landladies. One day, he cut his hair and shaved his beard, and they went to South America. He and his wife had been happy on Chiloe. She had recently died.

'I would not have lived in any other way,' he said.

Two lakes — Lago Huillinco and Lago Cucao — all but bisect the island, flowing one into the other, brown water into blue, and out into the Pacific. The lakes are the Styx of Chiloe. The souls of the dead are supposed to assemble at the village of Huillinco. The Boatman then ferries them to their destination.

The road to Huillinco was white and wound through fields of ripe grain. Winnowers shouted greetings as I passed. Silvery, shingled houses were encircled by pines and poplars. Hansel and Gretel would be happy to live here.

Under a tree of waxy white flowers a fat young man sat eating blackberries. Hector Dyer Garcia was returning from the races. He had lost money.

'Do you know Notting Hill Gate?' he asked.

Around the turn of the century, Alfred Dyer-Aulock jumped ship and landed in the arms of a Chilote girl. On his deathbed, he told his family to write to their English cousins. They did not know how to do this. Hector dreamed of an unclaimed inheritance in a London bank.

'Or I shall have to go to Venezuela,' he said.

We walked slowly, stopping at a blue cottage to drink cider with a woodcutter's family. At dusk, we came to Huillinco — a cluster of houses, a jetty and the silver lake beyond. Evangelists with nasal voices were droning to a guitar.

Hector crept into his house as though visiting the scene of a crime. He had a wife. She was twice his size and twice his age. Shrieking abuse — between mouthfuls of cheese — she drew out his painful confession. He had lost on the horses the money intended for groceries.

I spent the evening with Hector and his friends, playing dominoes in the bar.

In the morning a milky fog smothered the settlement. Across the lake came the sound of rowlocks and the muffled bark of a dog. A man, rubbing the sleep from his eyes, said the ferry to Cucao would come at three in the afternoon.

I walked along the lake shore, amid mimosas, wintergreen and flame trees. Emerald humming-birds sucked at trumpets of scarlet honeysuckle. One shrub had bright purple berries. The country smelled of burning.

347

At three, the village sighted the ferry, a black speck at the far end of the lake. Horses with panniers were tethered alongside the jetty.

The people of Cucao disembarked their produce: bales of black wool, mussels, and trusses of seaweed and shallots. The Boatman was a tiny man with glistening brown skin and an almost circular mouth. He was one of the last pure-blood Chonos Indians.

Besides myself, the only passenger for Cucao was Dona Lucerina, a firm-jawed woman swathed from head to foot in black. She owned the only hostel in the village.

The Boatman had started the guttering outboard when two boys ran to the shore carrying a white wood coffin. They were red-eyed from crying. They had gone to fetch a priest for their dying mother: he had refused to come. They sat a night and a day outside the priest's house: he refused to come. Then word came she was dead; still he wouldn't come. The weather was hot. The mother was rotting, unburied and unshriven.

'When did she die?' demanded Dona Lucerina.

'Friday.'

'At what hour?'

'Ten in the morning.'

'Heart?'

'Lungs.'

'Ah!' She gave a knowing smile. 'Tuberculosis!

'Bad diet. For tuberculosis you must drink milk. Then the disease cannot enter the house.'

'She was ill for years,' said the younger boy.

'She should have drunk more milk when she was young.'

The boat glided into Lago Cucao. The Boatman dropped the boys on a beach of white stone. We watched them, two black figures carrying the coffin to their homestead, through the dead trees.

At Cucao there were two wooden churches on a meadow: they might have been built by Early Celtic monks. Kingfishers flew back and forth. The Boatman tied up beside a row of cottages. I paid him my obol. Dona Lucerina led the way along a sandy path: we brushed our legs against giant-leaved gunnera.

We climbed the headland. The setting sun coloured the Pacific rollers a milky golden green. The sands along the bay were black. A fishing boat, crossing the bar, was a black crescent in the foam. Dona Lucerina's house was long and low, with a roof of shingles and planked walls painted cream.

'All mine!' she gestured along the beach. 'Two hundred hectares, the house, and mines of gold. I have to sell it. My husband is sick.'

In the dark green kitchen sat her lodger, Don Antonio: a straight-backed old man with dark eyes glittering through a fuzz of eyebrow.

'Tell the young man some stories,' said Dona Lucerina. 'He wants to hear stories.'

In soft and musical Spanish, Don Antonio told of the Basilisk and the Fiura, the Sirens and the Pincoya.

'Ah! I love the Pincoya.' Dona Lucerina clapped her hands.

The Pincoya was a sea-nymph: a laughing girl who encouraged the shellfish to multiply. Sometimes you saw her dancing on the sands, her dress of seaweed shimmering with pearls and her flaming hair streaming in the wind.

'Tell him another, old man,' she said. 'Tell him about the King of the Land.'

'Long ago,' Don Antonio began, 'Cucao had everything — cows, horses, sheep, goats, everything — and the rest of Chiloe had nothing. One day a sheep was born with three horns, and its fame spread. A stranger came to see the sheep and stayed the night. In the morning the people woke to find all their animals gone. They followed the tracks and came to a river. There was an old man sitting on the bank.

'"Have you seen the thief who stole our animals?" they asked.

349

' "That was no thief," the man said. "That was the King of the Land."

'And ever since the people of Cucao have nothing and the rest of the island is rich.'

'And another one!' said Dona Lucerina. 'Tell him about Millalobo.'

'Do you remember the cottages by the landing-stage?' he asked.

'I do.'

'In the second cottage,' he went on, 'there lived a family — mother, father, daughter. We knew them well . . .

'One day the mother told the girl to fetch some water for coffee from the spring . . . *por un cafecito no mas*. The girl did not want to go: there was a stranger, she said, in the village. But the mother insisted and the girl did not come back. The mother called and called and searched everywhere. She came to the spring and there was blood . . . blood all around . . . *para sangre*. The neighbours said yes, they had seen a stranger. He was as tall and fair as you are, Englishman. The mother knew that Millalobo had taken her daughter . . .

'A year later the girl came back with a baby in her arms. The woman was thrilled with her grandson, and rigged up a cradle. One morning, the daughter left the house, warning her mother not to look at the child. "Remember what I said, Mother," she repeated as she closed the door. But the woman was aching to see her grandson and rolled back the coverlet. From the waist down the baby was a seal. Then it changed into a star and bounced around the room, and out of the window, buzzing like a horse-fly.

'The girl heard the buzzing. She knew her husband had bewitched the child and sent it to live in the sky. She roamed the seashore crying "Cucao! Cucao!" She walked into the water and slid under the surface . . .

'Millalobo built a palace for her at the bottom of the lagoon. Once a year he frees her and she floats to the surface, and when she sees the meadow and the churches, she breaks into song:

' "Cucao! Cucao! Cucaoooooooooooo!" '

'Now tell him about the Boatman,' Dona Lucerina insisted.

Don Antonio was tired now: but he stood at the window and pointed to a chain of three black rocks like stepping stones at the far end of the bay.

'Those rocks', he said, 'are the Boatman's Landing. I once knew a man who laughed at the story of the Boatman. He stood on one of the rocks and shouted, "Boatman! Boatman!" — and the Boatman came.'

Night fell over Cucao. A full moon lit the surf. The fire of some gold panners burned a hole in the darkness. I walked along the sands. I approached the Boatman's Landing but I resisted the temptation to call.

1988

II

TALES OF
THE
ART WORLD

THE DUKE OF M——

Long ago, when I worked at Sotheby's, the art auctioneers, two seedy Swiss brought in prehistoric gold treasure: torques, bangles, hair-rings, plaquettes. They said it came from Middle Europe, but I knew it was Iberian. We gave a receipt and they left.

In the library we had a book on Iberian prehistory. I found several of the pieces illustrated, listed as the property of a Fundación Don Juan de Valencia in Madrid.

By means of the international operator I got through to the foundation and asked to speak to the curator.

'You have the gold?' he called in an excited voice. 'This is wonderful! It was stolen from us. Keep it! We will tell Interpol ... Excuse me, what did you say your name was? Mr Cha? ... Chat ... ? Chatwin! We will contact you. THANK you!'

Next morning, around eleven, the receptionist put through a call to my desk to say that the Duke of M—— was waiting in the office.

He was a white-haired grandee of the old stamp. He wore the black hat only a grandee can wear. I showed him into a waiting-room and went to fetch the gold from the safe.

Trembling with excitement, the Duke of M—— picked up the objects, one by one. Nothing was lost.

'I cannot tell you how grateful I am,' he said. 'You have no idea what I have been through. These Swiss came posing as archaeologists and we allowed them to study the collection.

They stole it. I am responsible for the foundation. I would be in terrible disgrace if the gold was not found.'

We agreed it should go back to the safe, and we would wait instructions from Interpol.

The Duke of M—— gave me his card and asked me to call on him if I came to Madrid.

On the way out we passed the Chairman of Sotheby's who was talking to the expert on Spanish painting. I saw the expert murmuring to the Chairman, who pressed forward to introduce himself.

'I've always heard about your wonderful collection of pictures . . .'

'Always' was thirty seconds beforehand.

'But you must come and see them,' said the Duke of M——.

He took from his wallet a second card: 'Whenever you come to Madrid, I shall be delighted to give you luncheon.'

Several years passed. I quit Sotheby's — Smootherboys as a friend likes to call it. I spent one winter kicking around the Western Sahara. In April my wife joined me for a two-week trip in Morocco.

On the runway at Casablanca was the Royal Air Maroc Caravelle that would take us to Paris with a connecting flight to London. But there was also an Iberian Airlines jet due to leave for Madrid twenty minutes earlier.

'Quick!' I said to Elizabeth. 'Let's go to the Prado and look at pictures.'

The airport staff hustled us aboard.

It was freezing in Madrid. We stayed in a poky hotel and shivered. Next morning, I called the Duke of M—— to ask if I could see the Don Juan de Valencia Foundation.

'You must come to lunch,' said the Duke of M——. 'Can you manage today?'

'I don't think we can,' I said. 'We've come from the Moroccan desert and we've got no respectable clothes.'

'We'll find you clothes,' he said. 'My sons have plenty of suits. But what size is your wife?'

'She's short,' I said, 'and slim.'

'We shall find something. We expect you at a quarter to one.'

We pressed the doorbell. The butler showed us into separate bedrooms. In mine there was a selection of grey suits, a row of black shoes, shirts, socks, cufflinks and silver silk ties.

I was dirty. I washed and dressed. I was terrified of mucking up the basin. I met Elizabeth in the hallway. She wore an emerald dress by Balenciaga. We went in to join the guests.

In the salon there were several paintings by Goya and, in the dining-room, a magnificent set of Guardis. The conversation was brilliant, the lunch delicious. After three months of eating food with my fingers, my table-manners were hardly up to it.

'I've left Sotheby's,' I said to the Duke of M——.

'I'm glad to hear it,' he smiled. 'We had a most disagreeable experience with a man from there. Wilson, I think his name was. He called to ask if he could see my collection. Of course, after *our* agreeable experience, I invited him to lunch. But he started to tell me the price my Guardis would fetch at auction. I had to show him the door.'

'In the middle of lunch?'

'Yes.'

'Tell me,' I asked. 'Did Interpol catch the thieves?'

'They did . . .'

Afterwards, in our borrowed clothes — which we borrowed for three more days — we went to the house of a very old lady, who had been among the guests.

She was a famous art historian and expert on Zurbarán. She showed us into her bedroom. The walls were white. There was a four-poster bed with a white coverlet but no curtains. There was a crucifix. On the bed-table were a rosary and a breviary. On the wall facing the bed hung a panel about four feet square: of *Saint Veronica's Veil* by El Greco.

1988

THE BEY

Among my first jobs at Sotheby's was that of porter in the Department of Greek and Roman Antiquities. Whenever there was a sale I would put on my grey porter's uniform and stand behind the glass vitrines, making sure that prospective buyers didn't sticky the objects with their fingers.

One morning there appeared an elderly and anachronistic gentleman in a black Astrakhan-collared coat, carrying a black silver-tipped cane. His syrupy eyes and brushed-up moustache announced him as a relic of the Ottoman Empire.

'Can you show me something beautiful?' he asked. 'Greek, *not* Roman!'

'I think I can,' I said.

I showed him a fragment of an Attic white-ground lekythos by the Achilles Painter which had the most refined drawing, in golden-sepia, of a naked boy. It had come from the collection of Lord Elgin.

'Ha!' said the old gentleman. 'I see you have The Eye. I too have The Eye. We shall be friends.'

He handed me his card. I watched the black coat recede into the gallery:

Paul A—— F—— Bey
Grand Chamberlain du Cour du Roi des Albanis

'So,' I said to myself. 'Zog's Chamberlain.'

He was true to his word. We became friends. He would turn up in London on some business of Albanians in exile. He fretted about Queen Geraldine in Estoril. He regretted that King Leka in Madrid had to earn his living in real-estate.

He spoke of the works of art that had been his. He had sold his Fauve Braques and paintings by Juan Gris *en bloc* to the Australian art collector, Douglas Cooper. He spoke of the excellent pheasant shooting in his ancestral domain. He had never been to Albania but had spent his life between Switzerland and Alexandria. Did I know, he once asked, that the government of Enver Hoxha was a homosexual cabal?

'At least, that's what they tell me.'

I soon realised that the Bey was not a buyer but a seller. His straitened circumstances forced him from time to time to dispense with a work of art. Would I, he enquired rather sheepishly, be interested in acquiring some odds and ends from his collection?

'I certainly would,' I said.

'Perhaps I could show you a few things at the Ritz?'

I had next to no money. The Directors at Sotheby's assumed that people like myself had private incomes to supplement our wretched salaries. What was I to do? Exist on air? I earned myself a little extra by trafficking in antiquities — until the Chairman told me to stop. It was wrong for members of the staff to deal in works of art because they actively hindered a possible sale at auction.

I felt this was unfair. Almost everyone in the art business seemed to be at it.

But with the Bey my conscience was clear. He refused to sell anything at auction. I don't think he could bear the idea of his things being handled on viewing day by the hoi polloi, by people who did *not* have The Eye. Besides, he gave me everything as a present. Spread out over his bed at the Ritz would be a cluster of exquisite objects: an Archaic Greek bronze, a fragment of a Mosan chasse, a Byzantine cameo, an Egyptian green slate palette of pre-dynastic period, and many others.

'Would you like them?' he asked anxiously.

'I would.'

'In that case I give them to you! Between two friends who have The Eye there can be no question of money.'

I would wrap the treasures in tissue paper and, taking them to a dealer friend, find out how much I could get for them. I always tried to keep one or two for myself.

A day later the phone would ring. 'Chatwin, could you spare a few moments to have a drink with me?'

'Of course I could, Bey.'

We would meet in the Ritz Bar.

'Chatwin, I've one or two little favours to ask you. You know how tiresome it is to move funds around Europe. Banks are so unobliging these days. I find I've overspent on this visit. I wonder if you could settle a few things for me.'

'Of course, Bey.'

'I've been a bit extravagant at the tailor. Three or four suits. Four pairs of shoes at Lobb's. And there's the poor old Bentley! She had to have a new radiator.'

'I'll see what I can do,' I said.

I went to the tailor and asked for the Bey's bill. I went to Lobb. I discovered from Jack Barclay the cost of the radiator. The Bey's prices were never excessive; but, in the best Oriental tradition, we always had a haggle at the end. Otherwise, the deal would not be a deal.

'Chatwin, I wonder if you could have a word with the Ritz cashier? I thought of leaving for Switzerland on Saturday week.'

'Out of the question, Bey. I suggest this Monday.'

'Alas, that cannot be. On Tuesday Lady Turnbull is giving a cocktail for the Anglo-Albanian Society. As Chamberlain, I have to attend.'

'Wednesday then?'

'Wednesday it shall be.'

'And no more phone calls after today?'

This went on for two or three years. Nowadays, I sometimes thumb through the catalogues of an American museum, or an exhibition of ancient art, and there, illustrated full-plate, will be an object or a painting that passed from the Bey to myself: 'A unique Cycladic marble vessel . . . ', 'A Pentellic marble head of a youth from a late fifth-century Attic stele . . . ', 'A white marble head of a Putto, attributed to Desiderio di Settignano . . . ', 'A painting of Christ Mocked, in tempera on linen, by a follower of Mantegna, possibly by Melozzo da Forli . . . '

We have one object left from the Bey's collection: my wife's engagement ring. It is a Greek electrum ring of the late fifth century BC. The Bey bought it in 1947 from a Cairo dealer called Tano. I believe it comes from the Tell-el Mashkuta Treasure, most of which is now in the Brooklyn Museum.

The intaglio has a wounded lioness levering with her mouth and forepaw the hunter's spear from her flank. Not entirely suitable as an engagement present, but I think it the loveliest Greek ring I ever saw.

I write about the Bey because people of his kind will never come again. His life, I suspect, was a bit of a sham. The Eye was always young and pure.

1988

THE FLY

For a year, when I was twenty-two, one of my dearest friends was an old man called Bertie Landsberg. There was a sixty-year gap in our ages. He was a Brazilian of German-Jewish descent. He had been raised by black wet-nurses and in his eyes there was a tropical languor. His family had a lot of 'useless' land, 'something the size of Belgium'.

He went to Trinity College, Cambridge, and then to Paris. He commissioned Matisse to paint a Cubist portrait of his sister, Yvonne. His mother would not pay for the painting. Picasso drew him. He bought and restored one of the loveliest and most melancholy houses in the world, Palladio's Villa Malcontenta on the Brenta Canal near Venice.

I took him to the Venice Biennale. We admired Giacometti. He did not like Ashile Gorky. When we came to the Soviet Pavilion, he said: 'At least it has an awful vitality.'

He taught me that works of art, if they are to live, should never be bought or sold, but given or exchanged. This, to a boy flogging pictures at Sotheby's, was news. He gave me a lovely fragment of an Archaic Greek marble. I sold it in one of my crises, and have felt guilty ever since.

Bertie's wife, Dorothea, had been a Boston spinster stranded in Venice after America came into the War. He took her to Brazil. He showed her the Baroque towns of Minhas Gerais, Ouro Preto and Conghoñas do Campo.

The rooms in Brazilian country hotels are compartments in which to sling a hammock. One night, Bertie complained

362

over the wall: 'There must be a hole in my mosquito net. I'm being bitten to death.'

'Take mine,' said Dorothea.

'This', Bertie said to himself, 'is a woman I could marry.'

My future wife, Elizabeth, was American. On hearing her tell a story, I, too, felt this was a woman I could marry.

Her great friend at Radcliffe was the daughter of the Director of the National Gallery in Washington. These were the years when a very rich couple, the W——'s, had installed themselves on Fifth Avenue in an apartment of French *boiseries* and royal French marquetry furniture. Among the pictures they had a Vermeer, bought on the advice of art experts. The Director of the Gallery thought it good for his girl's education if she saw this legendary collection. Elizabeth went along for tea. Understandably, Mrs W—— was agitated. Elizabeth, although short-sighted, registered her disapproval of the sheets of plate-glass laid over the marquetry. Both girls were ravenous after the train trip from Boston. They went through one plate of cucumber sandwiches and caused consternation by asking for another.

Elizabeth looked up and said, 'Look! There's a fly.'

'There can't be,' Mrs W—— cried. 'It can't have got in' — unless the air-conditioning and humidifying systems had broken down.

'There is,' said Elizabeth, shooing the fly from the sand-wiches.

'It must have come in with you.'

1988

MY MODI

It is 1944 in New York and Miss Lillie, alias Lady Peel, 'Lady Parlequipeel', is sauntering down Madison Avenue in her inevitable embroidered mobcap. She is a big hit in the musical *Seven Lively Arts* at the Ziegfeld Theatre. The war is still on and the art business is slow. Showbiz is booming. I haven't a clue to what time of year it was. Let us imagine it was spring. She passes the galleries along Madison Avenue and a picture takes her eye.

'Lawdie Gawdie!' It's the Valentin Gallery.

She sweeps in.

The assistant sweeps her into Mr Valentin's office. He rises to his feet. 'Miss Lillie. I am honoured you come to my gallery.'

'The room', says Bea, 'was covered in plum velvet and there was a plum velvet easel.' 'Mr Valentin,' she begins, 'my friend Vincent Price tells me you have a beautiful painting by M . . . Mo . . . Mo . . . '

'Modigliani.'

'Well, let's shorten it to Modi.'

The assistant goes to the shelves behind the plum velvet curtain and pulls out a painting of a young Belgian boy. He has a mass of blond curls and rosy cheeks; he wears a sand-coloured jacket; I forget the other details.

'Is that a Modi?'

'It is, Miss Lillie.'

'I never saw anything so frrrightful in my life. If that's a

Modi, I'm leaving!'

She sweeps out.

On the threshold she turns to Mr Valentin.

'And how much were you proposing to ask me for the Modi?'

'Miss Lillie. I have always been a great admirer of yours. I was suggesting fifteen thousand dollars.'

'Fifteen thousand *dollars*! You can keep it! I could offer you seventy-five hundred, but fifteen thousand!'

'Miss Lillie, if you really like the picture, I give it for seventy-five hundred.'

She goes back to the plum-coloured office and writes out a cheque. Since the war is still on, Mr Valentin agrees to keep it and ship it when hostilities are over.

He shipped Modi in a crate. It went upstairs into the attic of Bea's house on the river at Henley-on-Thames and she forgot about it.

The first time I saw Bea and the Modi was in 1963 when the Chairman of Sotheby's came into our office with Bea, the Modi and Bea's American friend and protector.

He said we would store the picture indefinitely. It would be insured for fifty thousand pounds.

That Sunday I went for lunch and supper at Henley. We laughed, sang and Bea played the piano. I was Noel and she was Gertie. We had perfect pitch:

> If you were the only girl in the world
> And I were the only boy,
> There would be such wonderful things to do.
> There would be such wonderful dreams come true
> If you were the only girl in the world
> And I were the only boy.

The last I heard of the Modi was a telephone call from the Chairman's secretary about ten years later asking me if I knew the details of the insurance on the Modigliani and whether

Beatrice Lillie signed the insurance form. Her protector had turned up one day at Sotheby's and asked for the picture back. The porter, supposing it to have been left there last week, let him have it. He took it down the road to Christie's where it sold for over two hundred thousand pounds.

The money went to pay her nursing bills.

I hope that Bea in her dotage in New York remembered the rosy-cheeked Belgian boy.

When you have written five books, people begin to comment on your style. They have compared my bleak, chiselled style with Hemingway, Lawrence (D.H., thank God, not T.E.). Yes, they are my writers. For bleak passages I have also looked hard at *Hedda Gabler*.

But, I was a boy who, at the age of eight, sang 'The Stately Homes of England' to the wind-up gramophone. I sang 'Mad Dogs and Englishmen' in falsetto: after puberty, having an extra male hormone or two, I couldn't get my tongue around Dig . . . arig . . . arig . . . arig . . . arig . . . adoo. For writers who want to write dialogue, I can recommend nothing better than the breakfast scene in *Private Lives*.

Of course, I longed to meet the Master — and did so. It was his last lunch party in London before he crept off to die in Jamaica. The hostess was Anne Fleming, widow of Ian. The other members of the cast were Merle Oberon, Lady Diana Cooper, myself and him. I laughed so much the grouse came down my nose. He and Lady Diana did a dialogue about how, in the 1920s, they appeared in Chicago, he in *The Vortex*, she in *The Miracle*.

On the way out from lunch he said, 'I have very much enjoyed meeting you, but unfortunately, we will never meet again because very shortly I will be dead. *But* if you'll take one parting word of advice, "Never let anything artistic stand in your way."'

I have always acted on this advice.

1988

BIBLIOGRAPHICAL NOTE

The stories and articles in this book originally appeared, some in a different form, in the following publications:

A Coup: *Granta 10*; The Albatross and Chiloe: *Granta 24*; Until My Blood Is Pure and Nadezhda Mandelstam: A Visit: *Bananas*; Madeleine Vionnet, Maria Reiche: The Riddle of the Pampa, André Malraux, George Costakis: The Story of an Art Collector in the Soviet Union, Heavenly Horses, Shamdev: The Wolf-Boy, The Very Sad Story of Salah Bougrine and On the Road with Mrs G.: *Sunday Times*; Konstantin Melnikov: Architect: American *House & Garden*; Werner Herzog in Ghana: *Interview*; Rock's World: *New York Times*; Nomad Invasions: *History Today*; Donald Evans and Ernst Jünger: An Aesthete at War: *New York Review of Books*; On Yeti Tracks: *Esquire*. A Lament for Afghanistan was first published as the introduction to the Penguin edition of *The Road to Oxiana* by Robert Byron; Howard Hodgkin was first published as a 'portrait of the artist' to accompany the catalogue for the Tate Gallery exhibition 'Howard Hodgkin's Indian Leaves'.

The Volga is reprinted by permission of the *Observer*. The lines quoted from the *Cantos* of Ezra Pound are reprinted by permission of Faber and Faber Ltd. Lyrics from 'If You Were the Only Girl in the World' by Clifford Grey are used by permission of Redwood Music Limited, 14 New Burlington Street, London W1X 2LR.

Also available in Vintage

Bruce Chatwin

THE SONGLINES

'Extraordinary...a remarkable and satisfying book'
Observer

'He is such a fine and original writer. A white nomad himself, Chatwin's affinity with the footloose tribes of the endless outback yields one of the most affectionate portraits yet of a race ravaged by the alcohol that so many other Australians privately hope will become a self-administered Final Solution'
Daily Mail

'The Songlines emerge as invisible pathways connecting up all over Australia: ancient tracks made of songs which tell of the creation of the land. The Aboriginals' religious duty is ritually to travel the land, singing the Ancestors' songs: singing the world into being afresh. *The Songlines* is one man's impassioned song'
Sunday Telegraph

'Chatwin is not simply describing another culture; he is also making cautious assertions about human nature. Towards the end of his life Sartre wondered why people still write novels; had he read Chatwin's he might have found new excitement in the genre'
Edmund White, *Sunday Times*

VINTAGE

Also available in Vintage

Bruce Chatwin

UTZ

'This shiny little novel is not just about pretty porcelain figurines but about dirty great issues of life and creativity'
The Times

'Bruce Chatwin knows his *objets d'art*, and the writing has the warmth of a double fascination – of the collector's fascination with portable art, and with the author's fascination with collectors as a species'
John Harvey, *Sunday Telegraph*

'With Chatwin, the real excitement derives from an intellectual drama, in dialogues about art as a surrogate creation, a robbery of divine power, and art collecting as idolatry...For Chatwin, ideas are the supreme fictions'
Peter Conrad, *Observer*

'For my money, Chatwin is the greatest stylist writing in England today...Not a word is wasted in the telling of this tale. Each sentence is fashioned, polished, and put into place with microscopic care'
Nicholas Shakespeare, *Daily Telegraph*

VINTAGE

Fagan Mechanical

Mid West Mechanical

C D Jones
Warehouse
— get names
from them.